HELLENISTIC ARCHITECTURE AND HUMAN ACTION

sidestonepress

HELLENISTIC ARCHITECTURE AND HUMAN ACTION

A Case of Reciprocal Influence

ANNETTE HAUG, ASJA MÜLLER

SCALES OF TRANSFORMATION I 10

Published by Sidestone Press, Leiden
www.sidestone.com

Imprint: Sidestone Press Academics

Layout & cover design: CRC 1266/Carsten Reckweg and Sidestone Press
Cover image: Sanctuary of Zeus in Labraunda. Photo: Asja Müller, reproduced by kind permission of Olivier Henry, director of the Labraunda excavations.

ISSN 2590-1222

ISBN 978-90-8890-909-2 (softcover)
ISBN 978-90-8890-910-8 (hardcover)
ISBN 978-90-8890-911-5 (PDF e-book)

The STPAS publications originate from or are involved with the Collaborative Research Centre 1266, which is funded by the Deutsche Forschungsgemeinschaft (DFG, German Research Foundation; Projektnummer 2901391021 – SFB 1266).

Preface of the editors

With this book series, the Collaborative Research Centre 'Scales of Transformation: Human-Environmental Interaction in Prehistoric and Archaic Societies' (CRC 1266) at Kiel University enables the bundled presentation of current research outcomes of the multiple aspects of socio-environmental transformations in ancient societies by offering this new publication platform. As editors, we are pleased to be able to publish monographs with detailed basic data and comprehensive interpretations from different case studies and landscapes as well as the extensive output from numerous scientific meetings and international workshops.

The book series is dedicated to the fundamental research questions of the CRC 1266 dealing with transformations on different temporal, spatial and social scales, here defined as processes leading to a substantial and enduring reorganization of socio-environmental interaction patterns. What are the substantial transformations that describe human development from 15,000 years ago to the beginning of the Common Era? How did the interaction between natural environment and human populations change over time? What role did humans play as cognitive actors trying to deal with changing social and environmental conditions? Which factors triggered the transformations that led to substantial societal and economic inequality?

The understanding of human practices within the often intertwined social and environmental contexts is one of the most fundamental aspects of archaeological research. Moreover, in current debates, the dynamics and feedback involved in human-environmental relationships have become a major issue looking at the sometimes devastating consequences of human interference with nature. Archaeology, with its long-term perspective on human societies and landscapes, is in the unique position to trace and link comparable phenomena in the past, to study the human involvement with the natural environment, to investigate the impact of humans on nature, and the consequences of environmental change on human societies. Modern interlinked interdisciplinary research allows for reaching beyond simplistic monocausal lines of explanation and overcoming evolutionary perspectives. Looking at the period from 15,000 to 1 BCE, the CRC 1266 takes a diachronic view in order to investigate transformations involved in the development of late Pleistocene hunter-gatherers, horticulturalists, early agriculturalists, early metallurgists as well as early state societies, thus covering a wide array of societal formations and environmental conditions.

The volume *Hellenistic Architecture and Human Action* brings the built space into focus perceived as arena for action particularly in the ritual sphere. The book is the outcome of the International Colloquium 'Hellenistic Architecture and Human Action - A Case of Reciprocal Influence' held in Kiel in 2018. We are very thankful to the editors Asja Müller and Annette Haug for their engagement during the conference and the preparation of this volume. Many thanks go also to the graphic illustrators Anna Carina Lange and Carsten Reckweg for the deep engagement in this publication. We also wish to thank Karsten Wentink, Corné van Woerdekom and Eric van den Bandt from Sidestone Press for their responsive support in realizing this volume and Hermann Gorbahn for organizing the whole publication process.

Wiebke Kirleis and Johannes Müller

Contents

Part 3: Beyond sanctuaries: the agora

Acknowledgements

This volume seeks to provide new insight into social-environmental interactions and, more specifically, into the interrelation between architecture, its landscape setting, and human action. It compiles the outcomes of the conference 'Hellenistic Architecture and Human Action – a Case of Reciprocal Influence' that took place in Kiel, 30/10 – 01/11/2018. It was part of a research project dealing with socio-environmental interactions in the Eastern Mediterranean that was realised in the context of the Collaborative Research Centre 1266, 'Scales of Transformation – Human-Environmental Interaction in Prehistoric and Archaic Societies', based at the Christian-Albrechts-Universität Kiel (Germany). The DFG funded both the conference and this volume's preparation and printing (DFG, German Research Foundation – Projektnummer 2901391021 – SFB 1266).

We would like to thank the institutions and people whose contribution enabled the conference to take place as well as allow for the publication of its results: Corné van Woerdekom and Karsten Wentink, founders of Sidestone Press; Carsten Reckweg, graphic designer of the CRC, for processing the volume's illustrations; and, Sixt Baumann, Marieke Gottschalk, Rebecca Hannemann, Daniel Nieswand and Iria Schmidt from the Institute of Classics, department of Classical Archaeology, at the University of Kiel, who ensured a smooth running of the conference and also prepared the following publication.

Introduction: Hellenistic Architecture, Landscape, and Human Action

Annette Haug[1], Asja Müller[2]

The understanding of human practices in a social and environmental context is one of the most fundamental issues of archaeological research. The Hellenistic age (4th to 1st century BCE) constitutes a key historical moment when a profound change in the human-environmental relationship occurs. Central features that contribute to the creation of specific spatial qualities include both architecture and man-made material arrangements, on one hand, and natural 'landscape' elements (*e.g.* mountains/rocks, waters, caves, *etc.*), on the other. As architecture occupies a specific, naturally-defined place, architecture and landscape necessarily relate to each other. However, the elements linking and arranging those physical entities belong to the realm of the social. Both the landscape setting and architecture organise and structure human agency and perception. These two categories comprise the central categories of spatial appropriation that are intrinsically related and refer to each other. Agency depends on perception, while perception is formed by actions.

In the Hellenistic period, the human-environmental relationship undergoes profound changes. We can speak of an extensive aestheticisation of the architecturally-shaped environment. In other words, architectures much more explicitly refer to the human agent's perception and action. This affects the design of single architectures, the creation of architectural complexes, and finally also the relationship between architecture and nature/landscape.

This interdependency of architecture and agent is achieved by specific strategies of visual staging such as axiality, symmetry, terracing, and rhythmisation. All these strategies are already known before the Hellenistic age. However, they then gain a new quality by their systematic combination. The present volume seeks to explore this interrelationship between architecture, landscape, and the human agent in greater detail. This will allow for a more specific understanding of Hellenistic architecture and its social implications.

[1]Christian-Albrechts-Universität zu Kiel
Johanna-Mestorf-Straße 5
24118 Kiel
Germany
ahaug@klassarch.uni-kiel.de

[2]Freie Universität Berlin
Fabeckstraße 23-25
14195 Berlin
Germany
asja.mueller@fu-berlin.de

Research history

The concept of built space, adopted for the present volume, stresses the links between physical components of built space (architecture and landscape) and social components (agency and perception). We thus discuss the history of research with regard to the interrelationship between these four elements.

Architecture in isolation versus architectures in context

Since earliest times, the study of Hellenistic architecture has focused on questions of typology, dating, or cultural influences – or all of them. This holds true for a broad array of excavation reports concerning well-preserved Hellenistic architectural complexes. These informed us about pioneering work in the excavation and documentation of Hellenistic architecture and established a steady foundation on which further studies would firmly rest. During this phase of consolidation at the late 19th and early 20th centuries, the central focus was clustering Hellenistic architectural complexes, as proved by Theodore Fyfe's *Hellenistic architecture: an introductory study* (1936). This was followed by major reference works such as Gottfried Gruben's *Die Tempel der Griechen* (1966; see also Fedak 1990; Nielsen 1994). This line of research was drawn into the early 21st century with contributions by Frederick Winter or Marie-Cristine Hellmann (Winter 2006; Hellmann 2002; 2006; 2010).

However, already in 1986, Hans Lauter's noted publication *Die Architektur des Hellenismus* (1986) had developed a second line of research. Lauter did not limit his study to Hellenistic architecture in isolation but also took into account questions of natural setting, urbanistic interrelations, as well as the architecture's influence on ancient viewers (Lauter 1986, pp. 287-304). Nonetheless, the springboard of his approach was the architectural setting, and he didn't consider specific forms of action.

It was not until the end of the 20th century that studies on architectural complexes considered the landscape setting in a more explicit way, going beyond landscape as a challenge or obstacle to be taken into account when realising architecture (compare Bergquist 1967, especially p. 67). This holds true for the proceedings of several conferences: *Stadt und Umland* (Schwandner and Rheidt 1999) focusing on the interplay between urban space and *chora*; *Natur – Kult – Raum*, focusing on the cultic function of natural features in sacred spaces (Sporn *et al.* 2015); and *Entdeckungen der Landschaft: Raum und Kultur in Geschichte und Gegenwart* (Kasper *et al.* 2017), taking a broader interdisciplinary approach to landscape, architecture, and human existence.

As these contributions show, the different physical components that constitute the lived world (architecture and landscape) are intrinsically related. However, the interrelatedness gains complexity when human bodies and practices are taken into account.

Human practices

Human practices have been subject to research for a long time. The reconstruction of practices was usually based on written sources without taking into account their spatial qualities. This holds true for a large number of studies on ancient cults and ritual action. We can, for example, cite works about incubation and healing rites, making only limited use of the archaeological contexts: *Greek incubation rituals in Classical and Hellenistic times* (von Ehrenheim 2015). The same holds true for many works about Hellenistic-Roman processions and festivals: Ellen Rice's dissertation *The grand procession of Ptolemy Philadelphus* (1983); the doctoral work of Jens Köhler, *Pompai: Untersuchungen zur hellenistischen Festkultur* (Köhler 1996); and the edited volume *The moving city: processions, passages and promenades in ancient Rome* (Östenberg *et al.* 2016). Compared to the archaeological context, there was still a preponderance of literary sources, but there were also two major conferences publications connected to the CRC 619, 'Ritual Dynamics' based in Heidelberg (Germany): *Ritual dynamics and religious change in the Roman Empire* (Hekster *et al.* 2009) as well as *Ritual dynamics in the ancient Mediterranean* (Chaniotis 2011).

Yet, discussing human practices in isolation entails the same shortcomings as discussing architecture in isolation: the emerging picture is reduced to one single (in this instance, social) component, without grasping the spatial dimension of those actions.

The social dimension of architecture: mental concepts (semantics, identity, memory)

The separation of the typological analysis of architectural remains, on one hand, and the study of human practices through the works of ancient authors on the other, began dissolving from the 1990s onwards. Under the influence of contemporary practice theory (Bourdieu 1977; Foucault 1978; Giddens 1984), research in Classical Archaeology also developed an interest in questions of human 'action'.

Such research analyses the social, political, religious, but also economic connotations of architectures which are, of course, activated by their human perceivers. We may draw upon the research project 'Die hellenistische Polis als Lebensform'. One of several conferences organised by the project resulted in the conference volume *Stadtkultur im Hellenismus* (Matthaei 2014) that looks at the interplay between urban architecture and society.

This line of research gave rise to several studies that considered human agency in the more abstract sense of identity, leading to a group of conferences, which examined architecture as text, communicating and thus negotiating identity: *Die Karer und die Anderen* (Rumscheid 2009), *From Pella to Gandhara: hybridisation and identity in art and architecture of the Hellenistic East* (Kouremenos *et al.* 2011), *4th century Karia: defining a Karian identity under the Hekatomnids* (Olivier 2013), and *Contextualizing the sacred in the Hellenistic and Roman Near East: religious identities in local, regional and Imperial settings* (Raja 2017). On the level of cities and cityscapes, we refer once again to conference proceedings that arose from the project 'Die hellenistische Polis als Lebensform': *Stadtbilder im Hellenismus* (Matthaei 2009) and *Urbane Strukturen und bürgerliche Identität im Hellenismus* (Matthaei and Zimmermann 2015).

Another way of constructing identity by means of evoking a shared past was initiated by Pierre Nora's influential studies *Les lieux de mémoire* (Nora 1984; 1986; 1992). From the turn of the millennium onwards the concept of 'sites of memory' was absorbed into antiquity studies and led to a broad variety of conference volumes and edited books: *Die römische Welt: Erinnerungsorte der Antike* (Stein-Hölkeskamp and Hölkeskamp 2006), *Die griechische Welt: Erinnerungsorte der Antike* (Stein-Hölkeskamp 2010), *Griechische Heiligtümer als Erinnerungsorte: Von der Archaik bis in den Hellenismus* (Haake 2011), and *Cityscapes and monuments of Western Asia Minor: memories and identities* (Mortensen and Poulsen 2017).

The insight that the construction of identity is strongly spatially-based soon led to a related branch of research. Now, the appropriation of landscape by means of architecture in order to display claims of ownership and power came into focus. This aspect was discussed in the conference volumes *Macht der Architektur: Architektur der Macht* (Schwandner and Rheidt 2004) and *Manifestationen von Macht und Hierarchien in Stadtraum und Landschaft* (Pirson 2012) as well as Christina Williamson's dissertation *City and sanctuary in Hellenistic Asia Minor:*

constructing civic identity in the sacred landscapes of Mylasa and Stratonikeia in Karia (Williamson 2012).

Drawing upon the relationship between mental categories and architecture is certainly the first step into the exploration of built space's dimensionality. However, clinging to those rather static forms of agency necessarily means omitting another important characteristic of built space: its dynamic.

Architecture and agency

Studies focusing on the interplay between architecture and more dynamic forms of social behaviour involving movement begun with a colloquium titled *Stadtbild und Bürgerbild im Hellenismus* (Wörrle and Zanker 1995). However, the point of departure for most contributions was building complexes such as *gymnasia* or *bouleuteria* which were considered to be 'containers' of specific functions. The same holds true for studies deliberately linking certain ritual practices to certain forms of architecture, as Inge Nielsen's *Cultic theatres and ritual drama* (2002). Only most recently have there been attempts to look at such contexts from the perspective of different kinds of conventionalised human practice and sequences of actions.

One approach is the systematic analysis of 'movement in space' as suggested by Henrik Boman's dissertation *Movement in space: an architectural analysis of public space in Archaic to Hellenistic Greece* (2003) or the proceedings of the conference *Die Architektur des Weges: Gestaltete Bewegung im gebauten Raum* (Kurapkat *et al.* 2014). Walking as a cultural practice is also addressed in the edited volume *Rome, Ostia, Pompeii: movement and space* (Laurence and Newsome 2011) and Jeremy Hartnett's thesis *The Roman street: urban life and society in Pompeii, Herculaneum, and Rome* (2017). Furthermore, coherent sets of religious activity as processions and their relationship to architecture increasingly receive attention: indicatively, Maggie Popkin's dissertation *The architecture of the Roman triumph: monuments, memory, and identity* (2016); the conference proceedings *Excavating pilgrimage: archaeological approaches to sacred travel and movement in the Ancient World* (Kristensen and Friese 2017); and the edited volume *Ascending and descending the Acropolis: movement in Athenian religion* (Friese *et al.* 2019).

Looking at the relationship between architecture and mobile forms of agency allowed for understanding the dynamics of built space. Yet, one dimension is still missing, despite being a direct consequence of a dynamic space concept: moving in space entails constantly changing forms of perception.

Architecture and perception

Perception, as agency, is also tackled in the more recent studies. From a predominant literary-based point of view, this was accomplished by a series of edited books appearing under the umbrella title *The senses in antiquity*: synaesthesia, smell, sight, touch, taste and sound (Butler and Purves 2013; Bradley 2015; Squire 2016; Purves 2018; Rudolf 2018; Butler and Nooter 2019). However, the potentialities of such an approach were soon realized by archaeological research as well, and several colloquia focusing on sensual perception soon resulted in a broad variety of conference publications and individual studies: *Making senses of the past: toward a sensory archaeology* (Day 2013), *Archaeology and the senses: human experience, memory, and affect* (Hamilakis 2014) and *Senses of the empire: multisensory approaches to Roman culture* (Betts 2017). In addition, research increasingly analyses urban contexts with regard to 'sensescapes' as can be seen in the conference proceedings *Stadterfahrung als Sinneserfahrung in der römischen Kaiserzeit* (Haug and Kreuz 2016).

With regard to the growing popularity of architecture studies focusing on ancient vision, one may think of the edited volume *Licht und Architektur* (Heilmeyer and

Hoepfner 1990) but also the much more recent conference volume *Licht – Konzepte in der vormodernen Architektur* (Schneider and Wulf-Rheidt 2011). This goes hand in hand with the development of suitable tools for visual analysis such as 3D models. As an example, we may refer to the volume *Visualizing cityscapes of Classical Antiquity: from early modern reconstruction drawings to digital 3D models* (Piccoli 2018).

It's important to keep in mind, however, that focusing on sight and certain viewpoints without considering actions connecting them, risks bringing rigidity back into the space concept. The dimensions of built space can only be fully explored when perception is being correlated with (dynamic) agency.

This volume's approach

The discussion of the history of research reveals that the gap between architecture and human practices began dissolving from the 2010s onwards. However, most studies and edited books published to date have either a very broad focus, looking at ancient architecture by means of case studies in general, or focus on Roman cityscapes in particular. Hellenistic architecture is still studied mainly with regard to very specific, static aspects such as identity, memory, and power relations. The present volume seeks to shift the focus. It addresses the complex interrelationship of architecture, object worlds, and landscape elements in their concrete spatial and material configuration with forms of human agency and (bodily routed) perception.

Most of the contributions will deal with sanctuaries, for different reasons. First, sanctuaries provide a 'coherent' architectonic context. They possess a 'border' (*temenos*), and inside this 'segregated' area, architecture and 'equipment' (altars, votives, *etc.*) are arranged to form 'ensembles'. This holds true even if the single constituents are erected consecutively. Second, sanctuaries are the *locus* of a coherent set of 'religious'/'ritual' actions. In other words, the context of agency also shows a certain consistency. Third, sanctuaries can be located inside as well as outside cities, thus exemplifying built space within a stronger urban embedding or less so. In many cases, their location is chosen with regard to a specific landscape or urban setting. Sanctuaries are thus particularly suitable for an analysis of the interplay of sacred architecture, other kinds of public architecture, and landscape with regard to aspects of agency and perception.

This first section presents three sanctuaries that are investigated archaeologically by the authors as significant case studies: the sanctuary of Artemis Limnatis at Messene, the Sanctuary of the Great Gods at Samothrace, and the Thesmophorion in Pella. They are characterised by a different 'embedding' with regard to the city space; they differ with regard to their landscape embedding, but also with regard to their cultic features. The sanctuary of Artemis Limnatis is located outside the urban area of Messene, but inside the city wall. The sanctuary of the Great Gods of Samothrace lies outside the city of Samothrace, in a valley. However, this mystery cult had 'international' importance and was neither visually nor functionally connected to the city. The Thesmophorion is located on a hill above the city of Pella, a certain 1150 m of the city centre's agora; it is however unclear if inside or outside the city-walls. Instead, it lies in a remote place, in a valley on the north coast of the island.

With regard to the sanctuary of Artemis Limnatis in Messene, **Stefan Feuser, and Maria Spathi** show that the central temple is adjoined by four buildings that define the borders of the natural (only slightly altered) 'sanctuary plateau'. High foundations allow the buildings to adjust to the orographic situation, whereas a (low) terrace retaining wall supports the lower level with water installations. The buildings possess different orientations but are orthogonally aligned, taking up the orientation of the urban street grid. This concept was not understandable to the approaching worshipper but the symmetry became visible for the worshipper entering the sanctuary from an elevated position. The conceptual nexus with the city is thus made visible. From this entry point onwards, it was the natural terrain that 'guided' the visitor through the sanctuary.

Bonna Wescoat, Susan Blevins, Maggie Popkin, Jessica Paga, Andrew Ward, Michael Page and William Size focus on the tension between movement and rest within the sanctuary of the Great Gods in Samothrace. The architecture 'channelled' and organised movement and vision. This experience became particularly prominent when crossing the torrents – two of them framing the sanctuary and one cutting through it. The landscape features provided a differentiated experience of lightness and darkness, flatness and steepness. The monuments hover: statue bases flank the ways, but also the prostyle facades and retaining walls, thus creating a certain coherence and guiding the spectator through the sanctuary. The theatre and the stoa provided spaces for rest: gathering spaces that gained a specific importance in the course of festivals and processions.

Soi Agelidis identifies the so-called Thesmophorion in Pella as a place of worhship for Demeter, Kore, but also Hades, and dates it to the third quarter of the 4th century BCE. The circular enclosure was not visible from afar despite its location on a hill. Once the worshippers reached the cult area, they descended into the mudbrick enclosure where they met the altar in the middle of the round. The choice of materials enhanced the experience of entering 'the earth'. In contrast to the sanctuary of the Great Gods, the Thesmophorion provided the experience of a limited, enclosed space.

With regard to the three case studies, it becomes evident, that landscape elements are architecturally enhanced to create a specific ritually-loaded experience. The visual and atmospheric effect changes from site to site, from cult to cult.

The articles in the second section provide overarching principles of sanctuary design that go beyond the uniqueness of every single spot. Starting with papers dedicated to sanctuaries with a more 'monumental' set of architectures, the section simultaneously widens the focus from limited spaces (*pronaoi*, partly subterranean sanctuaries) to architectural ensembles (sanctuaries extending on hill slopes, panhellenic sanctuaries). The last article, in contrast, looks on a very different configuration of architecture and landscape, sacred caves, and the ways these natural spaces were transformed by a limited amount of human (architectural) intervention.

Philipp Kobusch focuses on the usage of *pronai* in Hellenistic temples by analysing their visual appearance in relation to the surrounding buildings and by analysing their architectural disposition and their equipment. During the Hellenistic period, peripteral temples went out of fashion and at the same time, interest in the visual aspect of the *pronai* – thus the frontal appearance of the temple – grows. The new visual staging corresponds to a new functional interest. Even though *pronaoi* possess a uniform architectural layout, their uses differ. They can function as treasuries or waiting rooms but also as a *locus* for cult activities. It is by minor installations such as barriers, fences, stone benches, or tables, that space is visually ordered and adjusted to specific uses.

Christina Williamson's approach to the perceptual qualities of Hellenistic sanctuaries is aesthetic. She analyses strategies of intensification of (spatially-bound) religious experience: the use of a specific landscape setting, architectural forms of staging, as well as the staging of the epiphany of the god, and cognitive arousal via festivals. She considers such a sublime impression on the viewer as a specifically Hellenistic desire.

Asja Müller suggests a typological approach by contrasting secluded sanctuaries located at a single level and entangled sanctuaries developing on different levels. These two categories are exemplified by four case studies: the Asclepieion of Athens and the sanctuary of Demeter in Pergamon as examples of more secluded sanctuaries; the sanctuary of Zeus in Labraunda and the sanctuary of Hera in Pergamon as examples of more entangled sanctuaries. She analyses how these two contrasting 'basic' opportunities of architectural design with the same landscape setting (hill slopes) are related to different forms of movement and perception – different routes within a sanctuary, a different orientation of buildings, a different prospective quality, and different contact zones of architecture and landscape.

The contribution of **Jessica vant'Westeinde** changes the perspective and focuses on written sources that allow for an understanding of the mental conception of sanctuaries. The choice of Aemilius Paullus' travel through Greece (and Greek sanctuaries of panhellenic reputation) allows for a comparison of two authors who refer to that journey: the Greek author Polybius and the Roman author Livy. This reveals how sanctuaries are perceived and acted upon as spaces of identity, memory, political and military superiority and inferiority, of *graecitas* and *romanitas*, of tourist interest, but of course also as religious spaces. Perception is thus transformed into mental categories.

At the end of the section, **Katja Sporn** focuses on a specific category of Hellenistic sanctuaries that follow different aesthetic and functional concepts: cave sanctuaries. While built sanctuaries 'occupy' the natural space, Sporn discusses, how different man-made activities transform the natural space of a cave into a sacred place: altars and cult statues are not prerequisites but can be introduced into the caves while other features are niches, benches and water basins, inscriptions and, in front of the caves, terraces, paths, and steps. Consequently, caves follow a different logic of sacrality, of architecture and 'nature'.

The third section provides an outlook that goes beyond sanctuaries by examining a particularly important urban context: *agorai*. These can be organised as more or less coherent building complexes, however, they are characterised by a functional 'openness'. Situated in the centre of the town, their urban embedding is much stronger.

Dirk Steuernagel's contribution analyses the Upper Agora in Ephesos – one of at least two *agorai* of the city. It received its architectural monumental layout at the turn of the 2nd century BCE. He finds plausible its use as a public-official state as inscriptions hint to the existence of a *bouleuterion* and a *prytaneion*. However, the bench seats in the interior of the South Stoa as well as under open sky on the east side of the square suggest a place to stay, communicate, and behave as spectators. By its framing of 'spectator' devices, the agora turns into a performative space which could be explained by a processional route traversing the area.

To summarise the results of these chapters, we may state that Hellenistic building complexes are characterised by a tight and apparently conscious mutual relationship between architecture and human action that goes beyond the singularity of individual sites. The connection of physical and social components is detectable on every layer of built space, being it general modes of design (Müller), religious experience (Williamson) and mental concepts (van 't Westeinde), specific characteristics of a particular site (Feuser *et al.*; Wescoat *et al.*; Agelidis), or even a certain building unit (Kobusch). As the contributions of Sporn and Steuernagel show, this interdependence is neither restricted to highly architecturalised spaces, nor to sacred buildings *per se*, but seems to transcend all space-transforming activity. As these chapters prove, past action and perception, although long faded, were so deeply inscribed into the physical remains of the Hellenistic age that we may (partially) recover them, even where no textual sources assist. This conference volume may therefore be seen as a contribution to the growing awareness that architecture and human action are entangled to such a degree that the one cannot be fully understood without the other.

Acknowledgements

The research for the paper is partially funded by the Deutsche Forschungsgemeinschaft (DFG, German Research Foundation – Projektnummer 2901391021 – SFB 1266).

References

Bergquist, B. 1967. *The Archaic Greek temenos: a study of structure and function*. Lund: Gleerup.

Betts, E. (ed.) 2017. *Senses of the empire: multisensory approaches to Roman culture*. e-publication: Taylor and Francis.

Boman, H. 2003. *Movement in space: an architectural analysis of public space in Archaic to Hellenistic Greece*. Thesis (PhD). University of Göteborg.

Bourdieu, P. 1977. *Outline of a theory of practice*. Cambridge: Cambridge University Press.

Bradley, M. (ed.) 2015. *Smell and the ancient senses*. London: Routledge.

Butler, S. and Nooter, S. (eds.) 2019. *Sound and the ancient senses*. London: Routledge.

Butler, S. and Purves, A. (eds.) 2013. *Synaesthesia and the ancient senses*. Durham: Acumen.

Chaniotis, A. (ed.) 2011. *Ritual dynamics in the ancient Mediterranean*. Stuttgart: Franz Steiner Verlag.

Day, J. (ed.) 2013. *Making senses of the past: toward a sensory archaeology*. Carondale: Southern Illinois University Press.

von Ehrenheim, H. 2015. *Greek incubation rituals in Classical and Hellenistic times*. Liège: Presses Universitaires de Liège.

Fedak, J. 1990. *Monumental tombs of the Hellenistic Age: a study of selected tombs from the pre-Classical to the Early Imperial Era*. Toronto: University of Toronto Press.

Foucault, P.M. 1978. *Dispositive der Macht:* Über *Sexualität, Wissen und Wahrheit*. Berlin: Merve.

Friese, W., Handberg, S., Kristensen, T.M. (eds.) 2019. *Ascending and descending the Acropolis: movement in Athenian religion*. Aarhus: Aarhus University Press.

Fyfe, F. 1936. *Hellenistic architecture: an introductory study*. Cambridge: University Press.

Giddens, A. 1984. *The constitution of society: outline of the theory of structuration*. Cambridge: Polity.

Gruben, G. 1966. *Die Tempel der Griechen*. München: Hirmer.

Haake, M. (ed.) 2011. *Griechische Heiligtümer als Erinnerungsorte: Von der Archaik bis in den Hellenismus*, Erträge einer internationalen Tagung in Münster, 20.-21. Januar 2006. Stuttgart: Franz Steiner.

Hamilakis, Y. 2014. *Archaeology and the senses: human experience, memory, and affect*. New York: Cambridge University Press.

Hartnett, J. 2017. *The Roman street: urban life and society in Pompeii, Herculaneum, and Rome*. Cambridge: Cambridge University Press.

Haug, A. and Kreuz, P.-A. (eds.) 2016. *Stadterfahrung als Sinneserfahrung in der römischen Kaiserzeit*. Turnhout: Brepols.

Heilmeyer, W.-D. and Hoepfner, W. (eds.) 1990. *Licht und Architektur*. Tübingen: Ernst Wasmuth Verlag.

Hekster, O., Schmidt-Hofner, S., Witschel, C. (eds.) 2009. *Ritual dynamics and religious change in the Roman Empire*. Leiden: Brill.

Hellmann, M.-C. 2002. *Les principes de construction*, L'architecture grecque 1. Paris: Librairie Générale Française.

Hellmann, M.-C. 2006. *Architecture religieuse et fúneraire*, L'architecture grecque 2. Paris: Librairie Générale Française.

Hellmann, M.-C. 2010. *Habitat, urbanisme et fortifications*, L'architecture grecque 3. Paris: Librairie Générale Française.

Kasper, M., Korenjak, M., Rollinger, R., Rudigier, A., (eds.) 2017. *Entdeckungen der Landschaft: Raum und Kultur in Geschichte und Gegenwart*. Wien: Böhlau Verlag.

Köhler, J. 1996. *Pompai: Untersuchungen zur hellenistischen Festkultur*. Frankfurt am Main: Lang.

Kouremenos, A., Chandrasekaran, S., Rossi, R. (eds.) 2011. *From Pella to Gandhara: hybridisation and identity in the art and architecture of the Hellenistic East*. Oxford: Archaeopress.

Kristensen, T.M. and Friese, W. (eds.) 2017. *Excavating pilgrimage: archaeological approaches to sacred travel and movement in the Ancient World*. London: Routledge.

Kurapkat, P.I., Schneider, U., Wulf-Rheidt, U. (eds.) 2014. *Die Architektur des Weges: Gestaltete Bewegung im gebauten Raum*, Internationales Kolloquium in Berlin, 8.-11. Februar 2012. Regensburg: Schnell & Steiner.

Laurence, R. and Newsome, D.J. 2011. *Rome, Ostia, and Pompeii: movement and space*. Oxford: Oxford University Press.

Lauter, H. 1986. *Die Architektur des Hellenismus*. Darmstadt: Wissenschaftliche Buchgesellschaft.

Matthaei, A. (ed.) 2009. *Stadtbilder im Hellenismus*, Die hellenistische Polis als Lebensform 1. Berlin: Verlag Antike.

Matthaei, A. (ed.) 2014. *Stadtkultur im Hellenismus*, Die hellenistische Polis als Lebensform 4. Heidelberg: Verlag Antike.

Matthaei, A. and Zimmermann, M. (eds.) 2015. *Urbane Strukturen und bürgerliche Identität im Hellenismus*, Die hellenistische Polis als Lebensform 5. Heidelberg: Verlag Antike.

Mortensen, E. and Poulsen, B. (eds.) 2017. *Cityscapes and monuments of Western Asia Minor: memories and identities*. Oxford: Oxbow Books.

Nielsen, I. 1994. *Hellenistic palaces: tradition and renewal*. Aarhus: Aarhus University Press.

Nielsen, I. 2002. *Cultic theatres and ritual drama: a study in regional development and religious interchange between East and West in antiquity*. Aarhus: Aarhus University Press.

Nora, P. 1984. *La République*. Les lieux de mémoire 1. Paris: Gallimard.

Nora, P. 1986. *La Nation*. Les lieux de mémoire 2. Paris: Gallimard.

Nora, P. 1992. *Les France*. Les lieux de mémoire 3. Paris: Gallimard.

Österberg, I., Malmberg, S., Bjørnebye, J. (eds.) 2016. *The moving city: processions, passages and promenades in Ancient Rome*. London: Bloomsbury Academic.

Olivier, H. (ed.) 2013. *4th century Karia: defining a Karian identity under the Hekatomnids*. Paris: de Boccard.

Piccoli, C. 2018. *Visualizing cityscapes of Classical Antiquity: from Early Modern reconstruction drawings to digital 3D models*. Summertown: Archaeopress.

Pirson, F. (ed.) 2012. *Manifestationen von Macht und Hierarchien in Stadtraum und Landschaft*, Wissenschaftliches Netzwerk der Abteilung Istanbul im Rahmen des Forschungsclusters 3 „Politische Räume“ des Deutschen Archäologischen Instituts. İstanbul: Ege Yayınları.

Popkin, M.L. 2016. *The architecture of the Roman triumph: monuments, memory, and identity*. Cambridge: Cambridge University Press.

Purves, A.C. (ed.) 2018. *Touch and the ancient senses*. London: Routledge.

Raja, R. (ed.) 2017. *Contextualizing the sacred in the Hellenistic and Roman Near East: religious identities in local, regional and Imperial settings*. Turnhout: Brepols.

Rice, E. 1983. *The grand procession of Ptolemy Philadelphus*. Oxford: Oxford University Press.

Rudolf, K.C. (ed.) 2018. *Taste and the ancient senses*. New York: Routledge.

Rumscheid, F. (ed.) 2009. *Die Karer und die Anderen*, Internationales Kolloquium an der Freien Universität Berlin, 13.-15. Oktober 2005. Bonn: Habelt.

Schneider, P.I. and Wulf-Rheidt, U. (eds.) 2011. *Licht – Konzepte in der vormodernen Architektur*, Internationales Kolloquium in Berlin, 26. Februar-1. März 2009. Regensburg: Schnell & Steiner.

Schwandner, E.-L. and Rheidt, K. (eds.) 1999. *Stadt und Umland: Neue Ergebnisse der archäologischen Bau- und Siedlungsforschung*, Bauforschungskolloquium in Berlin, 7.-10. Mai 1997. Mainz am Rhein: von Zabern.

Schwandner, E.-L. and Rheidt, K. (eds.) 2004. *Macht der Architektur: Architektur der Macht*, Bauforschungskolloquium in Berlin, 30. Oktober - 2. November 2002. Mainz am Rhein: von Zabern.

Sporn, K., Ladstätter, S., Kerschner, M. (eds.) 2015. *Natur – Kult – Raum*, Akten des internationalen Kolloquiums, 20.-22. Jänner 2012. Paris/London/Universität Salzburg/Wien: Österreichisches Archäologisches Institut.

Squire, M. 2016. *Sight and the ancient senses*. London: Routledge.

Stein-Hölkeskamp, E. (ed.) 2010. *Die griechische Welt: Erinnerungsorte der Antike*. München: Beck.

Stein-Hölkeskamp, E. and Hölkeskamp, K.-J. (eds.) 2006. *Die römische Welt: Erinnerungsorte der Antike*. München: Beck.

Williamson, C.G. 2012. *City and sanctuary in Hellenistic Asia Minor: constructing civic identity in the sacred landscapes of Mylasa and Stratonikeia in Karia*. Thesis (PhD). University of Groningen.

Winter, F.E., 2006. *Studies in Hellenistic architecture*. Toronto: University of Toronto Press.

Wörrle, M. and Zanker, P. (eds.) 1995. *Stadtbild und Bürgerbild im Hellenismus*, Kolloquium, 24.-26. Juni 1993 München. München: Beck.

Notes on contributors

Annette Haug - Institute of Classical Studies / Classical Archaeology, CAU Kiel (present). Studies of Classical Archaeology, Art History and Prehistory in Heidelberg and Paris; binational PhD Heidelberg and Paris 2003; Habilitation Leipzig 2009; LMU München Heisenberg Fellow; Full Professor of Classics, especially Classical Archaeology at the Christian-Albrechts-Universität zu Kiel 2012-; Co-Coordinator of the Kiel Graduate School 'Human Development in Landscapes' 2016-.

Asja Müller - Institute of Classical Archaeology, Freie Universität Berlin (present). Studies of Classical Archaeology, Prehistoric Archaeology, Experimental Archaeology and Egyptology at Leipzig and Exeter (UK); PhD Kiel 2017; Postdoc Research Fellow CRC 1266, project E3 at the Institute of Classical Studies / Classical Archaeology, CAU Kiel, 2016-2017; Travel Scholarship of the German Archaeological Institute 2017-2018; Assistant Professor at the Institute of Classical Archaeology, Freie Universität Berlin 2018-.

Part 1

Three sanctuaries as case studies

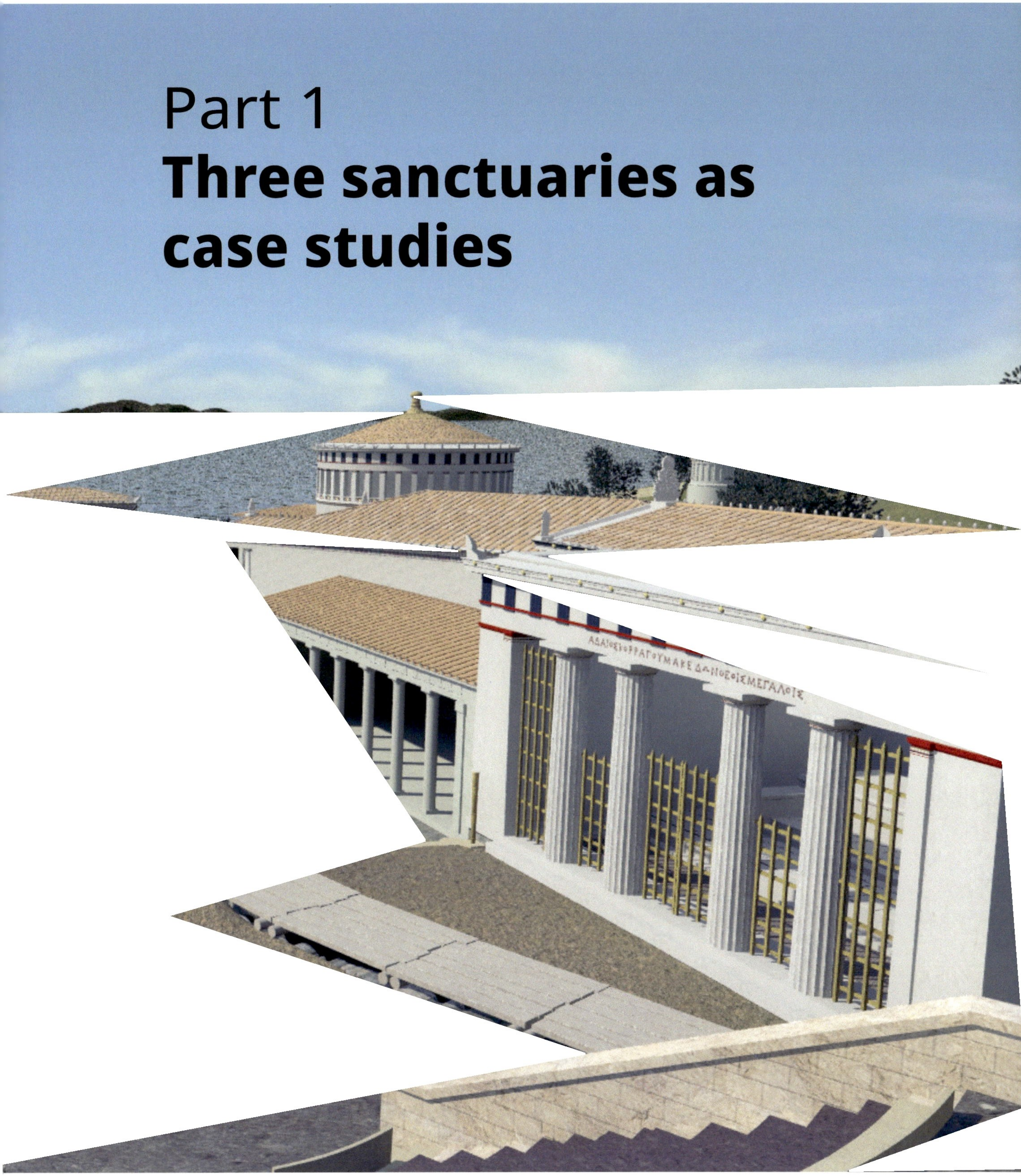

The Sanctuary of Artemis Limnatis in Messene: Natural Setting and Human Action

Stefan Feuser[1], Maria Spathi[2]

Abstract

Shortly after the founding of Messene in 369 BCE, the sanctuary of Artemis Limnatis was established on the south-eastern flank of Mount Ithome on a prominent rock spur. Based on the latest results of research carried out in the sanctuary, the article outlines the topography within the sanctuary and obtains a fresh look at how the different buildings were situated in the temenos and integrated into the natural landscape. Key questions are how the materiality of the architectural space altered the natural terrain and how the materially defined space of the sanctuary interrelated with the human action (worshipper/visitors approaching and moving within the sanctuary).

Keywords: Messene, Artemis, Sanctuary of Artemis Limnatis, Mount Ithome

Ancient Messene in the south-west Peloponnese is a crystallization point in the history of ancient Greece. The founding of the city in 369 BCE was a political act that marked the end of Sparta's long-standing predominance and was thus an ideological act. For the choice of the location as well as the topographic conception of the city of Messene, Mount Ithome was not only relevant as a fortification bulwark – it was associated with the revolt against Sparta in the 5th century BCE and considered a symbol of resistance (Luraghi 2008, p. 10) – but also as a traditional place of worship. The cult of Zeus Ithomatas on Mount Ithome's peak can be traced to before the new city's founding (Themelis 2004). The sanctuary of Artemis Limnatis and the so-called sanctuary of Eileithyia and the Kouretes (Spathi 2017) (Fig. 1) were founded on its southern slope. The sanctuary of Artemis Limnatis is located on the south-eastern flank of Ithome on a prominent rock spur outside the urban area but within the fortification wall. The fortification wall at Messene encompassed a large area of cultivated and pastoral land, which included the south slope of Mount Ithome with its sanctuaries (Müth 2010, pp. 57-83). The sanctuary's main building is the anta temple of Corinthian style, south of which are the remains of four smaller buildings

[1]Christian-Albrechts-Universität zu Kiel
Johanna-Mestorf-Str. 5
24118 Kiel
Germany
feuser@klassarch.uni-kiel.de

[2]Society of Messenian Archaeological Studies
33 Psaromiligkou Str
105 53 Athens
Greece

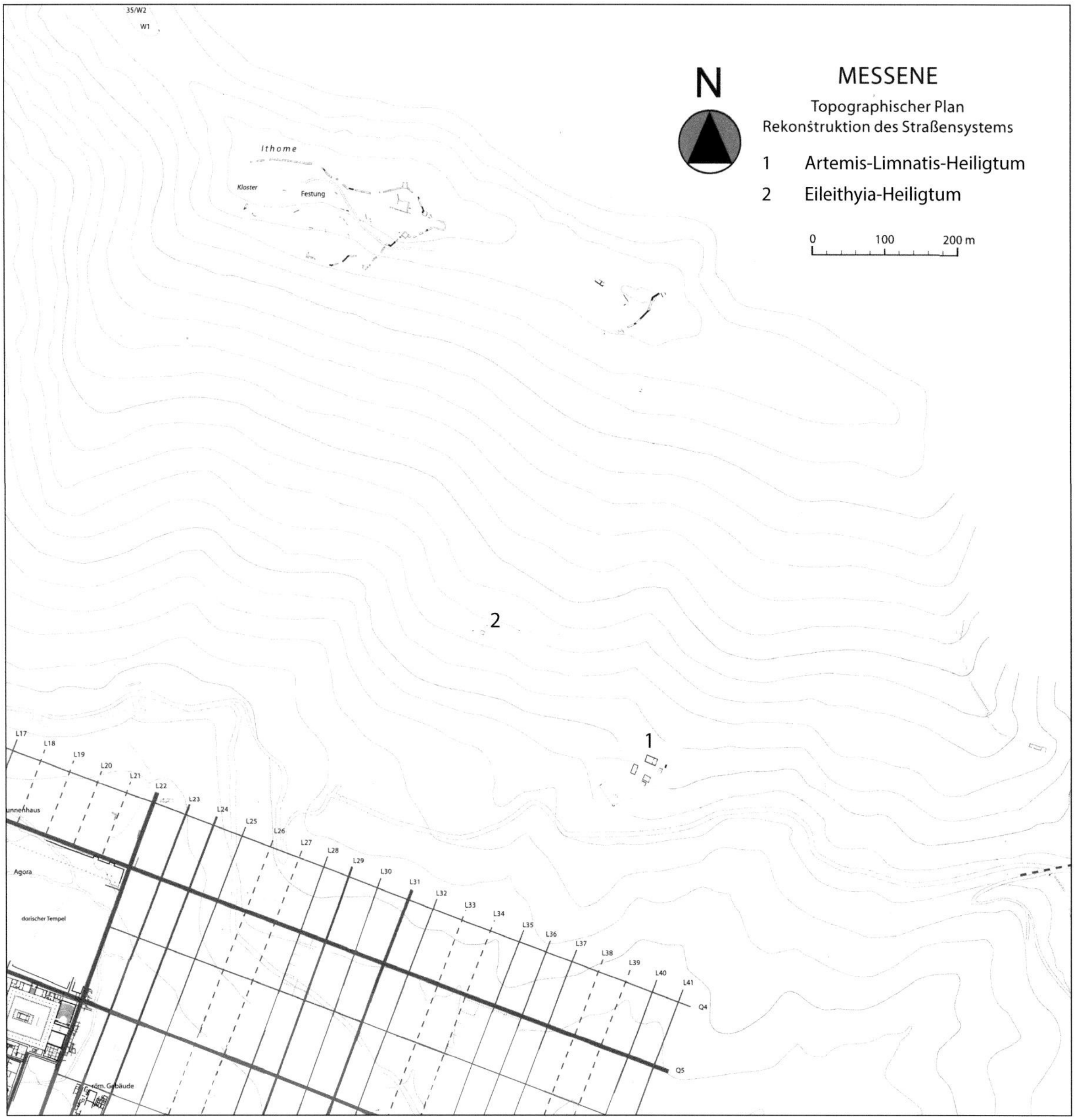

Figure 1. Messene. Plan of the city and Mount Ithome (Müth 2007, plan 1).

of different sizes arranged rectangular to the temple and tentatively interpreted as banquet buildings for ritual feasts (Wannagat and Linnemann 2017) (Fig. 2). About 15 m below there is a large terrace with what seems to be a small fountain house not aligned with the other buildings of the sanctuary.

The Artemis-Limnatis sanctuary was discovered in the early 19th century by Philip Le Bas. He concentrated primarily on the temple's excavation. Le Bas published his short report in 1844 in the 'Voyages et recherches archéologiques en Grèce et en Asie Mineure' (Le Bas 1844, pp. 426-432) and dated the temple 'postérieure d'au moins cent cinquante ans à la fondation de Messène' (Le Bas 1844, p. 427). The plan of the sanctuary was not published until 1888 (Reinach 1888, pp. 134-138). Through these publications, the sanctuary found its way into the specialist literature on Hellenistic architecture without ever having been seen or examined again (Lauter 1986, pp. 194-195). Only a comprehensive cleaning of the area in 1988 under Petros Themelis made the ruin accessible again. In the course of this work, previously unrecognized buildings directly below the temple came to light. This was the first indi-

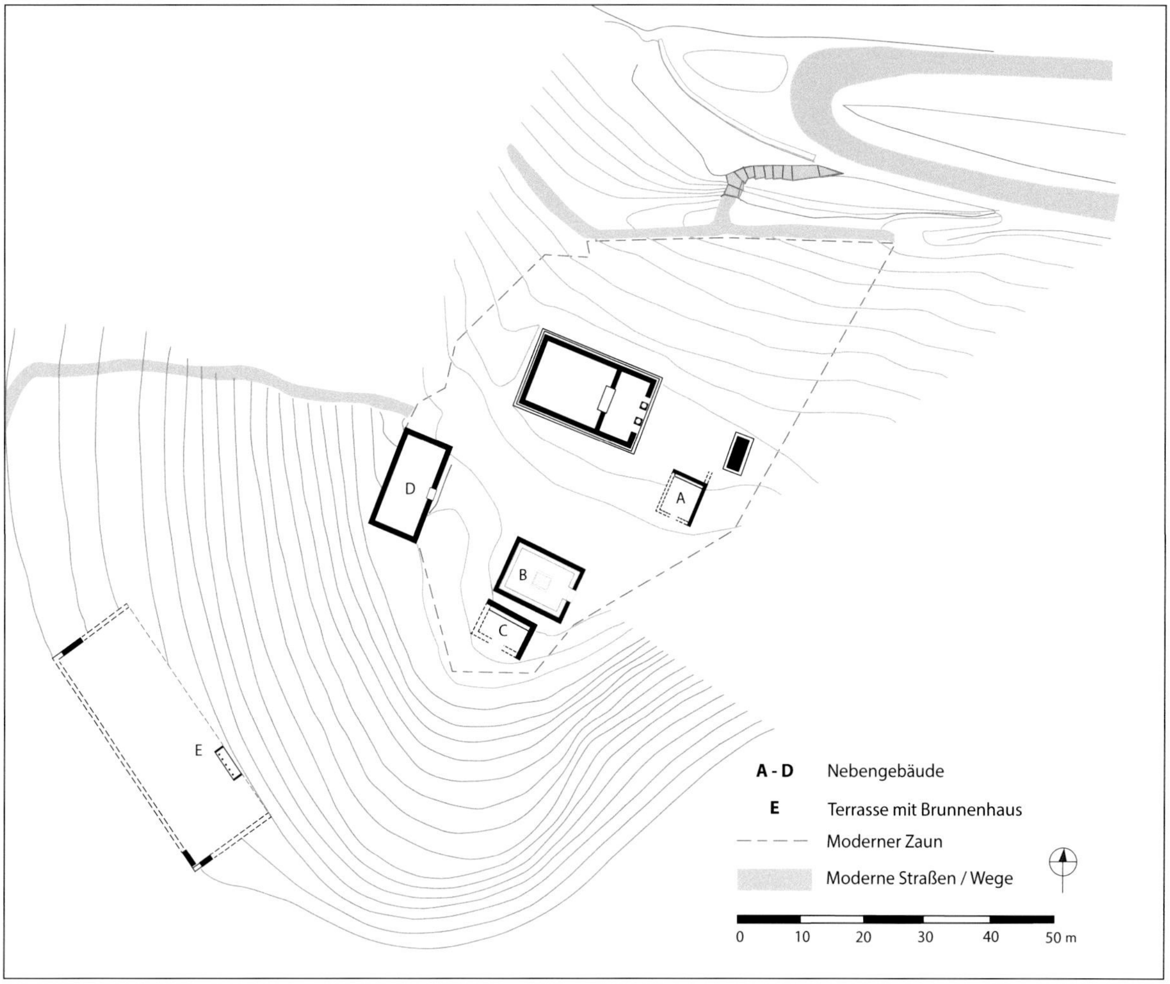

Figure 2. Messene. Plan of the Artemis Limnatis sanctuary (Wannagat and Linnemann 2017, p. 42 Fig. 3).

cation of the complex structure of the sanctuary with its various adjoining buildings. In 2006, Themelis also completely cleared the area of the Artemis temple with an intensive surface cleaning. In addition, small-scale excavations were carried out in the temple area, during which many small finds came to light (Themelis 2006; 2008).

In this chapter, we present the latest results of the research carried out in the sanctuary of Artemis Limnatis. We also outline the topography within the sanctuary and suggest an updated chronology. On this basis, we obtain a fresh view of how the different buildings were situated in the *temenos* and integrated in the natural landscape. Furthermore, we will acquire knowledge of how these buildings shaped the approach towards the sanctuary from the centre of the city as well as the movement within the sanctuary in this rather steep terrain. The sanctuary's founding in Early Hellenistic times as well as its location on a steep mountain ridge make the Artemis Limnatis sanctuary an important case study for the interrelationship between architecture, landscape, and human action.

The sanctuary of Artemis Limnatis: location, topography and buildings

The sanctuary of Artemis Limnatis lies on the south eastern slope of Mount Ithome on a prominent rocky spur at a height of approx. 500 m above sea level. The sanctuary's terrain slopes downwards with a steep gradient from north to

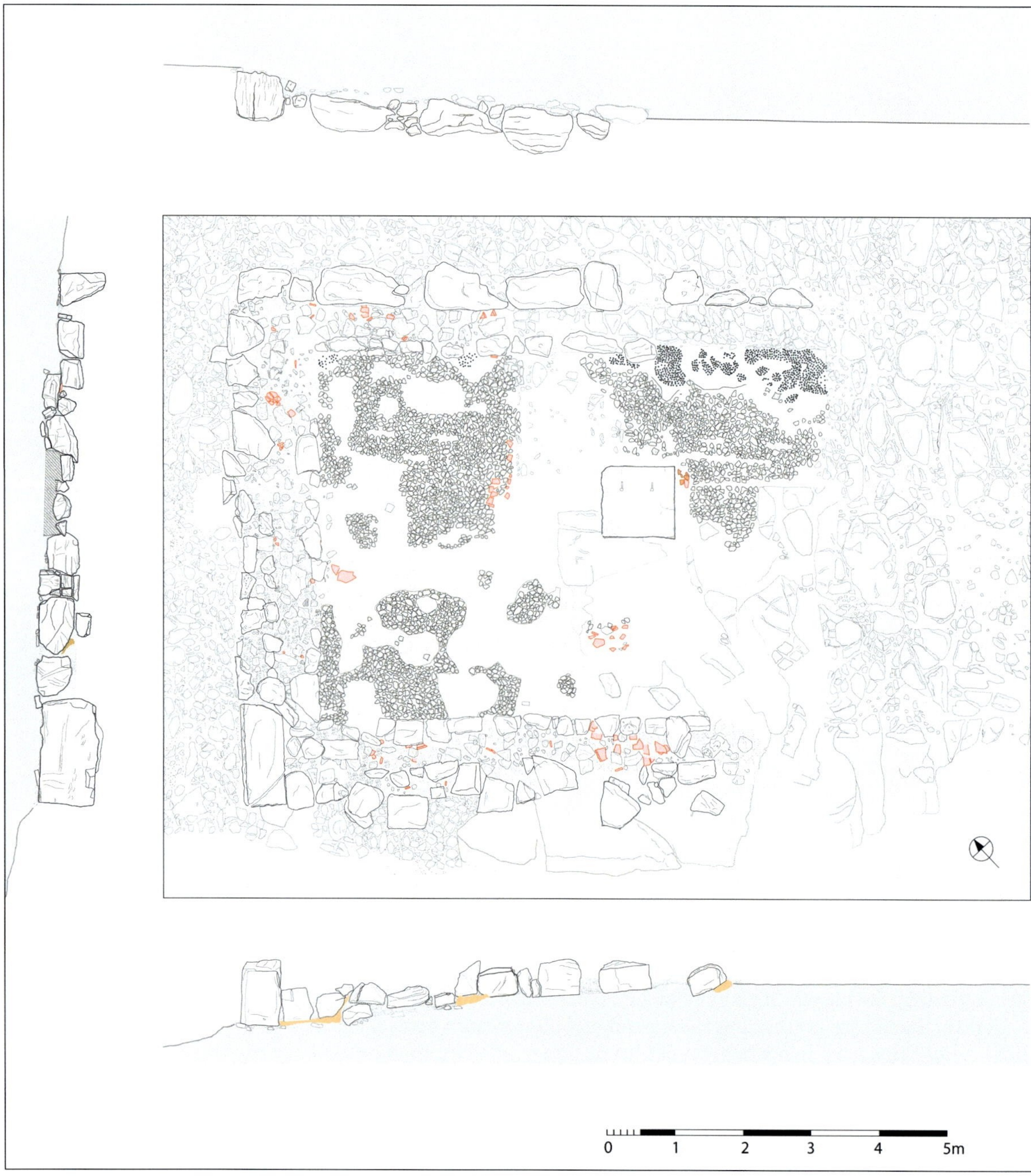

Figure 3. Messene. Building B. Ground plan and views. Remnants of the pebble mosaic are indicated by black dots in the north-eastern part of the interior (Wannagat and Linnemann 2017, p. 48 Fig. 15).

south. The difference in height between the Artemis temple and the southern end of the spur with buildings B, C, and D is up to five metres (Fig. 2).

The sanctuary is located outside the urban area but within the ring of the city wall. It is placed at a distance of about 800 m as the crow flies from the agora and 600 m from the Laconic gate, the city's main gate to the east. Due to its topographical position, the sanctuary was visible from the city centre further below and from the city's *chora* in the south.

The identification of the sanctuary with that of Artemis Limnatis is confirmed by a Hellenistic inscription found by Le Bas in the ruins of the temple and which names two Limnatis priestesses (*IG* V, 1, 1442). A second inscription, discovered in the Agora, mentions an 'ιέρειαν Λιμν[ατιδος] Αρτέμιδος' (*IG* V, 1 1458). Le Bas also brought to light three more manumission inscriptions, one of which preserves the name of Limnatis (*IG* V, 1, 1470, 1471, 1472).

The main building of the sanctuary is a Corinthian-style temple *in antis* oriented not exactly to the east, but turned about 25 degrees to the south-east. The temple measures 16.70 x 10.60 m and has two Corinthian columns *in antis*, a deep *pronaos*, and a wide *sekos*. The cult statue was located in the middle of the *sekos*, set atop a limestone base (fragments of the cult statue, now lost, were found by Le Bas). Approximately 15 m to the east, a rectangular altar was situated in line with the temple. South of the temple lie the remains of four adjoining buildings (A-D) of different sizes. The adjoining building A is located directly to the south-east of the temple and has a long rectangular floor plan. Buildings B and C are parallel to each other at the southern end of the ridge spur. Building D is located south-west of the temple at the edge of the plateau. About 15 m below there is a terrace with what seems to be a fountain house (E).

Building B was excavated in 2012 and 2013 (Wannagat and Linnemann 2017). The building has a width of approx. 7.50 m and a length of approx. 10.00 m (Fig. 3). Since the walls of the north, south, and west sides are completely closed, the entrance must have been located on the eastern side of the building. However, the precise location of the entrance on the east side and its layout are unclear. Inside the building, a podium runs along the interior with a depth of at least 62-70 cm. The floor was elaborately decorated with an ornamental pebble floor. Both building B's size and orientation parallel to the Artemis temple hint at the interpretation of a second temple within the sanctuary. Furthermore, it seems to be a characteristic feature of the temples within Messene, as a continuous stone bench also runs along the interior of the Eleithyia temple, (Spathi 2017) and appears in the sanctuary of Artemis Orthia along the walls of the side rooms (Themelis 1994, pp. 111. 122 Figs. 10. 12). However, the depth of the surrounding podium as well as the lack of an altar – building B's eastern front was so close to the steep slope that there was no space available for an altar – both suggest that building B was used as an assembly building lavishly decorated with a pebble floor (Wannagat and Linnemann 2017). The further study of the finds from the building's excavation will eventually clarify its use.

Building D is located along the south-western part of the *temenos* at the edge of the natural plateau on top of a rocky protrusion (Fig. 4). The building is rectangular in shape, measuring 11.25 x 6.25 m (Fig. 5). It was made of local limestone. Its walls consist of two facings: an interior facing made of irregular stones and an exterior pseudo-polygonal one. A threshold was found *in situ* in the middle of the building's eastern side, where the entrance was located. In 2016, the excavation of the area in front of the south-eastern corner reached 2.5 m in depth and revealed its foundations on the natural rock. Building D was erected on the western edge of the plateau in such a way that high substructures made of irregular ashlar masonry were necessary for the south and west sides. Due to the steep landscape, the western and southern walls of the building define the limits of the *temenos* to the lower lying terrain.

The space between the temple and adjoining buildings is not levelled by terrace walls but follows the natural slope relief.

About 15 m beneath the rock spur with the temple and the other buildings lies an approx. 40 x 10 m large terrace with a small spring house (6 x 2 m) in its southern part. To the east lies the cavity of the natural bedrock which produced water until the 1980s. Against the slope of the hill, the terrace consists of two retaining walls. To the west, the terrace is stabilized by two layers of ashlars. The foundations of a building structure in the north-eastern part could be the remains of a second fountain.

Figure 4. Messene. Artemis-Limnatis sanctuary. Building D. View from north-east with the agora in the background (photo: Deltev Wannagat).

The sanctuary of Artemis Limnatis: chronology

The earlier excavation and landscaping campaigns in the sanctuary of Artemis Limnatis yielded a quantity of pottery (mostly tableware) and terracotta figurines as well as various bronze finds. Most of the pottery and terracotta finds date from the late 4th to the 2nd century BCE. In addition to this tentative timeframe of the sanctuary's lifetime, the excavations in building D in the 2018 campaign revealed further important information about the date of the sanctuary's foundation. The architectural decoration of the temple was dated by Ralf Schenk to the end of the 3rd century BCE, however, this assessment was solely based on the drawings of Le Bas and not on an examination of the fragments (Schenk 1997, pp. 19-18).

The bulk of the ceramic assemblage was found north of Building D: some samples were unearthed during the excavation along the eastern side of the building and a few inside the building at the NW corner. The pottery consists mostly of tableware. Many fragments of plates came to light, among them a fish-plate and some examples featuring a broad rim with thickened edge (Rotroff 1997, pp. 146-149 Figs. 50. 51). The latter has its origin in the middle of the 5th century in Athens and can be traced through the Early Hellenistic period (Rotroff 1997, pp. 146-149 Figs. 50. 51). Additionally, there are fragments (mostly rims) of black-glazed plates with a projecting rim and plates with a horizontal rilled rim. This final type began being manufactured in Athens around 375 BCE (Rotroff 1997, Figs. 54. 55). At least one example has rouletting on its interior.

Figure 5. Messene. Artemis-Limnatis sanctuary. Building D. Ground plan (drawing: Nadine Marcinczik; graphic post-production: Detlev Wannagat and Brigitte Meyer).

Apart from the plates, there are also several fragments of echinus bowls, a type common from the 4th century onwards (Rotroff 1997, Figs. 62. 63) and of smaller bowls, the so-called footed saltcellars popular during the 4th century that survived into the Hellenistic period (Rotroff 1997, p. 167 Fig. 65). A large number of drinking vessels was also recovered, such as black-glazed *skyphoi* with horizontal handles, plain rim and ribbed body of the Attic type (Rotroff 1997, p. 94 Fig. 12), and many examples of *kantharoi* with moulded foot, plain or moulded rim, convex body below and a concave body above (Rotroff 1997, p. 83 Figs. 4. 5). Some examples from Messene have a ribbed lower body and 'Westslope' decoration between the handles. A single example of a one-handler was also found, a type popular in Athens during the 4th century that survived into the early years of the 3rd century (Rotroff 1997, pp. 155-156 Fig. 71). The example from Messene is somewhat different: the rim is moulded, the handle almost round-shaped, and the base lower than the Athenian one-handlers (for an example from Patras, see Petropoulos 2005, p. 66 Fig. 7).

Lastly, some near-whole vessels were found at the northwest corner of building D scattered around two Corinthian rooftiles. A black-glazed *kantharos* with moulded foot, plain rim, flat resting surface with a scraped groove and spur handles; another *kantharos*, similar to the baggy-type from Athens (Rotroff 1997), but with its upper body more concave and the lower un-grooved, a ring foot; and two black-glazed round-mouth juglets. They are similar to the Attic *chytridia* (Rotroff 1997, pp. 103-105 Figs. 16-18), but the handle does not rise high above the rim and they have a ring foot instead of a rather flat bottom. Quite a lot of small fragments of mould-made bowls, popular in the Peloponnese – main/primary site of production – were found not only in the sanctuary but also in various excavations throughout the city (Themelis 2005, pp. 95-106). There also came to light lids with knobs and miniature vessels, mostly *krateriskoi*. The latter type has been found at other sanctuaries in Messene, while in the so-called sanctuary of Eileithyia and the Kouretes, the majority consist of miniature *hydriai* (Spathi 2017). Generally, the aforementioned types of pottery were common and popular in the Greek world from the end of the 4th century into the first half of the 3rd century BCE, and some of them derived from classical types originating from Athens.

The excavation also yielded many *terracottas*, mostly figurines of Artemis. The goddess is generally represented standing, wearing a short chiton with an animal skin draped over, while a *stephane* rests on her head. Most of the terracotta dates from the Early Hellenistic period to the 2nd century BCE.

The findings from the sanctuary of Artemis Limnatis therefore suggest that it was founded shortly after the city. The majority of the finds can be dated from the Early Hellenistic period to the 2nd and 1st centuries BCE. It seems that from the beginning of the 2nd century BCE onwards, the city centre became more important with the establishment of the Asklepieion (on the extension of the Asklepieion in the first half of the 2nd century BCE, see Birtacha 2008 and Hayashida *et al.* 2013), whereas the sanctuaries on the slope of Mount Ithome began to play a secondary role in the political and religious life of the city. By the 2nd century AD at the latest, the Artemis Limnatis sanctuary was either no longer in use or of only minor importance, as Pausanias does not mention the sanctuary in his detailed descriptions of Messene, although he visited the summit of Ithome.

Materiality – The interrelation of architectural and natural space in the Artemis Limnatis sanctuary

The sanctuary of Artemis Limnatis is an interesting example of how the architectural space was set into the natural terrain with only slight adaptations thus creating a sacred space unique in its pristine appearance. On the south-facing ridge of the mountain spur, on which the sanctuary of Artemis Limnatis was located, only remarkably minor alterations to the natural landscape relief can be seen at present. The temple and altar were built on an extremely narrow surface that was not, or at best only very slightly, artificially enlarged. The temple was partially built with substructure walls, which remained visible, in order to level it out. (Fig. 6).

In view of the narrow surface on which the temple and altar were placed, the minor interventions in the structure of the spur back are particularly striking. The lack of a suitable building site can be clearly seen in the foundations of both the temple and building D. To level the temple, some of its long southern side and narrow western side were built with foundations that were visible as retaining walls. This concept of high foundations with partial backfill for the purpose of levelling and creating a building site was even more striking with building D, the largest of the ancillary buildings, where the south and west sides are also characterised by high retaining walls. These terraced measures for the extension of the building site are limited to the actual building areas on the hilltop; in the other parts of the sanctuary the rock spur's, the relief was not altered by building measures and level areas between the buildings were not created by such measures (Fig. 7).

There were no terraces laid out, but rather the architecture was integrated into the existing topography by using natural surfaces and elevations in a purposeful manner. At the same time individual building walls served as retaining walls and enabled the gradient to be equalised at certain points. Natural space requirements thus defined the dimensions of the buildings on the sanctuary's upper terrace, at least in their basic features.

Despite the steep topography, the buildings are orthogonally aligned (Fig. 2). Furthermore, even though the sanctuary is located outside the urban area, the temple and the adjoining buildings are aligned to the street grid (on the reconstruction of the street grid, see Müth 2007, pp. 235-278). The temple is not exactly oriented to the east, but turned about 25 degrees to the south-east, which is not due to the local topograph-

Figure 6. Messene. Artemis-Limnatis sanctuary. View from building D to the temple of Artemis (photo: Detlev Wannagat).

ical situation. In addition, the other adjoining buildings of the sanctuary take up this orientation. An orientation of the temple to the street grid is remarkable, since, as a result of the steep topography, none of the streets or *insulae* could have reached up to the Artemis Limnatis sanctuary. Therefore, the buildings of the sanctuary cannot have been aligned to one of the streets during the building process. Their erection must have been preceded by a conscious measurement and orientation to the street grid.

With terrace E, however, the case seems to be somewhat different as the architectural intervention into the natural topography appears to be more profound. In the south-eastern corner of the terrace, the rock spur has been worked off and a well house was erected, from which only the upper edge of the roofing of flat stone slabs is visible today. To the north, west, and south, shallow retaining walls create a level ground of approximately 40 x 10 m. These retaining walls had a height of no more than three layers of ashlars. Located in front of the towering rock spur and buildings on the upper terrace, these retaining walls were barely visible from a distance. Furthermore, terrace E took advantage of a natural plateau at this point of the topography and was not set on steep ground. Thus, the retaining walls' purpose was to establish an enclosed, level surface and not to create impressive views.

The question of whether the upper terrace with the temple and adjoining buildings and terrace E with the well house belong to one sanctuary has not yet been satisfactorily answered. The spatial proximity of the buildings to each other speaks in favour of a uniform complex. However, this argument is countered by the fact that the buildings on the lower and upper terraces are oriented differently. In addition, there is no direct access between them, as the steep terrain prevents a transition between the two terraces. Rather, it can be assumed that the sanctuary of Artemis Limnatis was limited to the upper terrace and that the temenos was primarily separated by the steep terrain. The lower

Figure 7. Messene. Artemis-Limnatis sanctuary. Western façade of building D with the collapsed south-western corner from west (photo: Detlev Wannagat).

terrace could have been a smaller source sanctuary at the entrance to Mount Ithome. Whatever this may be in detail, in the following analysis Terrace E shall also be taken into consideration since worshippers crossed it to approach the sanctuary of Artemis Limnatis on the upper terrace. Thus, the lower terrace is important for questions on how the sanctuary was approached. When comparing the Artemis Limnatis sanctuary in Messene to contemporary sanctuaries of the late 4th and early 3rd century BCE such as the Asclepieion of Athens, the sanctuary of Demeter in Pergamon or Sanctuary of Zeus in Labraunda, differences are apparent (for a detailed discussion of these sanctuaries, see Müller, in this volume). Whereas for the latter the steep topography was deeply altered by creating terraces to gain level building ground for temples, stoai, and banquet buildings, in the Artemis Limnatis sanctuary the steep terrain was left unchanged. The sacred space was wide and open, with only few architectural entities structuring it. While in the other sanctuaries the boundaries were clearly marked by walls and gates, the limits of the Artemis Limnatis sanctuary – the natural edge of the plateau – were obscured and only visible when directly approaching them.

Space – Approaching the sanctuary

The worshippers approached the sanctuary from the city centre of Messene with the agora and the other main buildings. Except for building A, all other buildings of the sanctuary were visible from a distance. However, their symmetry was not visible to the viewer. During their ascent, the pilgrims saw the ensemble of building D with the temple of Artemis behind it over all other structures. The fact that both

Figure 8. Messene. Artemis-Limnatis sanctuary. View from west with Artemis temple and altar in the centre, building D to the right on lower ground (photo: Detlev Wannagat).

buildings' high retaining walls faced south-west made the sanctuary appear as if it had been erected on terraces (Fig. 8).

Ascending the lower flank of Mount Ithome, building D and the Artemis temple were always visible to the worshippers. Despite its size, terrace E made no visible impression on those approaching the sanctuary because of its lack of high retaining walls. Before arriving at the upper plateau, the worshippers first entered terrace E and had access to at least one fountain house – presumably for ritual purification. With a size of 40 x 10 m, the terrace provided space for a large group of people to perform rituals. When facing Mount Ithome from below, only building D in the Artemis Limnatis sanctuary would have been visible. In the other direction the worshippers saw the prospect of the lower lying city centre.

The worshippers left terrace E from its eastern end and followed the ascending terrain to the north. The recently established digital elevation model has now shown that a slight depression – today hidden under the Macchie – runs up the slope to the north directly east of the rock spur (Fig. 9). Most probably, this was the path that worshippers took when ascending Mount Ithome. While following this narrow path, the visitors could see the Artemis temple on their left.

The precise location of the entrance to the sanctuary is unknown. Due to the topography, it must have been located to the altar's north-east so that the temple, altar and adjoining buildings lay below the visitors. The steep gradient makes it very unlikely that the entrance was further south. An approach from the north is also implausible as the terrain is rising steeply north of the temple and altar. The architectural layout of such an entrance cannot yet be verified with certainty. An elaborately designed *propylon* is, however, unlikely as the borders

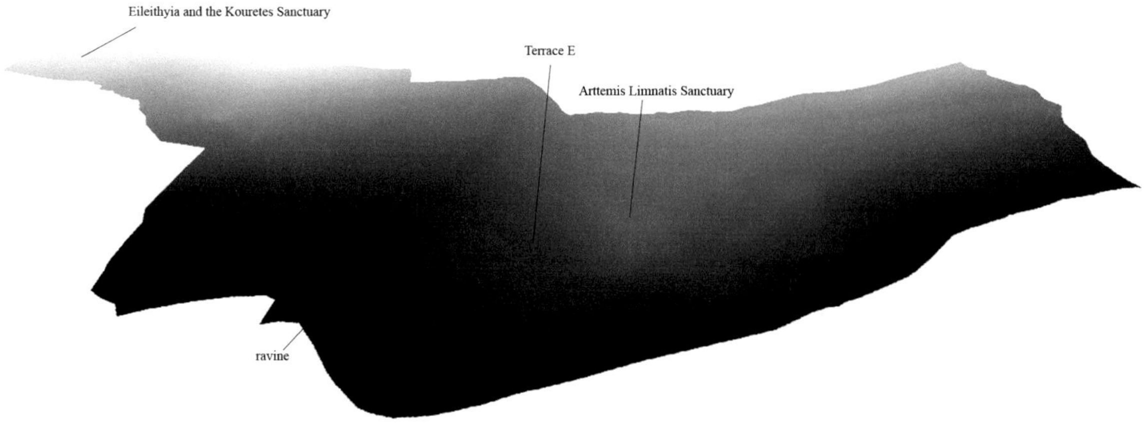

Figure 9. Messene. Artemis-Limnatis sanctuary. Digital terrain model of the Artemis Limnatis sanctuary and its surroundings (Florian Bauer, Kilian Etter and Juri Klusak, Institute of Geography of the Christian-Albrechts-University of Kiel, Chair of Landscape Ecology and Geoinformatics).

of the sanctuary seemed to have been mainly defined by its steep terrain and the slopes, thus an architecturally-defined delimitation of the temenos is unlikely.

Movement within the sanctuary

Presumably, the worshippers entered the sanctuary on higher ground from the north-east of the altar. The symmetric layout of the sanctuary was visible from this elevated position. The first buildings the visitors arrived at were the altar and the temple as theses were the sanctuaries' focal points of worship. From there, the adjoining buildings A, B, and D were visible. Only building C was hidden behind building B. From the altar and the temple, the worshippers basically had the choice between different ways of moving in the sanctuary. However, the natural terrain and the orientation of the building's entrances both guided them: from the altar and the temple, building A could be reached easily within a few steps. Its entrance, however, was oriented towards the south so that visitors had to move downwards first. From building A, the entrance of building B was visible. The natural terrain guided the worshippers to the southern end of the spur, where buildings B and C stood. The entrances to these two buildings, however, were not oriented towards the same direction so that visitors had to move around building B's northern and western façade to access building C through its south-facing entrance. From there the worshippers could walk over to building D which is situated on the same level as the entrance to building C but approx. 2 m lower than building B and approx. 5 m lower than the temple. Thus, the combination of the natural terrain and the materially-defined space – the position of the buildings – functioned as a guide for people coming to the sanctuary.

The positioning of the entrances of the adjoining buildings not only led the visitors through the sanctuary, but also fostered the physical experience of the steep terrain. With buildings A and C, the entrances were placed in such a way that visitors first had to walk down the slope and around the corner of the respective building before they finally reached the entrance, moving slightly up the terrain again. The entrances to buildings B and C are oriented towards the edge of the plateau where the visitors had to walk on restricted and precarious grounds. This orientation was deliberately chosen because access would have been possible without any problems from another path. Moving to the different buildings in the sanctuary created a unique physical experience of the topographical situation that may have been part of the sacred and sublime experience (for constructing the sublime in Hellenistic sanctuaries, see Williamson, in this volume). Furthermore, the views of the landscape from buildings B and C, interpreted as banquet buildings, were another reason for the awkward orientation of their entrances.

Views of the landscape were thus an integral part of the design of the sanctuary. Visually, the sanctuary had an open character so that views into the surrounding landscape were possible from each point within it. As pointed out, the entrances to the adjoining buildings were oriented in such a way that visitors approaching them had multiple views of the lower lying city and the surrounding hills. For worshippers entering the sanctuary from the northeast, these views were the backdrop in which the temple and the adjoining buildings were set. While the sloping terrain and adjoining buildings guided visitors through the sanctuary, it is not known how the worshippers left the sanctuary. An exit could have existed north of building D from where it was possible to further ascend Mount Ithome to the so-called sanctuary of Eileithyia and the Kouretes to the north-west and the sanctuary of Zeus Ithomatas on top. Another option is that worshippers walked the path back up and left the sanctuary through the presumed entrance in the north-east.

Conclusion

Our recent archaeological work revealed that the sanctuary of Artemis Limnatis was established in Early Hellenistic times shortly after the foundation of Messene. It lies on the south-eastern slope of Mount Ithome on a prominent rocky spur with only remarkably minor alterations to the natural landscape relief. The temple, the altar, and the four adjoining buildings were erected on extremely narrow surfaces that were not, or at best only very slightly, artificially enlarged. The temple as well as building D were partially built with substructure walls. Thus, the architectural space was set into the natural terrain with only slight adaptations. The sacred space was wide and open with only few architectural entities structuring it. Its limits – the natural edge of the plateau – were obscured and only visible when directly approaching them.

With its temple, the four adjoining buildings, and the terrace on lower grounds, the sanctuary is an example of how architecture was set into the natural topography in order to create different impressions for people approaching it and for those moving within it. When seeing the sanctuary from Messene's city centre and approaching it from the south-east, the staggered architecture of building D and the Artemis temple with its lofty retaining walls gave the impression of a sanctuary erected on terraces. This façade was created for those viewing or approaching the sanctuary from the city centre in the south-west. However, for those moving within the sanctuary, the Artemis temple and the four adjoining buildings were set and integrated in the natural topography of Mount Ithome with only slight alterations of the natural terrain.

As the terrain in the sanctuary was not levelled, and with a difference in height of approx. 5 m between the temple and the adjoining buildings C and D, movement within the sanctuary was a physical exercise. The positioning of the entrances to these buildings further fostered the physical experience of the steep terrain as visitors had to descend and ascend several times and walk close to the plateau's edge to approach the buildings' entrances. Without any architectonical boundaries, visual connections to the lower lying city and prospects into the surrounding landscape were an integral part of the sanctuary's design. These landscape views were visual backdrops for the temple and the adjoining buildings.

Acknowledgements

Our first thanks go to Petros Themelis and his colleagues for the opportunity to carry out the work presented here within the framework of his excavation project in Messene. The work in the Artemis Limnatis sanctuary has been funded by the Fritz Thyssen Foundation (2011/2012), the University of Rostock (2016), private donors, and in 2018 by the CRC 1266 Scales of Transformations (funded by the Deutsche Forschungsgemeinschaft

[DFG, German Research Foundation – Projektnummer 2901391021 – SFB 1266]). Our sincere thanks go to all persons and institutions for their support.

The UAV survey and the subsequent generation of the digital elevation model were carried out in 2018 by Florian Bauer, Kilian Etter, and Juri Klusak from the Institute of Geography of the Christian-Albrechts-University of Kiel, Chair of Landscape Ecology and Geoinformatics. Torben Kessler, Christian-Albrechts-University of Kiel, Institute of Classics / Classical Archaeology assisted the UAV survey. Nadine Marcinczik, Berlin, produced amongst others the drawings of adjoining building D in the campaign 2018. We would like to express our warmest thanks to the aforementioned for their dedicated work in Messene.

References

Birtacha, P. 2008. Το Ωδείο καί το ανατολικό πρόπυλο του Ασκληπιείου. Athen: Hē en Athēnais Archaiologikē Hetaireia.

Hayashida, Y., Yoshitake, R., Ito, J. 2013. *Architectural study of the stoas of the Asklepieion at Ancient Messene*. Fukuoka: Kyushu University Press.

Lauter, H. 1986. *Die Architektur des Hellenismus*. Darmstadt: Wissenschaftliche Buchgesellschaft.

Le Bas, P. 1844. Voyages et recherches archéologiques en Grèce et en Asie Mineure. *Revue Archéologique* 1 (2), 426-432.

Luraghi, N. 2008. *The Ancient Messenians: construction of ethnicity and memory*. New York: Cambridge University Press.

Müth, S. 2007. *Eigene Wege: Topographie und Stadtplan von Messene in spätklassisch-hellenistischer Zeit*. Rahden/Westf.: Verlag Marie Leidorf GmbH.

Müth, S. 2010. Fortifikationskunst und Repräsentation an der Stadtmauer von Messene, in: Lorentzen, J., Pirson, F., Schneider, P.I., Wulf-Rheidt, U. (eds.). *Aktuelle Forschungen zur Konstruktion, Funktion und Semantik antiker Stadtbefestigungen*, Kolloquium 9.-10. Februar 2007 Istanbul. Istanbul: Ege Yayınları, 57-83.

Petropoulos, M. 2005. Το βόρειο νεκροταφείο των αρχαίων Πατρών: Οικόπεδο οδού Πουκεβίλ 25-27, in: Greece. 6. Ephoreia Proistorikōn kai Klasikōn Archaiotētōn (ed.). *Ελληνιστική κεραμική από την Πελοπόννησο*. Athens: ΥΠΠΟ, ΣΤ΄ ΕΠΚΑ, 59-72.

Reinach, S. 1888. *Voyages archéologiques en Grèce et on Asie Mineure sous la direction de M. Philippe Le Bas*. Paris: Firmin-Didot et Cie.

Rotroff, S.I. 1997. *Hellenistic pottery: Athenian and imported wheelmade table ware and related material*, Agora XXIX. Princeton: American School of Classical Studies at Athens.

Schenk, R. 1997. *Der korinthische Tempel bis zum Ende des Prinzipats des Augustus*. Rahden/Westf.: Verlag Marie Leidorf GmbH.

Spathi, M. 2017. The votive offerings from the sanctuaries of Ancient Messene as an indication of the cultic identity: The Example of the Sanctuary of Eileithyia and the Kouretes on Mount Ithome, in: Themelis P., Spathi, M., Psaroudakis, K. (eds.). *Sanctuaries and cults of Ancient Messene: from the pre-Classical to the Byzantine Period*. Athens: Society of Messenian Archaeological Studies, 55-92.

Themelis, P. 1994. Artemis Ortheia at Messene: the epigraphical and archaeological evidence, in: Hägg, R. (ed.). *Ancient Greek cult practice from the epigraphical evidence*, Proceedings of the 2nd International Seminar on Ancient Greek Cult organized by the Swedish Institute at Athens, 22-24 November 1991. Stockholm: Svenska Institutet i Athen, 101-122.

Themelis, P. 2004. Cults on Mount Ithome. *Kernos* 17, 143-154.

Themelis, P. 2005. Η ελληνιστική κεραμική της Μεσσήνης, in: Greece. 6. Ephoreia Proistorikōn kai Klasikōn Archaiotētōn (ed.). *Ελληνιστική κεραμική από την Πελοπόννησο*. Athens: ΥΠΠΟ, ΣΤ΄ ΕΠΚΑ, 95-106.

Themelis, P. 2006. Ανασκαφή Μεσσήνης. *Πρακτικά της εν Αθήναις Αρχαιολογικής Εταιρείας*, 31-67.

Themelis, P. 2008. Ανασκαφή Μεσσήνης. *Πρακτικά της εν Αθήναις Αρχαιολογικής Εταιρείας*, 31-50.

Wannagat, D. and Linnemann, J. 2017. Ein Versammlungsgebäude im Heiligtum der Artemis Limnatis von Messene, in: Themelis, P., Spathi, M., Psaroudakis, K. (eds.). *Sanctuaries and cults of Ancient Messene: from the pre-Classical to the Byzantine Period*. Athens: Society of Messenian Archaeological Studies, 29-54.

Notes on contributors

Stefan Feuser - Institute of Classical Studies / Classical Archaeology, CAU Kiel (present). Studies of Classical Archaeology, Ancient History and Pre- and Protohistory in Münster and Berlin; PhD Münster 2008; Habilitation Rostock 2017; Temporary Professor (5 years) of Classical Archaeology at the Christian-Albrechts-Universität zu Kiel 2016-; Coordinator of the Strategic Partnership „Ancient Cities“ (ERASMUS+) 2017-.

Maria Spathi - Society of Messenian Archaeological Studies (present). Studies of Classical Archaeology and History in Athens; PhD Würzburg, 2006; Research Fellow at the University of Rostock; Research Fellow at the DAI (German Archaeological Institute) in Berlin; Lecturer at the University in Crete; Archaeological Service, Greek Ministry of Culture.

Interstitial Space in the Sanctuary of the Great Gods on Samothrace

Bonna D. Wescoat[1], Susan Ludi Blevins[2], Maggie L. Popkin[3], Jessica Paga[4], Andrew Farinholt Ward[5], Michael C. Page[6], William Size[7]

Abstract

The interstitium, a network of fluid-filled spaces forming a coherent organ of translocation within the body, maps well onto our investigations of the Hellenistic Sanctuary of the Great Gods on Samothrace. The cognate interstitium of spaces, pathways, and viewscapes within the sanctuary share a similar flexible and connective coherence. Through examining experiential aspects of passages leading from the entrance to the Central Sanctuary, across the seasonal torrent, and to the theatre and terrace in front of the Stoa, we argue that the interstitial network within the sanctuary emerges as a critical mediator of the reciprocal relationships between architecture, landscape, and human actors in the construction of sacred space.

Keywords: Samothrace, interstitium, sacred landscape, experience, materiality

[1]Emory University
M40 Carlos Hall
GA 30322 Atlanta
United States of America
bwescoa@emory.edu

[2]Dexter Southfield School
20 Newton Street
MA 02455 Brookline
United States of America
sludi@emory.edu

[3]Case Western Reserve University
Mather House 318
OH 44106 Cleveland
United States of America
maggie.popkin@case.edu

[4]William & Mary
Morton Hall 324
VA 23185 Williamsburg
United States of America
jpaga@wm.edu

[5]William & Mary
Mortan Hall 334
VA 23185 Williamsburg
United States of America
alward01@wm.edu

[6]Emory University
Department of Environmental Sciences
400 Dowman Drive
GA 30322 Atlanta
United States of America
michael.page@emory.edu

[7]emeritus, Emory University
Department of Environmental Sciences
GA 30322 Atlanta
United States of America
wsize@emory.edu

Figure 1. Samothrace. Sanctuary of the Great Gods (Evros, Greece). Digital model of the reconstructed sanctuary (model: American Excavations Samothrace).

In 2018, scientists published new findings suggesting that the fluid-filled network of connective tissue found throughout the human body, called the *interstitium*, is sufficiently coherent in structure and function to be defined as an organ – the largest – of the body (Benias *et al.* 2018). This previously unacknowledged 'highway of moving fluid', once articulated, displays a unity of structure and function across the body; according to one of the co-authors, 'Once you see it, you can't unsee it' (Howard 2018). Scientists further assert that it is impossible to understand the mechanical properties of any tissue in the human body without understanding the functional potential of the *interstitium*, for the *interstitium* and the tissues it connects are interdependent. Understanding the *interstitium* as an organ of translocation within the human body tracks well with emerging strategies for investigating and understanding ancient Greek sacred environments. To translate the hermeneutic metaphor into architectural terms, we envision the *interstitium* as composed of the pathways, nodes, marginal spaces, and surrounding landscape that are traversed by and frame human action within the built environment. Such categories find a place in Kevin Lynch's 1960s seminal work arguing that urban images are composed of paths, edges, districts, nodes, and landmarks (Lynch 1960). Lynch's theories found fertile ground in work on the ancient city examining the experiential impact of buildings and the urban spaces that connect them (e.g., Favro 1996; 2014); and increasingly studies of sacred space privilege the kinesthetic passages (e.g., Hollinshead 2015). We emphasize the organic capacity of these connectors and construe their tension within the natural environment as determining factors in the efficacy of sacred space. By taking the 'connective tissue' between buildings – that is, the spaces, kinaesthetic passages, and viewscapes – as components equal to the natural landscape and the buildings themselves in the construction, function, and experience of sacred space, we necessarily privilege human action as the essential constituent binding architecture and landscape. One such place that repays this approach is the Sanctuary of the Great Gods on Samothrace (Figs. 1 and 2).

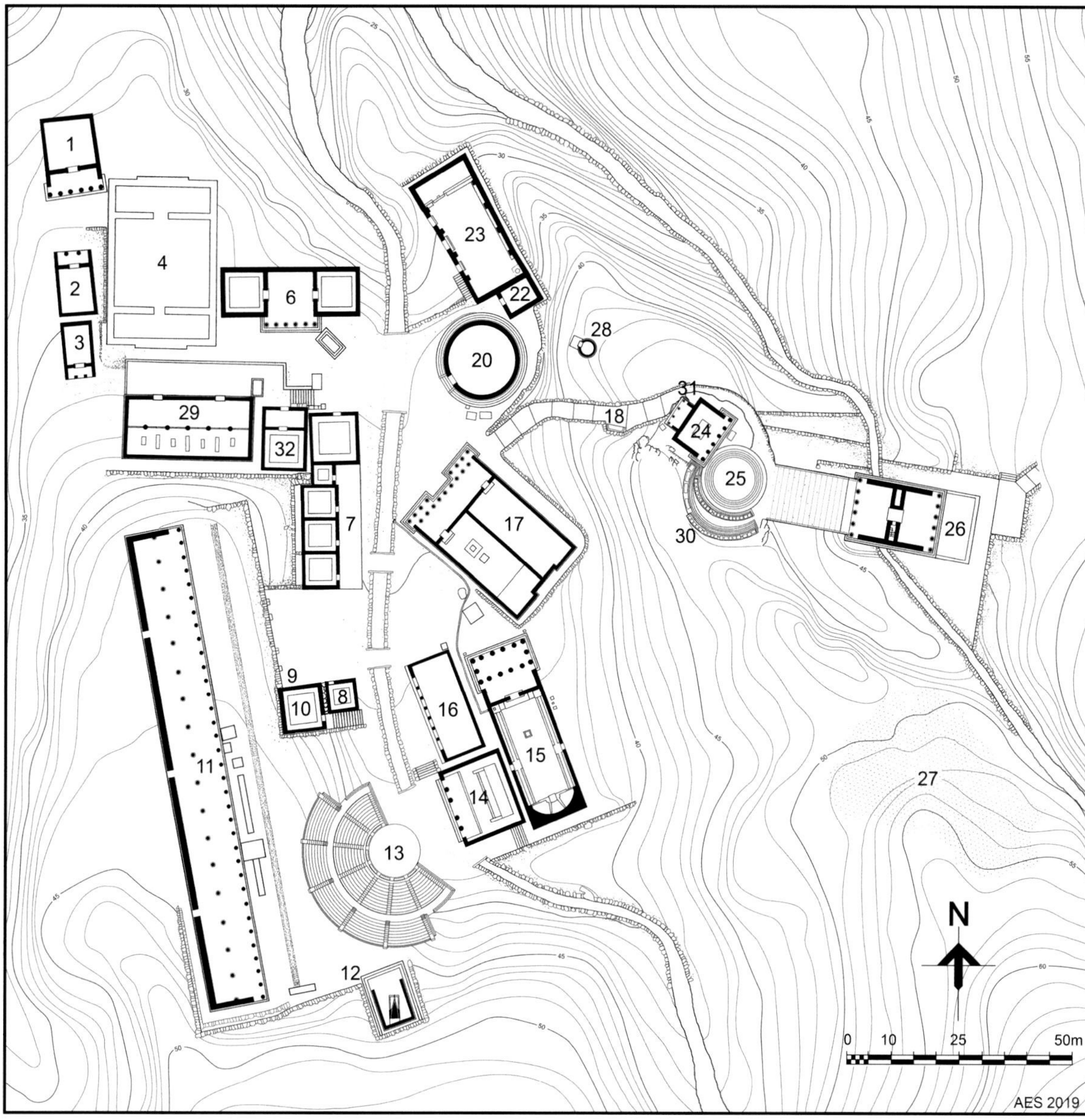

Figure 2. Samothrace. Sanctuary of the Great Gods (Evros, Greece). Restored plan of the sanctuary. 1, 2, 3 Unidentified Late Hellenistic buildings; 4 Unfinished Early Hellenistic building (Building A); 6 Milesian Dedication; 7, 8, 10 Dining rooms; 9 Archaistic niche; 11 Stoa; 12 Nike Monument; 13 Theatre; 14 Altar Court; 15 Hieron; 16 Hall of Votive Gifts; 17 Hall of Choral Dancers; 18 Sacred Way; 20 Rotunda of Arsinoe II; 22 Sacristy; 23 Anaktoron; 24 Dedication of Philip III and Alexander IV; 25 Theatral Circle; 26 Propylon of Ptolemy II; 27 South Nekropolis: 28 Doric Rotunda; 29 Neorion; 30 Stepped Retaining Wall; 31 Ionic Porch; 32 Hestiatorion (plan: American Excavations Samothrace).

The Sanctuary of the Great Gods is a strikingly evocative place, even within the dramatic landscape of the windswept, northern Aegean island of Samothrace. Nestled in a valley on the northern coast of the island where the slopes of the Agios Giorgios ridge broaden to meet the sea, the sanctuary was built across plateaus and valleys formed by seasonal torrents that frame and bisect the *temenos*. From its vantage in the north-eastern Aegean, the island and its sanctuary were well poised to communicate with Thrace and Anatolia as well as the Greek islands and mainland through pilgrimage, travel, and trade. Although the cult shows signs of activity in the 7th century BCE, it rose to prominence in the Hellenistic and Early Imperial periods. Travelers from across the Mediterranean braved the arduous sea journey to the island to be initiated into the sanctuary's famous mystery cult (Dimitrova 2008), whose secret rites offered both physical protection at sea and moral benefit (for ancient *testimonia*, see Lewis 1959, pp. 102-114 nos. 226-241). Vital to the Samothracian community and patronized by royal, elite, and ordinary people alike, the Sanctuary of the Great Gods offers a powerful instance of how multiple social communities shaped an extraordinary sacred environment.

While the secret initiatory rites remain opaque to us, we can gain some sense of the experience by following human movement through the sanctuary's rugged terrain. A complex nexus of spaces, passages, and viewscapes defined an *interstitium* that reached the key destinations, not always following the path of least resistance. Our ongoing research in the sanctuary explores how these components helped construct visitors' experiences, based on the premise that each intervention – the construction of a building, the erection of a monument, the levelling of earth, the bridging of a ravine – must be understood in relationship to and as part of the intricate topography of the sanctuary and the movements of visitors within it. Augmenting archaeological investigation with 3D modelling, both in fixed platform animation and in real-time interactivity, has offered a powerful tool for visualizing and assessing the sanctuary's interstitial space, which ultimately emerges as a critical mediator of the reciprocal relationships between architecture, passage, landscape, and human actors.

From our exploration of several regions in the sanctuary, key themes emerge. First, we argue that in the interstitial spaces of the sanctuary, one set of human actors – makers (patrons and Samothracian overseers and masons) – simultaneously exploited landscape and architecture to shape an evocative experience for another set of actors – users (prospective initiates, *theoroi*, and other visitors). Second, we consider how human interaction with the environment – be it through manipulation of lighting, materials, or architectural constructions – affected the sanctuary's experiential potential. Finally, we argue that builders in the sanctuary purposefully created permeable, transitional zones between interstitial spaces and the bounded interior spaces of architectural structures, much as the human *interstitium* has matrix walls with permeable sections that allow communication between the *interstitium* and other human tissue.

Experiential opposites and the Eastern Hill: entering and leaving, descent and ascent, light and shadow

The powerful reciprocity between landscape, architecture, and human action originally rose to the forefront of our research initiative in response to the remarkable entrance complex spanning from the Propylon of Ptolemy II to the Eastern Hill (Fig. 2, nos. 24-26. 30-31). The complexities of the landscape and its subtle manipulation by Samothracian builders to achieve powerful experiential and visual effects over half a millennium could only be understood as a series of initiatives and responses centred on the actions of entering and leaving the sanctuary. The advent of new technologies allowed us to query this reciprocity – spatially, visually, and temporally – using 3D modelling and computer graphics. This work has been presented elsewhere (Wescoat 2012; 2017a; 2017b; 2020); we include it here insofar as it established the groundwork for exploring other regions of the site from a similar vantage.

Time of day, direction of action, and degree of knowledge profoundly affected a visitor's experience. Even though the visitor followed the identical interstitial path, entering the sanctuary – at night, in anticipation of the rites of initiation that heretofore had been kept secret, and descending from the Propylon of Ptolemy II to the

Figure 3. Samothrace. Sanctuary of the Great Gods (Evros, Greece). Digital reconstruction of the Sacred Way at night, looking west into the sanctuary (model: American Excavations Samothrace).

centre of the sanctuary where the primary cult buildings were sequestered – would have been fundamentally different from the experience of leaving the sanctuary – in the light of day, ascending the Sacred Way, and with knowledge of the initiatory rites. So much is obvious but not sufficiently called out in discussions of ritual experience: direction and lighting influenced what visitors could see at any moment along the path; the momentum of their bodies moving down (or up) the steep Sacred Way affected where and how they looked at their surroundings; turns in the pathway created and subverted expectations; and spaces along the route constricted and expanded, thus affecting whether visitors could walk in groups or only proceed in single file (on movement generally, see Hollinshead 2015).

Anticipation of the rites of initiation kept visitors who entered at night (Fig. 3) focused on what lay before them: first the Propylon of Ptolemy II (26); then the plunging descent on stepped ramp into the sunken *orchestra* of the Theatral Circle (25), framed by tiers of bronze statues (30) and the marble 'exedra' dedicated by of the successors of Alexander the Great, Philip III, and Alexander IV, to the Great Gods (25). A second passage took visitors around the sharp outcropping of bedrock and into another stepped ramp (18), from which they would see the Doric gallery of the Rotunda of Arsinoe (20) and, in the distance, the Stoa. The space tightened both visually and physically as visitors reached the valley floor. A turn to the north opened into a narrow triangular *plateia* before the principal cult building, the Hall of Choral Dancers (17) (see Paragraph: Materiality, landscape, and human interaction in the Sanctuary, p. 57).

Initiates following this path had to wend their way over the sanctuary's rugged terrain and through this tangle of monumental buildings in darkness. Artificial lighting would have been essential to practical navigation. Unsurprisingly, then, numerous ancient sources describe torches as characteristic of the Samothracian cult (Lewis 1959, pp. 72 no. 151; 77 no. 166; 89 no. 194), and evidence for lamps and torches abounds in the archaeological record. Samothracian monuments illustrate torches, and stone blocks with cut-outs to receive the bases of torches have been identified in the sanctuary, for example, in front of the Hieron (15) and east of the same building's *cella* (Lehmann 1969, Part 2, pp. 17-18). Excavations have also

Figure 4. Samothrace. Sanctuary of the Great Gods (Evros, Greece). Digital reconstruction of the Sacred Way during the day, looking east up to the Ionic Porch (model: American Excavations Samothrace).

Figure 5. Samothrace. Sanctuary of the Great Gods (Evros, Greece). Aerial view of the Central Sanctuary, central ravine, theatre, Nike Precinct, and terrace in front of the Stoa (photo: American Excavations Samothrace, Michael C. Page).

uncovered numerous terracotta and marble lamps. The sheer number of clay lamps, some inscribed as property of the Great Gods, suggests that initiates carried lamps at some point during the rites (Lehmann 1998, p. 40; Blevins 2017, pp. 387-394). Torches' and lamps' ability to reveal the world at night paralleled the revelation of the mysteries to the initiates as they moved through the sanctuary's *interstitium* and buildings.

Re-examining the interstitial passage by day and as a route out of the sanctuary offers additional explanations for key design features (Fig. 4). It is in going up the Sacred Way, with the optical advantage of daylight, that visitors were keenly aware of the Ionic Porch that commands the summit of the passage; from this vantage its floral-decorated coffer ceiling was best admired. The Corinthian order of the west façade of the Propylon of Ptolemy II (26), its intricate foliage now illuminated by the sun, had its greatest impact on the new initiates as they ascended the causeway to leave the *temenos*. The dedicatory inscription that was written on both sides of the building, however, underscored the palindromic nature of both the *propylon* and the path of the initiate. The Hellenistic monarch thus staked a claim on the favour of the Great Gods and the benefits of the initiation as pilgrims entered with anticipation and left the sanctuary with new prospects.

Controlling and bridging the torrent in the central valley

From its inception, the cult of the *Great Gods* was centred on the valley floor near the banks of a strong seasonal torrent (Fig. 5). The earliest archaeological deposits remain on the torrent's eastern side, but in the 4th century BCE we witness major development on the western bank and, with it, the need to cross the ravine. The torrent segregates the sacred buildings on its eastern bank from the dining and entertainment facilities to the west, but it did not serve as a simple zoning device. As will become clear, initiates could only reach key sacred monuments such as the Hieron (15) and Altar Court (14), as well as the theatre (13) and Nike Precinct (12), by crossing back and forth over the torrent multiple times and at several points. Understanding how such a fractured route became the *interstitium* that structured the kinaesthetic experience of visitors is vital to our understanding of the sanctuary.

An epigram celebrating the dedication of a bridge – likely on the road to Eleusis – describes how the bridge allows safe passage, even during winter floods, for initiates to the temple of Demeter (Antagoras of Rhodes, Paton 1916, 147). This inscription reminds us that sanctuaries were subject to the vicissitudes of the seasons, that access fluctuated, and that passages crossing waterways structured the approach to and movement within sanctuaries. Anthropogenic alterations to the central ravine in the Sanctuary of the Great Gods provide a stark reminder of these phenomena. Understanding the potency of the torrent is crucial to thinking about movement around and between sacred edifices.

The Sanctuary of the Great Gods rides the cusp of a geologic fault at the base of the rugged Agios Giorgios ridge. It is framed and divided by powerful seasonal torrents that have cut deep valleys into the colluvial plain as they converge just before reaching the sea. The outer two torrents articulate the natural boundaries of the sacred *temenos*; the third shapes the deep central valley that forms the heart of the sanctuary. While many Greek sanctuaries are proximate to water features, few are shaped by them as dramatically as the Sanctuary of the Great Gods.

The numerous and substantial ancient interventions in the ravine signal the urgency of controlling this powerful natural feature. The first phase of retaining walls, presumably Late Classical or Hellenistic in date, is clearly visible in several locations. These walls consist of a lining composed of basalt and trachyte boulders ranging from 10 cm to several meters in width, with only minor signs of tooling, laid in irregular courses (Fig. 6). Similar retaining walls are used to channel the torrent in the sanctuary's eastern ravine through the Propylon of Ptolemy II and to direct the stream that runs through the ancient city. This lining was later repaired with extensive Roman concrete rubble walls, at places well more than ten rough courses deep and partially composed of reused ashlars, held together by a durable hydraulic mortar (Fig. 7). These walls have become increasingly obscured by post-excavation fills, storm damage, and modern retaining walls (cf. McCredie *et al.* 1992, p. 251).

The multiple ancient interventions to control the path and force of water were readily apparent to 19th century excavators (Deville and Coquart 1867, plan 'Pont Génois'; Conze *et al.* 1875, pp. 31-32; 1880, Pl. 1) even though much was destroyed and the flood basin was a great deal wider. The path of the central ravine bends dramatically as it enters the sanctuary from the south, makes a sharp change in direction as it passes through the area between the Altar Court (14) and theatre (13), and then runs relatively straight through the remaining length of the sanctuary (Figs. 1. 2. 5). While the channel's current path, crafted in the 1950s, generally follows the ancient one and often rests on top of it, we are now in the process of determining the ancient course of the channel and identifying further remains of both the boulder and Roman

Figure 6 (opposite top). Samothrace. Sanctuary of the Great Gods (Evros, Greece). Central ravine, basalt boulder retaining wall, looking south (photo: American Excavations Samothrace).

Figure 7 (opposite below). Samothrace. Sanctuary of the Great Gods (Evros, Greece). Central ravine, Roman concrete and rubble retaining wall, looking west (photo: American Excavations Samothrace).

concrete walls (excavation diaries 1953, 1954, 1955). Three questions arise out of consideration of attempts to channelize this natural feature, in what is arguably the most extensive and sustained interaction between humans and terrain in the sanctuary: (1) to what degree was the course of the torrent altered through anthropogenic action, rather than simply controlled; (2) did the torrent feature in initiation or ritual action; and (3) how did visitors cross the torrent over the life of the sanctuary?

In the 1950s, Karl Lehmann restored a large covered channel between the Altar Court and theatre, creating a sense of seamless integration of the Central Sanctuary with the Western Hill (Lehmann 1960, plan; Lehmann and Spittle 1964, pp. 136-140 Fig. 117). Several decades later, James R. McCredie included a second bridge at the northern end of the sanctuary in the area where the massive Roman concrete landing had suggested a bridge to the earliest archaeologists (DeVille and Coquart 1867). These two bridges seemed sufficient prior to the discovery that the building in the heart of the sanctuary, formerly known as the Temenos, was twice as big as previously thought (Lehmann and Spittle 1982; Wescoat 2010, pp. 22-30; Marconi 2010). The newly named Hall of Choral Dancers (Fig. 2, no. 17) filled the central valley, essentially blocking access to the important cult buildings to the south, particularly the Hieron. With just two restored crossings, visitors could enter the sanctuary and cross to the western side of the valley, but they could not then reach the Hieron. The crossing between the theatre and Altar Court was equally unreachable given the theatre's placement and restored design (Lehmann 1998, plan 4).

In the 2002 reconstructed site plan, the issue was addressed by covering the entire central ravine from the theatre northwards to the Anaktoron, essentially erasing it (Wescoat 2010, Fig. 3.3). The result was a broad, easily negotiable valley. But this solution essentially eliminated one of the sanctuary's most powerful and defining natural features. It hid the impressive ancient channel walls, which, solely in terms of architectural mass, rival any of the more traditional monuments within the temenos. And it assumed that the central torrent was chiefly a natural hazard, thus obscuring the potential role this powerful natural force (and the ravine it carved) may have played in the control of movement and construction of ritual experience.

In 2016, we initiated a project re-envisioning the central ravine, its torrent, and the retaining walls built to control it as an integrated monument/phenomenon shaped by both natural and anthropogenic features, which by its very existence and massiveness generated and controlled sacred experience. As part of the project, we documented the several channels built within the ravine, identifying areas of vulnerability and more than 11 distinct phases of ancient and modern renovation. We hypothesized that the concrete and rubble section that collapsed into the modern ravine near the Rotunda of Arsinoe may have been remains of fallen bridging in the area of the massive concrete foundations west of the Rotunda known as the 'Pont Génois'. It turned out to be the collapsed retaining wall from the opposite side of the ravine, however. With the exception of the so-called Pont Génois, no other remains immediately indicated where and how the torrent may have been bridged.

While bridging solutions remain hypothetical for now, there are two strong possibilities for bridge construction. Given Samothrace's ancient forests, traditional bridging techniques used on the island provide a likely form of construction that would not leave a significant trace in the archaeological record: wooden beams carrying cross planks. A traditional bridge still in place over the torrent at Kerasia on Samothrace is constructed of wood beams set on boulder retaining walls and covered with cross planks. It is over a meter wide and about 7.5 m long, more than double the width of the central valley's torrent. Bridges within the sanctuary would likely have been considerably wider, but this kind of construction could easily have been replicated to form a broader passage. It is flexible and can be used opportunistically. It offers a good solution for bridging the torrent in both the Greek and Roman periods.

Stone vaulting is another possibility for the boulder wall phase. A corbel arched covering – used at several points in the neighbouring ancient city's walls – offers a more robust solution for bridging the channel during the Greek phase when boulder construction was used. The technique was used for stone bridges throughout Greece in the 4th and 3rd centuries, including at Eleutherna (Spratt 1865), and in drains, including a stretch of the Great Drain southwest of the Athenian Agora, at the Sacred Gate of the Kerameikos (Young 1951, p. 151; Lang 1968, pp. 22-24), and at Eretria (Krause 1972). At some sites, the corbelling is complete; at others, capstones complete the corbelling. Given the central torrent's irregular width and course, a barrel-vaulted tunnel is unlikely, even though Samothracian builders clearly demonstrated their knowledge and expertise with this technology in the barrel-vaulted tunnel that channelled the eastern torrent diagonally through the foundations of the Propylon of Ptolemy II (Frazer 1990, pp. 26-35. 228-230).

Even with several options for potential bridging techniques, it remains unclear how many bridges were needed, and where, between the 'Pont Génois' and the theatre. One additional bridge is absolutely necessary. In the absence of physical evidence, we simulated human movement to determine where visitors might have crossed the central ravine. Moving our non-linear model into a real-time gaming environment, using Unity 3D, with the camera set at eye level and following the known and extant paths, we modelled the kinaesthetics of movement from the base of the Sacred Way through the central valley to determine the most probable points of crossing needed to reach the several important buildings south of the Hall of Choral Dancers. We had the starting point of the crossing west of the Rotunda ('Pont Génois'), where the visitor would have reached the western bank. From there, we needed at least one bridge south of the Hall of Choral Dancers (17) to reach the Hieron (15) on the eastern bank. To get to the Hall of Votive Gifts (16) and Altar Court (14), the visitor had to cross back to the western bank. This could have entailed returning to the bridge just south of the Hall of Choral Dancers, proceeding up the valley, and crossing again in the region of the theatre. However, it may have been more convenient to have crossings both to the north and south of the Hall of Votive Gifts. This option opens to the possibility that an individual crossing may have signalled each building. The final crossing would connect the Altar Court to the theatre. The crossings remain hypothetical at this stage in our research; we have indicated on the plan and model two possible locations, with the wooden planking form of construction (Fig. 1-2).

These crossings may have developed over time as the sanctuary itself developed, but they suggest the exploitation of very limited space, and perhaps the intention to sequester a series of experiences related to rituals of the cult. The delimited spaces between monuments, torrent, and bridges funnel human action: from the base of the Sacred Way the space opens to the *prostyle* façade of the Hall of Choral Dancers, the entrance of the Rotunda, and the main bridge across the torrent, prompting movement in those directions. A similar funnel is at work for the Hieron, drawing the visitor up and into the narrowing space centred on the façade of the building. In addition to helping shape movement and kinaesthetic experience within the Central Sanctuary, the intermittent bridging would leave portions of the ravine visible and the torrent, when running, audible to the ancient pilgrims. Although an unpredictable component, the night-time sound of rushing water (particularly over the cascades near the theatre) would have amplified the initiatory experience, already heightened by the use of instruments, singing, and chanting (Clinton 2003, pp. 62-65; Wescoat 2017a, pp. 61-62).

Dedications in the Central Sanctuary

Dedicatory monuments constitute another type of human intervention in the delimited spaces of the Central Sanctuary between buildings, ravine, and bridges. The surviving bases and foundations allow us to understand how such monuments impacted visitors' movement. Dedications in the Central Sanctuary affect movement in two significant ways: constricting a thoroughfare and arresting movement by demanding a viewer's attention. At the base of the Sacred Way, for example, visitors were forced to turn immediately to their right, where they were confronted by two monuments, impossible to ignore, on the south side of the Rotunda of Arsinoe (20). The *orthostate* Monument C consists of a *c.* 2.65 m long moulded marble base that rested on a porous sandstone foundation. The dimensions of the base suggest at least two figures, tripod, or other dedication. A later monument is attested by a limestone foundation so close to Monument C that the foundations overlapped; both are visible in the Rotunda plan of the *in situ* remains (McCredie *et al.* 1992, pp. 241-244 Pl. 1). This proximity, even though other space was available, acknowledges that this location at the base of the Sacred Way was a prime opportunity for display. The grouping of dedications also caused visitors to pause as they entered the triangular node formed by the *plateia* between the Hall of Choral Dancers, Rotunda, and ravine. It simultaneously discouraged movement into the narrow space between the Rotunda and its retaining wall.

From this *plateia*, visitors could progress westward across the bridge proposed above. On the west bank, in the spatial node leading to the Milesian Dedication (6), two additional monuments claim attention and constrict pedestrian flow. Placed at an oblique angle to the Milesian Dedication, the monument foundation measuring 6.3 m by 3.0 m (Bouzek and Ondřejová 1985, pp. 14-17) must have supported a large-scale dedication. Directly across the path leading to the entrance of the Milesian Dedication and additional buildings to the west stood another monument supporting up to two statues; together these two monuments dramatically narrowed the width of the pathway. These monuments were carefully positioned not only to impact visitors' kinaesthetic movement, but also to take advantage of sightlines from the important monuments in the central valley. The smaller dedication stands across the ravine from the door of the Rotunda of Arsinoe. The monument surmounting the large foundation in front of the Milesian Dedication is directly on axis with the *prostyle* facade of the Hall of Choral Dancers. Given its dimensions and elevation, this monument would certainly have attracted visitors' attention from this major cult building. Such alignments demonstrate that patrons clearly were interested in having their dedications positioned to attract maximum attention, and the *interstitium*, far from being merely negative space, was elastic in its ability to absorb and display – as prescribed – along the specified routes it required visitors to traverse.

Physical and visual dynamics of the theatre, Stoa, and Nike Monument

Bearing these pathways in mind, we now move to the south-western area of the sanctuary currently under investigation: the zone formed by the theatre (13), Stoa (11), and Nike Precinct (12). The buildings of the Eastern Hill and Central Sanctuary are splendid marble structures mostly paid for by the royal and elite patrons around whom the history of the sanctuary has been written. Comparatively little attention has been paid to the role Samothracians themselves may have played in brokering the fame of the sanctuary and shaping its footprint. The Stoa, theatre, and Nike Monument architecture are made entirely of local materials; they offer an opportunity to see the Samothracians working as agents within their sacred space and exploiting the resources of their immediate natural environment to excellent effect. In this zone, we see the Samothracians' ingenuity in their creation of hybrid interstitial spaces: the theatre as architecture and *interstitium* and the open Stoa terrace as node and ambulatory pathway.

The Stoa and Nike Monument have been the subject of intensive excavation, but understanding how they work together and in relation to the Central Sanctuary demands a better grasp of the theatre. This structure was partially preserved at the time of the 1923 French-Czech excavation but had been largely destroyed by the time of Lehmann's first visit to the island in 1937 (Chapouthier *et al.* 1956; Bouzek and Ondřejová 1985, pp. 17. 19-25. 36-37. 78 Figs. 12-19. 43. 54; Lehmann and Spittle 1964, pp. 4-8). When we excavated in the area of the theatre in 2018, we were able to locate the foundations for the *orchestra*, the *socle* of the *diazoma* wall, one theatre seat *in situ*, basalt cobbling that served as the foundation for both the seats and the stairs, and the remains of the pipe that the French-Czech team had uncovered in the *diazoma*. While we have not, at this stage, determined the full extent of the *koilon*, we were able to confirm, with the help of the French-Czech plan, the position of the seats, staircases, *diazoma* and *orchestra*. We now have a better grasp of the orientation of the structure, the diameter of the *orchestra*, and, perhaps most important, the elevation of the *orchestra*, which is considerably higher than Lehmann and Denys Spittle proposed (Lehmann and Spittle 1964, pp. 136-141 Figs. 117. 122).

Above the theatre, Samothracian builders made substantial interventions in the sanctuary's topography on the Western Hill to construct the *c.* 104 m long Stoa, by cutting into the southern slope and using this earth to artificially extend the plateau *c.* 25 meters northward (McCredie 1965). The Stoa provided necessary covered gathering space for visitors apart from the sacred structures in the Central Sanctuary. Crucially, however, it also generated the largest interstitial space in the sanctuary: the terrace in front of the Stoa. This long and *c.* 15 m wide terrace was primarily accessed through the theatre, which allowed visitors to ascend to yet another triangular node bounded by the theatre, Nike Precinct, Stoa, and Orthostate Monument VI. As a man-made elaboration of the natural hill slope, the theatre existed in reciprocity and merged with the landscape. Serving not only as a place of gathering and viewing, but also as connective tissue linking lower elevation areas along the central ravine and the upper elevation of the terrace in front of the Stoa, the theatre design exploits the natural topography to maximum advantage for architectural, kinaesthetic, and visual purposes. We witness similar strategies at work in the Hellenistic world, *e.g.*, at Pergamon, where the Hellenistic theatre on the west slope of the upper Acropolis links the Sanctuary of Athena and upper Acropolis with the Sanctuary of Dionysos and a stoa at the foot of the theatre's *koilon* (Radt 2016, pp. 255-262).

Patrons of sculptural dedications also maximized the kinaesthetic and visual potential of the topography here, most dramatically in the case of the Nike. The statue is set back from the theatre's edge in a deep niche cut into the steep hillside yet elevated above the ground level of the plateau by the *krepis* of the building and the marble prow on which she alights. From this position, the statue can be seen both from the central valley and the terrace in front of the Stoa, but she disappears in close proximity to the theatre and only makes her reappearance gradually as the visitor's culminating reward for ascending the theatre.

As in other nodes in the sanctuary, the terrace in front of the Stoa was a desirable location for sculptural dedications. The surviving foundations of at least seven monumental statue bases (McCredie 1965; 1968; 1979) attest to the accumulation of grand dedications lining the Stoa façade (Figs. 8 and 9). Rising up above the roofline of the Stoa and visible from most vantage points within the sanctuary, one of the most impressive monuments on the Stoa terrace was the column monument of Philip V,

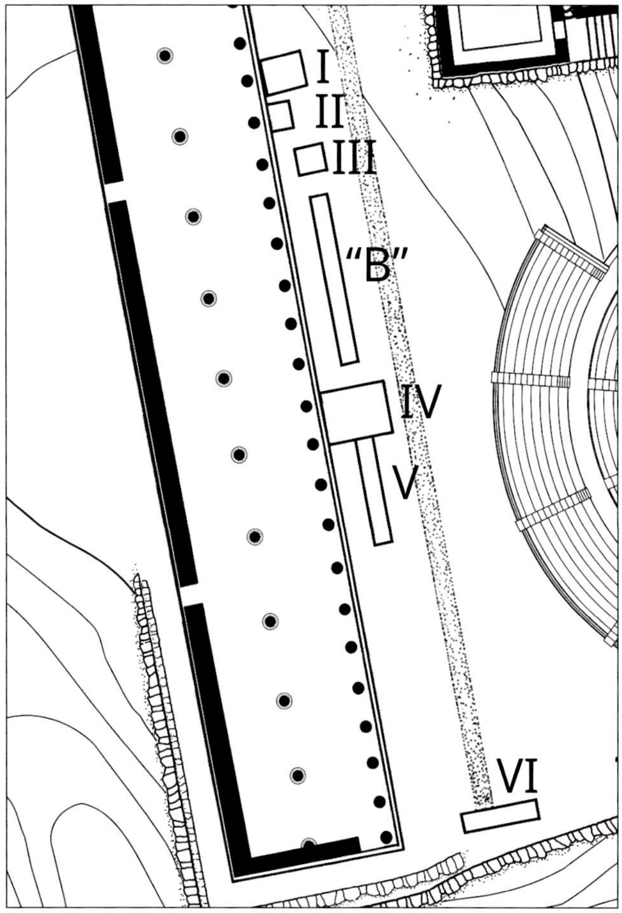

Figure. 8. Samothrace. Sanctuary of the Great Gods (Evros, Greece). Detail of the plan of the monuments in front of the Stoa (plan: American Excavations Samothrace).

dedicated by the Macedonians to the Great Gods around 200 BCE (McCredie 1979, p. 16 Pl. 8a). Marble fragments of an Ionic column found in the area indicate a second column monument on one of the adjacent foundations. Given its order, it likely would have risen higher than and thus potentially eclipsed the Column of Philip V. At least three *orthostate* monuments supporting paratactic sculpture ensembles are also attested: Monument VI, Monument V, and Foundation B (Conze *et al.* 1880, p. 51). With lower dimensions of 6.07 m by 1.7 m, Monument VI is the best preserved and the smallest of the *orthostate* monuments, running perpendicular to the Stoa's axis and roughly aligned with its south wall. Monument VI likely supported three to four statues and, based on cuttings in the surviving crown block, an object such as a tripod. In addition, two well-preserved *orthostate* monument crowns with cuttings for over life-sized male and female bronze statues, associated with Monument V, evoke the scale and grandeur of these dedications (Conze *et al.* 1880, Pl. 59).

A desire to manipulate the interstitial space and, therefore, visitors' movement and attention, surely played a role in the configuration of the monuments. If the Column of Philip V was located on Monument II abutting the foundation of the Stoa, as suggested by James McCredie (1979, p. 16), the fact that Monuments I and III project considerably past Monument II to intrude into the visitors' space suggests an effort to distinguish and privilege these monuments. In the Hellenistic world monuments tended to congregate around earlier important dedications (*e.g.* the *dromos* of the Sanctuary of Apollo at Delos; Dillon and Baltes 2013). As in the Central Sanctuary, dedicators strategically placed monuments on the terrace in front of the Stoa to vie for physical prominence, exploiting interstitial spaces for maximum visibility and impact on visitors.

Figure. 9. Samothrace. Sanctuary of the Great Gods (Evros, Greece). Digital model of the Stoa terrace, looking south toward the Nike Precinct (model: American Excavations Samothrace. Model of the statue of the Nike courtesy of the Musée du Louvre and Art graphique & Patrimoine).

The configuration of Foundation B, Monument IV, and Monument V (Fig. 8) manipulated the interstitial space to demand viewer attention in a different way. This row of dedications, stretching approximately 25 m, determined how visitors could enter the Stoa. After ascending the theatre visitors might pass in front of Monument VI to enter the Stoa through the southernmost section of the portico. To reach the next available opportunity for access to the Stoa, however, visitors were forced to progress north and enter the Stoa through two-meter-wide openings on either side of Foundation B. Visitors had no choice but to walk down the terrace and, presumably, view the statues of Monument IV and the flanking dedications. Integral components of the interstitial space, the dedicatory monuments prompted visitor movement northward along the Stoa, converting the spatial node bounded by the theatre, Nike Precinct, and Stoa into a pathway and propelling visitors toward expansive views. Given its unique prospect, the terrace in front of the Stoa offered a fitting space of transition for the newly initiated. In contrast to the beginning of the initiates' experience in the inwardly focused Theatral Circle, the expansive vistas from the Stoa's terrace encouraged visitors to pause and look north over the Aegean Sea, recalling their maritime approach to the island, and east over the Central Sanctuary, mentally re-enacting their recent physical and ritual journey.

Mediating zone of transition: prostyle design

Between the connective *interstitium* of physical and visual pathways and the sharply defined interiors of the Samothracian cult buildings, we find a third mediating zone of transition: the *prostyle* chamber. From a practical perspective, *prostyle* design is a highly effective architectural strategy for communicating a temple front façade while allowing for maximum interior space of variable depth. It thus can readily be adjusted to topography and function. But practicality is not a sufficient explanation for the super-abundance of *prostyle* facades defining deep liminal spaces we find in the Sanctuary of the Great Gods.

Eight of the major buildings in the sanctuary exploit this type of design, using Doric, Ionic, and Corinthian orders (Fig. 2, nos. 1. 6. 11. 15. 17. 24. 26. 31). The earliest, the Ionic winged porch on the Hall of Choral Dancers (17), is also the most elaborate and important (Lehmann and Spittle 1982 [but note change of design]; Wescoat 2010, pp. 27-30; Marconi 2010, pp. 107-136). Two *tetrastyle* wings set before a colonnade of nine columns *in antis* define a deep transitional space that mediates between the triangular *plateia* at the base of the Sacred Way and the two emphatically enclosed cult chambers within the building. The scale and depth of the space (over 19.5 m long and 5.5 m deep) suggests that it deserves to be called a *prostoon*, like the colonnaded porch of the Telesterion at Eleusis (*e.g.*, in *IG* II^2 1666; Shear 2016, pp. 161-196). The splendid marble coffered ceiling further defined the space as a locus of attention. The Doric Hieron (15), set close behind the Hall of Choral Dancers and at a slightly higher elevation, also had an unusually deep entrance area (Lehmann 1969, pp. 93-117). In the case of the Hieron, the porch is constrained between the long, impermeable lateral west wall of the Hall of Choral Dancers, and the projecting north end of the Hall of Votive Gifts (16), which effectively disguise the length of the Hieron and defines the only passage forward toward it. The porticoed space was subdivided into two open spaces by a second colonnade. However, like the Hall of Choral Dancers, a richly coffered ceiling both drew in viewers and enhanced the spatial integrity of the permeable space (Lehmann 1969). These two porches form gathering spaces and staging areas for the large enclosed halls that surely were central to the main rites of the cult (Wescoat 2010; Clinton 2017). For the visitor, reaching these deep porches signalled that one part of their translocation was achieved; a sense of accomplishment must also have been accompanied by a sense of anticipation for what lay within.

Other *prostyle* spaces within the sanctuary vary the experience. The exedra-like space of the Dedication of Philip III and Alexander IV (24) is not a spatial prologue to more secluded chambers; instead it creates a diversion along the sacred path. Its position and orientation command the attention of the visitor but also significantly deflect the interstitial passage of the Sacred Way (18) around the bedrock knoll into which the Theatral Circle (25) is embedded. In the Propylon of Ptolemy II (26), constructed some 40 years later (26) (Frazer 1990, pp. 43-47), the pair of *prostyle* chambers on either side of the door wall reclaim the primacy of the pathway by monumentalizing the action of both coming and going.

The identical size of the chambers offers equal gathering spaces, thus subverting a spatial hierarchy of experience. Spatially, being within and outside the *temenos*, and entering and leaving it become equally important. Difference instead is signalled by architectural order, with Corinthian the sacred-facing order and Ionic the public-facing display (Wescoat 2012; 2017b). The Milesian Dedication's Ionic *prostyle* chamber (6) offers yet another spatial experience, by providing a deep open hall between two 15-couch dining chambers (Wescoat 2015). The space is palatially generous as a staging area (note the 3-room suites of the palace at Vergina; Nielsen 1999, pp. 87-88); it offers a semi-open permeable space preceding the closed and presumably highly exclusive dining rooms.

Prostyle facades also offer an architectural feature that responds experientially to visitors' movements through the sanctuary in diurnal and nocturnal lighting conditions. During night-time initiation rites, the colonnaded facades of the sanctuary's monuments would have flickered beneath the light cast by torches and lamps. The dance of flames on white marble columns contrasted with the darkened recesses of

Figure. 10. Samothrace. Sanctuary of the Great Gods (Evros, Greece). Great central retaining wall (photo: American Excavations Samothrace).

porches. In daytime, as initiates moved back through the sanctuary, the sun would have glinted brilliantly off the marble columns but would also have illuminated the porch interiors, many with intricate coffered ceilings, that were shrouded in darkness the night before. Initiates saw the sanctuary in a new light, literally: sunlight. Their movement through space *and* time activated the *prostyle* architecture and surrounding landscape in different ways from night to day, from entry into the sanctuary to egress. In turn, this changed directional and luminous perspective embodied the internal changes the initiates had undergone during the night's rituals.

Materiality, landscape, and human interaction in the Sanctuary

While a wide variety of local materials were used for construction in the sanctuary, trachyte and basalt stand out as the materials that were highly visible in nature *and* in man-made monuments, leading us to conclude that Samothracian builders intentionally created visual resonances between these materials as they occurred in the landscape and as they appeared in built structures. These two rock types dominate the landscape: trachyte from the Agios Giorgios ridge and basalt boulders originally formed by pillows of molten rock that bubbled up from the seafloor and then were thrust up by tectonic action to form the mile-high peak of Saos (Heimann *et al.* 1972). The appeal of using carefully fitted basalt boulders or roughly worked trachyte to create building terraces, frame passages, channel torrents, and manipulate sharp changes in elevation and rough terrain lay in these stones' ability to blend into the natural landscape. In addition, the local basalts contain the mineral magnetite (Fe_3O_4), which interferes with earth's normal magnetism, creating a magnetic field strength in the sanctuary (one that causes a compass needle to sway dramatically depending on nearby rock types). This force was concretized and made transportable in the magnetized iron rings received by initiates as a token of their experience (Lewis 1959, pp. 8. 11. 96. 97. 99 nos. 20. 30. 212. 213. 219; Blakely 2012, pp. 61-64). While the earliest identifiable structure in the sanctuary (the retaining wall visible within the foundations of the Rotunda) was built using unworked basalt boulders, the technique was particularly exploited in the Late Classical and Hellenistic periods for large-scale hardscaping. One finds examples throughout the sanctuary: the retaining walls east and south of the Hall of Choral Dancers, south of the Hieron, northeast and southwest of the Stoa, south of the Neorion, and east of the Rotunda (rebuilt in the Roman period); the water channels in the central and east ravines; and in the passage of the Sacred Way (Wescoat 2017a, pp. 305-308. 330-336). Even in the great central retaining walls constructed in the late 3rd/early 2nd century BCE to enlarge the space immediately to the east of the Stoa, builders retained the polygonal mode, although here composed chiefly of polygonally worked trachyte stones set in a lattice of limestone ashlars (Fig. 10) (McCredie 1979, p. 9 Fig. 4d, although note difference in petrographic description). Although artifice is more readily apparent in this wall, the polygonal trachyte stones still blend with the natural landscape in colour and texture.

Acknowledging the practical value of working with immediately available material and generations of technical expertise, we nevertheless note that the Samothracians explored but did not pursue more conventional alternatives (*e.g.*, the ashlar retaining wall supporting the north side of the Neorion Terrace). They preferred the striking contrast and natural aesthetic of the massive and roughly textured boulder walls against the glittering buildings constructed in Thasian, Pentelic, and Proconnesian marble (Maniatis *et al.* 2012). Being closely allied materially, the boulder walls became an extension of the landscape, creating the impression that the landscape opened naturally to accept the buildings it supported. The polygonal design also appears as one of several archaisms chosen to give the sanctuary an air of greater antiquity than its Hellenistic floruit can claim. Moreover, the magnetic energy of the local rocks may have been felt, if not fully understood. In short, human manipulation of the sanctuary's natural materials created powerful visual, affective, and experiential connections.

Conclusion

In parallel to the characterization of the interstitial space in the human body as an organ with unique features that performs specific functions, we have emphasized the unique features and functions of interstitial space in the Sanctuary of the Great Gods that justify treating it as a single if flexible organ. Visitors to the sanctuary experienced key kinaesthetic moments along the *interstitium*: descending the Sacred Way to the Central Sanctuary, manoeuvring through the Central Sanctuary by criss-crossing the central torrent, ascending the theatre to the terrace joining the Nike Precinct and Stoa, and interacting with monuments in regions of sculptural display. As the carefully crafted pathways guided visitors through the sanctuary, *prostyle* facades, sculptural dedications, and boulder retaining walls provided visual and spatial continuity in the face of novel configurations of sacred space and architecture. In a sanctuary that does not adhere to more typically attested forms of Hellenistic spatial organization and visual staging such as axiality, symmetry, and systematic terracing, Samothracian builders seem to have purposefully connected areas of the sanctuary to create an experience in which visitors could negotiate the site's unexpected aspects as a fluid, unified whole, connected by the all-important interstitial spaces.

A critical means by which this continuity of experience was achieved lies in the fundamental reciprocity between the natural world and the sanctuary's interstitial spaces. This relationship generated the matrix within which humans and buildings co-existed. Architecture and landscape design theorists have characterized three modes of relationship between architecture and landscape: contrast, merger, and reciprocity (Rainey 1988). In a contrasting relationship, architecture and landscape are set side by side without integration or transition in order to emphasize the inherently different qualities of each. In a merging relationship, buildings that merge with the natural world appear as an integral part of the landscape. In a reciprocal relationship, the natural world and architecture are in dialogue with each other in a mutually constitutive relationship. It is precisely this reciprocal relationship that existed in the Sanctuary of the Great Gods.

The dynamic interplay of natural features and interstitial network of connective tissue impacted viewer experience in crucial ways. The pathways simultaneously respond to natural features (most notably the steep hills and deep central ravine) and buildings to create compelling views and sensory experiences that privilege interaction between humans and natural and man-made structures. Strategically positioned, non-axial pathways across steep changes in elevation created alternately constricted and expanded viewsheds, such as when descending or ascending the Sacred Way. The sanctuary's builders also eschewed axial orientation and, with the exception of the terrace in front of the Stoa, broad vistas in favour of continuously changing, yet equally staged, views created through bodily movement. The reciprocity is apparent in the framing retaining walls that draw on natural resources emerging from the landscape itself, and in natural and artificial light along these passages that illuminated and animated architecture, natural topography, and human action. The inherent reciprocity between landscape and architecture not only enlivened and enriched viewer experience but also indicates a preferred aesthetic for and deference to the natural world consistent with the nature of the cult.

The sanctuary's *interstitium* developed as the essential passage of translocation connecting architectural structures through transitional zones. In the natural environment, the boundaries where two ecosystems meet – for example, where ocean meets sand or forest meets grassland – are often the most fertile because of a confluence of resources from two environments. There are certainly flat, imposing, impermeable walls seemingly sealing off important interstitial spaces within the sanctuary, such as the southwest wall of the Hall of Choral Dancers partially enclosing the triangular space leading up to the Hieron. More striking, however, is the proliferation of *prostyle* architecture producing buildings at almost every turn adorned with colonnaded entrances that blurred distinctions between architectural and connective space. Strategically placed statue assemblages located against buildings but also jutting into ambulatory pathways created further complexity in the permeable zone between architecture and *interstitium*. Finally, hybrid spaces such as the theatre, which served simultaneously as built structure with a specific purpose and pathway from one sector to another, demonstrate the extraordinary flexibility afforded by spaces that combine interstitiality and architecture. Across the *interstitium* of the Sanctuary of the Great Gods, human action and movement bound together architecture and landscape, and constructed people's perceptions of both.

Acknowledgements

We would like to thank Annette Haug and Asja Müller for organizing this conference and bringing its papers to publication, and also the participants at the conference, whose papers and lively discussion helped shape our understanding. We owe a great debt to the many members of our field team, past and present, for their contributions, as well as to our 3D modelers, Ian Burr, Vincent Baillet, and Aryabrata Basu for their work in digitally recreating the sanctuary. We are grateful to Domna Terzopoulou of the Ephorate of Antiquities of Evros, Chryssa Karadima of the Ephorate of Antiquities of Rhodopi, and Dimitris Matsas (retired, ΙΘ΄ Ephorate of Prehistoric and Classical Antiquities, Komotini) for their support of our research on Samothrace.

References

Benias, P.C., Wells, R.G., Sackey-Aboagye, B., Klavan, H., Reidy, J., Buonocore, D., Miranda, M., Kornacki, S., Wayne, M., Carr-Locke, D.L., Theise, N.D. 2018. Structure and distribution of an unrecognized interstitium in human tissues. *Scientific Reports* 8 (4947) [online]. Available from: https://doi.org/10.1038/s41598-018-23062-6 [accessed 29 June 2019].

Blakely, S. 2012. Toward an archaeology of secrecy: power, paradox, and the Great Gods of Samothrace. *Archaeological Papers of the American Anthropological Association* 21 (1), 49-71.

Blevins, S.L. 2017. Lamps, in: Wescoat, B.D. (ed.). *The monuments of the Eastern Hill,* Samothrace: excavations conducted by the Institute of Fine Arts of New York University 9. Princeton: American School of Classical Studies at Athens, 387-394.

Bouzek, J. and Ondřejová, I. 1985. *Samothrace: 1923/1927/1978. The results of the Czechoslovak excavation in 1927 conducted by A. Salač and J. Nepomucký and the unpublished results of the 1923 Franco-Czechoslovak excavations conducted by A. Salač and F. Chapouthier*. Prague: Univerzita Karlova.

Chapouthier, A., Salač, A., Salviat, F. 1956. Le theatre de Samothrace. *Bulletin de correspondance hellénique* 80, 118-146.

Clinton, K.M. 2003. Stages of initiation in the Eleusinian and Samothracian Mysteries, in: Cosmopoulos, M.B. (ed.). *Greek mysteries: the archaeology and ritual of ancient Greek secret cults*. New York: Routledge, 50-78.

Clinton, K.M. 2017. Two buildings in the Samothracian sanctuary of the Great Gods. *Journal of Ancient History* 5 (2), 323-356.

Conze, A., Hauser, A., Benndorf, O. 1880. *Neue archäologische Untersuchungen auf Samothrake*. Vienna: Druck und Verlag von Carl Gerold's Sohn.

Conze, A., Hauser, A., Niemann, G. 1875. *Archäologische Untersuchungen auf Samothrake*. Vienna: Druck und Verlag von Carl Gerold's Sohn.

Deville, G. and Coquart, E. 1867. Rapport sur une Mission dans l'île de Samothrace. *Archives des Missions Scientifiques et Littéraires* 4, 2nd ed., 254-278.

Dillon, S. and Baltes, E.P. 2013. Honorific practices and the politics of space on Hellenistic Delos: portrait statue monuments along the dromos. *American Journal of Archaeology* 117 (2), 207-246.

Dimitrova, N. 2008. *Theoroi and initiates in Samothrace: the epigraphic evidence*, Hesperia Supplement 37. Princeton: American School of Classical Studies at Athens.

Favro, D. 1996. *The urban image of Augustan Rome*. New York: Cambridge University Press.

Favro, D. 2014. Moving events: curating the memory of the Roman triumph, in: Galinsky, K. (ed.). *Memoria Romana: memory in Rome and Rome in memory*. Ann Arbor: University of Michigan Press, 85-101.

Frazer, A.K. 1990. *The Propylon of Ptolemy II*, Samothrace: excavations conducted by the Institute of Fine Arts of New York University 10. Princeton: Princeton University Press.

Heimann, K.O., Lebkuchner, H., Kretzler, W. 1972. *Samothraki sheet, geological map of Greece*. Munich: Technische Hochschule München, Institut für Geologie.

Hollinshead, M.B. 2015. *Shaping ceremony: monumental steps and Greek architecture, Wisconsin Studies in Classics*. Madison: The University of Wisconsin Press.

Howard, J. 2018. *Newfound 'organ' could be the biggest in your body*. CNN [online]. Available from: https://edition.cnn.com/2018/03/27/health/new-organ-interstitium-study/index.html [Accessed 6 July 2019].

Krause, C. 1972. *Das Westtor: Ergebnisse der Ausgrabungen 1964-1968,* Eretria IV. Berne: Francke Verlag.

Lang, M.L. 1968. *Waterworks in the Athenian Agora*. Princeton: American School of Classical Studies at Athens.

Lehmann, K. 1960. *Samothrace: a guide to the excavations and the museum*. New York: J. J. Augustin.

Lehmann, K. 1998. *Samothrace: a guide to the excavations and the museum*. 6th ed., revised by J.R. McCredie. Thessaloniki: AAAltintzis.

Lehmann, K. and Spittle, D. 1964. *The Altar Court,* Samothrace: excavations conducted by the Institute of Fine Arts of New York University 4 (2). New York: Pantheon Books.

Lehmann, P.W. 1969. *The Hieron,* Samothrace: excavations conducted by the Institute of Fine Arts of New York University 3. Princeton: Princeton University Press.

Lehmann, P.W. and Spittle, D. 1982. *The Temenos*, Samothrace: excavations conducted by the Institute of Fine Arts of New York University 5. Princeton: Princeton University Press.

Lewis, N. 1959. *The Ancient literary sources,* Samothrace: excavations conducted by the Institute of Fine Arts of New York University 1. New York: Pantheon Books.

Lynch, K. 1960. *The image of the city*. Cambridge, Mass.: The Technology Press & Harvard University Press.

Maniatis, Y., Tambakopoulos, D., Ditsika, E., Wescoat, B.D., Matsas, D. 2012. The Sanctuary of the Great Gods on Samothrace, Greece: an extended marble provenance study, in: Garcia-Moreno, A.G., Mercadal, P.L, de Llanza, I.R. (eds.). *Interdisciplinary studies on ancient stone,* Proceedings of the IX Association for the Study of Marbles and Other Stones in Antiquity (ASMOSIA) Conference, 2009. Tarragona: Institut Català d'Arqueologia Clàssica, 263-278.

Marconi, C. 2010. Choroi, Theōriai and international ambitions: the Hall of Choral Dancers and its frieze, in: Palagia, O. and Wescoat, B.D. (eds.). *Samothracian connections: Essays in honor of James R. McCredie.* Oxford: Oxbow, 107-136.

McCredie, J.R. 1965. Samothrace: preliminary report on the campaigns of 1962-1964. *Hesperia* 34 (2), 100-124.

McCredie, J.R. 1968. Samothrace: preliminary report on the campaigns of 1965-1967. *Hesperia* 37 (2), 200-234.

McCredie, J.R. 1979. Samothrace: supplementary investigations, 1968-1977. *Hesperia* 48 (1), 1-44.

McCredie, J.R., Roux, G., Shaw, S.M., Kurtich, J. 1992. *The Rotunda of Arsinoe,* Samothrace: excavations conducted by the Institute of Fine Arts of New York University 7. Princeton: Princeton University Press.

Nielsen, I. 1999. *Hellenistic palaces: tradition and renewal.* 2nd ed. Aarhus: Aarhus University Press.

Paton, W.R. 1916. *Greek Anthology*, Vol. 3, Trans. Cambridge: Harvard University Press, Loeb Classical Library.

Radt, W. 2016. *Pergamon: Geschichte und Bauten einer antiken Metropole.* Munich: Philipp von Zabern in Wissenschaftliche Buchgesellschaft (WBG).

Rainey, R.M. 1988. Architecture and landscape: three modes of relationship. *Places* 4 (4), 4-6.

Shear, T.L. 2016. *Trophies of victory: public building in Periklean Athens*. Princeton: Princeton University Press.

Spratt, T.A.B. 1865. *Travels and researches in Crete* 2. London: J. van Voorst.

Wescoat, B.D. 2010. James R. McCredie and Samothracian architecture, in: Palagia, O. and Wescoat, B.D. (eds.). *Samothracian connections: Essays in honor of James R. McCredie*. Oxford: Oxbow, 5-32.

Wescoat, B.D. 2012. Coming and going in the Sanctuary of the Great Gods, Samothrace, in: Wescoat, B.D. and Ousterhout, R.G. (eds.). *Architecture of the sacred: ritual,* space, *and experience from Classical Greece to Byzantium*. New York: Cambridge University Press, 66-113.

Wescoat, B.D. 2015. Recalibrating Samothracian architecture, in: des Courtils, J. (ed.). *L'architecture monumentale grecque au IIIe s. a.C.* Bordeaux: Ausonius, 117-146.

Wescoat, B.D. 2017a. *The Monuments of the Eastern Hill,* Samothrace: excavations conducted by the Institute of Fine Arts of New York University 9. Princeton: American School of Classical Studies at Athens.

Wescoat, B.D. 2017b. The pilgrim's passage through the Sanctuary of the Great Gods, Samothrace, in: Christensen, T.M. and Friese, V. (eds.). *Excavating pilgrimage: archaeological approaches to sacred travel and movement from Classical Greece to Late Antiquity*, 9-10 May 2014 Aarhus University. New York: Routledge, 67-86.

Wescoat, B.D. 2020. Architectural documentation and visual evocation: choices, iterations, and virtual representation in the Sanctuary of the Great Gods on Samothrace, in: Sapirstein, P. and Scahill, D. (eds.). *New directions and new paradigms for the study of Greek architecture: interdisciplinary dialogues in the field*. Leiden: Brill, 305-321.

Young, R.S. 1951. An industrial district of Ancient Athens. *Hesperia* 20 (3), 135-288.

Notes on contributors

Bonna D. Wescoat - Art History Department and Program in Ancient Mediterranean Studies, Emory University, USA (present). PhD Oxford 1983; Samuel Candler Dobbs Professor of Art History at Emory University; Director of Excavations, Sanctuary of the Great Gods, Samothrace.

Susan Ludi Blevins - History Instructor, Dexter Southfield School, USA (present). MA 2007; PhD Emory 2013 in Art History and Archaeology; J.D. 1997, William and Mary School of Law.

Maggie L. Popkin - Department of Art History and Art, Case Western Reserve University, USA (present). MA 2005; PhD New York 2012 in Classical Art and Archaeology; Robson Junior Professor in the Humanities, Associate Professor at the Department of Art History and Art, Case Western Reserve University.

Jessica Paga - Department of Classical Studies, College of William & Mary, USA (present). AB Smith College 2005; PhD Princeton 2012; Assistant Professor at the Department of Classical Studies at the College of William & Mary.

Andrew Farinholt Ward - Visiting Assistant Professor, Department of Classical Studies, College of William & Mary, USA (present). PhD New York 2017 in Greek Archaeology and Art; Council of American Overseas Research Fellow 2018-2019.

Michael C. Page - Department of Environmental Sciences, Emory University, USA (present); Lecturer; Geographer, Digital Visualization Lab, Emory Center for Digital Scholarship.

William Size - Professor emeritus, Department of Environmental Sciences, Emory University, USA; Geologist.

Sanctuary Disposition and Cult Practice: The Thesmophorion in Pella

Soi Agelidis

Abstract

The so-called Thesmophorion in the Macedonian capital Pella is a unique building with respect to form and materiality. The wall of the round enclosure consists of ashlar masonry plastered with clay, two stairs lead down to the interior of the complex where openings are cut into the bedrock, and an altar is built in the middle of the round. The shape and materials as well as the sanctuary's location are significant for the ritual practice and the perception of the site by the worshippers. The discussion of these elements is set in relation to the development of Hellenistic architecture and the activity of the Macedonian royal family.

Keywords: Pella, Macedonia, Demeter, Kore, Hades

Hellenistic architecture features a wide variety in individual form as well as a tendency to monumentalisation. This is apparent especially, or even mainly, in the erection of various buildings in sanctuaries, whether in urban, suburban or rural spatial contexts. An exception in this respect is Macedonia. Here monumentalisation and architectural variety are likewise evident, but they are applied in *sepulcral*, domestic and political buildings, albeit not in religious. Although Macedonian kings donated temples, *stoai* and other edifices to sanctuaries abroad, *e.g.* in Delos or Priene, they seem to have had no interest to adorn the cities in their own realm with similar buildings. Not even their capitals Aigai and Pella are equipped with great, representative temples and sanctuaries (Christesen and Murray 2010, pp. 436-440). This feature might appear astonishing, since the kings initiated a complete rearrangement of the political, social and cultural realities in the Hellenic world, then again sheds a different light on the few existing sacred places established in Macedonia.

The case study for this paper will be the so-called Thesmophorion in Pella. The focus lays mainly on the impact of location and architectural form to the movement of worshippers, on the one hand, and the effect of landscape and materiality on the perception

Ruhr-Universität Bochum
Am Bergbaumuseum 31
D-44791 Bochum
Germany
soi.agelidis@ruhr-uni-bochum.de

of the people during the rituals, on the other. Due to the erection of the sanctuary at the beginning of the Hellenistic era, the situation at this very architectural complex could be indicative for the development of a 'typical Hellenistic architecture' in some aspects.

Current state of research

Pella: excavation and ancient city

In order to better understand the significance of ancient Pella for the Late Classical and Hellenistic world and obtain an overview of the current state of research as well as the extent of the available archaeological evidence, a few preliminary remarks are needed. Pella gained importance when king Archelaos (413-399 BCE) made the city Macedonia's capital instead of Aigai (Papakonstantinou-Diamantourou 1971, pp. 84-87. 209; Lilimbaki-Akamati and Akamatis 2003, pp. 13. 134). A great advantage of Pella was its access to the sea which persisted until the Thermaic Gulf dried up (Hdt. 7, 123; Thuc. 2, 99, 3-4; Papakonstantinou-Diamantourou 1971, pp. 7-24. 200-203; Lilimbaki-Akamati 2007a, p. 586). The city was excavated systematically in 1914-1915, 1957-1970, and 1976-1990 (Papakonstantinou-Diamantourou 1971, pp. 2-4. 199-200; Drougou 1992, p. 15). After 1991, the main objective of the Greek archaeological service's work was the restoration of the excavated buildings (Lilimbaki-Akamati and Akamatis 2003, pp. 120-127. 153-154; 2015). The layout of the Hellenistic city is clear since its central sections are known (Lilimbaki-Akamati and Akamatis 2003): the city centre with its rectangular street system, the *agora* (Akamatis 1999), some small sanctuaries (Lilimbaki-Akamati 1999; 2000), luxurious houses with exquisite furniture (Makaronas and Giouri 1989), the palace of the Argeads on the hill in the north of the city, parts of the city walls in the north, west, and east as well as *necropoleis* (Drougou 1992, pp. 15-26; Lilimbaki-Akamati 1994; Chrysostomou 1998; Lilimbaki-Akamati 2007b; 2008; Lilimbaki-Akamati and Akamatis 2014). The uncovered buildings show a clear chronological peak in the second half of the 4th and the 3rd centuries BCE concerning the public and private sector (Akamatis 1999, p. 31).[1]

At some distance from the archaeological site, in the middle of the modern village of Pella, a rescue excavation under the supervision of Maria Lilimbaki-Akamati in the early 1980s revealed a sanctuary that the excavator interpreted as a *Thesmophorion* (Lilimbaki-Akamati 1996). The complex lies on a hill near the city walls, although it is unclear whether it was inside or just outside the immured space because of uncertainty regarding the fortifications' precise course here.

Description of the excavated remains in the Thesmophorion

A circuit wall built of ashlar masonry surrounds an area of 10 m diameter (Figs. 1 and 2). This area lies below the level of the terrain outside the complex. The wall is 0.50 m wide; three courses of limestone ashlars are conserved to a maximum height of 1.50 m (Lilimbaki-Akamati 1996, pp. 19-22 Pls. 1b. 2a-b; Gelou 2012, pp. 104. 127 Fig. 269a-d.; 132 Fig. 280a-d). The narrowest course lies 15 cm beneath the level of the interior floor. The inner surface of the wall is plastered with clay. In some places,

1 Regarding the city's earlier phases, from the end of the 5th to the first half of the 4th century BCE, cf. Lilimbaki-Akamati 2007a. An extended burned layer containing finds dated up to the third quarter of the 4th century BCE indicates that the evident building boom at the end of the century was the reaction to greater fire destruction around 325 BCE. The rectangular street grid of the Classical city persisted in this phase (Lilimbaki-Akamati 2007a, pp. 592-593).

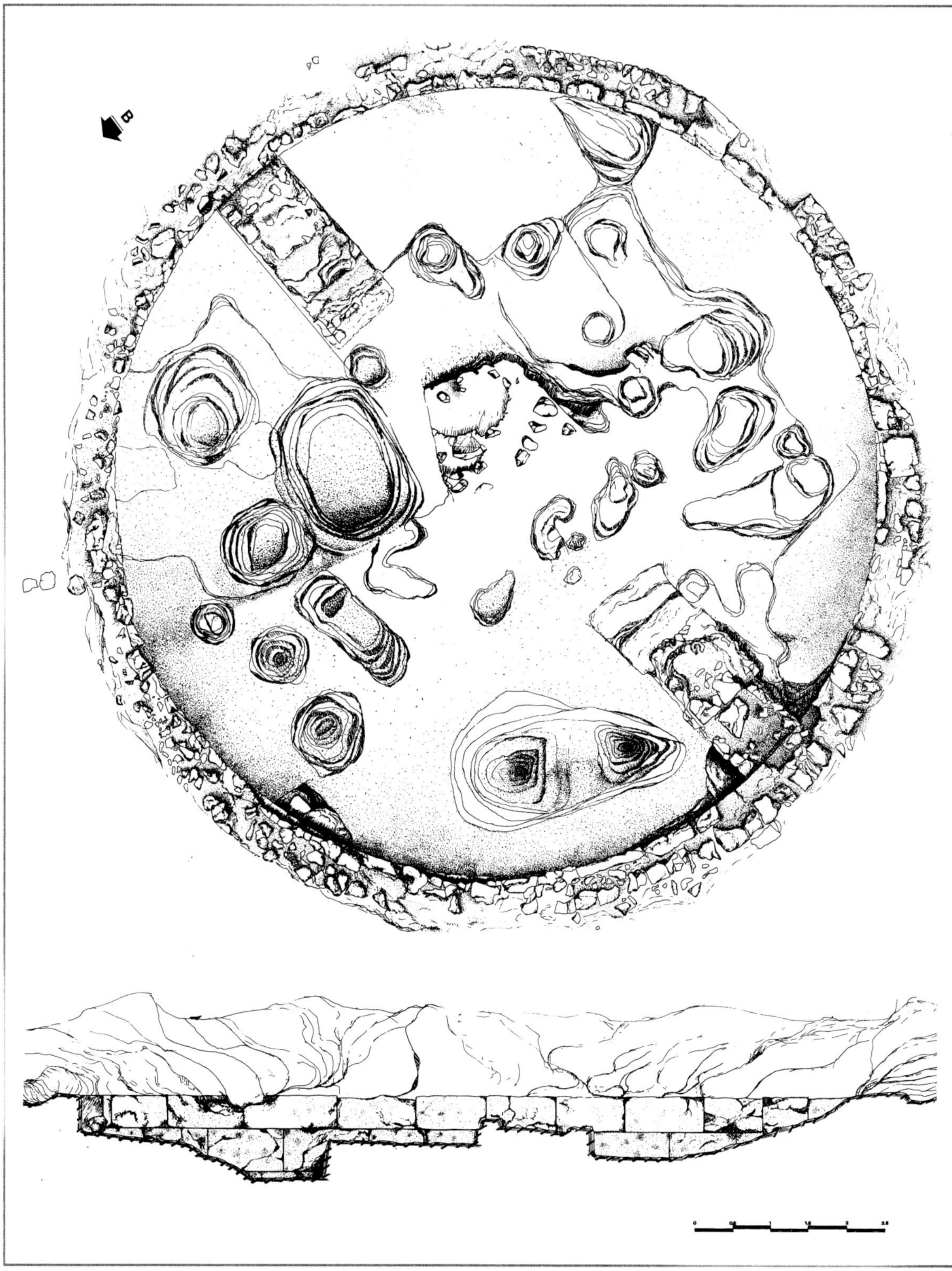

Figure 1. Pella, the so-called Thesmophorion. Ground plan and vertical section (Lilimbaki-Akamati 1996, p. 21 Fig. A).

Figure 2. Pella, the so-called Thesmophorion. View from Northeast (Lilimbaki-Akamati 1996, Pl. 1a).

Figure 3. Pella. Altar in the middle of the enclosure. (Lilimbaki-Akamati 1996, Pl. 5b).

a second layer of plaster is conserved; there, between the two clay layers, fragments of roof tiles are placed to achieve a better bonding of the plaster (Lilimbaki-Akamati 1996, p. 22 Pl. 3a-b; Gelou 2012, pp. 104-105 Pl. 3a-b). The outer surface of the wall is covered entirely by stone grit from the present upper surface to the bedrock (Lilimbaki-Akamati 1996, Pl. 4a; Gelou 2012, p. 105 Fig. 220). Moreover, on the exterior, the wall may have been covered by an earth fill up to its top (Lilimbaki-Akamati 1996, pp. 19-22) so only its upper surface was visible from the surroundings.

Inside the circle, two antithetic-built staircases in the east and west reach from the enclosure down towards the centre of the plain, enabling entrance to the structure. They are about 2.50 m long, one meter wide, and end in separate landings. Their construction and surface are identical with those of the circuit wall (Lilimbaki-Akamati 1996, pp. 22-23; Gelou 2012, pp. 105-106 Fig. 222).

The floor was built by an approximately 35 cm high layer of grit, identical with the material on the outer surface of the circuit wall. Irregular rectangular openings were cut into the floor at numerous spots that reveal pits inside the bedrock called *megara*. These *megara* were dug carelessly, without any pattern or regularity in their distribution, form, or size. The excavator describes rectangular openings sized 1.20-1.80 m x 70-90 cm with pits of 38-52 cm diameter and 40-70 cm depth (Lilimbaki-Akamati 1996, pp. 23-24; Gelou 2012, pp. 106-107).

In the centre of the immured area stands a rectangular installation, 1.40-1.90 m long and approx. 1.10 m high (Fig. 3). The position and form of the installation are indications suggesting an altar, which has been repeatedly renewed as shown by the subsequent nine layers of clay plaster and stone grit on top of each other to a total height of 75 cm. Above them, a 20 cm thick layer of stones sealed the altar. Numerous fragmented terracotta figurines were found between the single layers of stone grit and clay (Lilimbaki-Akamati 1996, pp. 23-24 Pl. 6a-b; Gelou 2012, p. 107 Figs. 224. 225). All this material was removed in order to collect the finds, thus finally revealing the stone platform and stone core of the altar.[2] They both probably consist of the bedrock; the platform still shows its natural form with a roundish shape and some steps, while the higher core was cut to be straightened – as indicated by the obvious horizontal and vertical edges as well as the rectangular cutting in the upper third.

To sum up the excavated situation: the complex consists of a circuit wall which shielded the interior from the outside, two staircases leading down towards the narrower level of the circular area, a regularly renewed altar, and numerous pits that were successively opened and used.

Architecture and materiality of the sanctuary

The excavated remains of the building and its furnishing allow a quite comprehensive reconstruction of the sanctuary in terms of architecture and materiality.

The circuit wall is an enclosure and not the pedestal of a mudbrick wall as one might think on sight. The main indication for this reconstruction is the lack of roof tiles in the excavation finds (Lilimbaki-Akamati 1996, p. 26). Moreover, due to the construction of the staircase and the fact that single steps were identified in the structure, it is most likely that the top step did not rise higher than the conserved top course of the enclosure – I would even reckon that it lay slightly below the upper surface of the wall.[3] With regards to the enclosure's construction, this would thus be sufficient as is and would not require a superstructure of a mudbrick wall.

---

2 The stone core and platform of the altar are clearly visible in the photographs of the publication, however they were not described in detail by the excavator (Lilimbaki-Akamati 1996, pp. 23-24).

3 The conservation of the building does not allow us to securely reconstruct the original height of the wall, nevertheless the ashlar fragments at the top of the enclosure – best visible to the north of the eastern staircase – indicate that a further narrow course completed the wall (Lilimbaki-Akamati 1996, Pl. 3b; Gelou 2012, pp. 127 Fig. 269a-b; 131-132 Figs. 279. 280a-d).

Figure 4 (above left). Terracotta figurines probably depicting Demeter or Kore (Lilimbaki-Akamati 1996, Pl. 18e-st).

Figure 5 (above right). Terracotta figurine depicting Nike (Lilimbaki-Akamati 1996, Pl. 13b).

Additionally, no traces of thresholds, neither *in situ* nor in a different spot, were found so the doors required for a closed building are not evident in the archaeological record. Finally, during the excavation no remains of elapsed mudbricks were detected in the filling of the enclosure, while the collapsed clay plaster of the inner surface could be clearly identified by the excavator along the lower part of the wall (Lilimbaki-Akamati 1996, p. 22).

The building's architecture finds no comparison in the Hellenistic time. Edifices of a round ground plan are rare anyway, and the few that do exist do not match the so-called Thesmophorion in either form or function (Lauter 1986, pp. 176-179): The Philippeion in Olympia was a proper tholos and served as a shrine for the statues of the royal family while the Arsinoeion in Samothrace was a roofed rotunda erected as an assembly room. Moreover, some rooms inside larger roofed complexes in Pella differ obviously in layout and purpose from our sanctuary, while other circular enclosures associated with chthonic rituals (cf. Robert 1939, pp. 229-232; Lilimbaki-Akamati 1996, pp. 25-26; Gelou 2012, pp. 108-111) diverge too much in their age from our case study to be correlated.

Under the circumstances we can hence consider the so-called Thesmophorion in Pella as a unique architecture. The evaluation of this intriguing edifice concerning its form, materiality, and function will follow the information about excavation finds and the structure's dating.

Small finds

The interpretation and dating of the complex are based on the small finds: mainly terracotta figurines, animal bones, and coins; some pottery, glass, and metal objects; and, numerous molluscs. The figurines lay on the floor and inside the layers of the altar, the animal bones inside the *megara*. Most of the bones were from goats, a species still intensively bred in the area; a few cow bones and even fewer piglet bones were also found (Lilimbaki-Akamati 1996, p. 24).[4] In the scarce pottery assemblage, small *hydriai* dominate – single or connected by a ring to a *kernos*.

4 In the Thesmophorion of Thasos unique figurines of piglets were found: their bellies are sliced open so their inner organs (*splachna*) are visible. This form of depiction is surely related to sacrifices made for the worshipped deities (Rolley 1965, pp. 470-471 Figs. 30. 31; Pingiatoglou 1999, p. 914).

Figure 6 (left). Terracotta figurine depicting Athena (Lilimbaki-Akamati 1996, Pl. 14a).

Figure 7 (right). Terracotta figurine depicting Artemis (Lilimbaki-Akamati,1996, Pl. 15g).

Figure 8 (below left). Heads of terracotta figurines depicting Hades (Lilimbaki-Akamati 1996, Pl. 23e-st).

Figure 9 (below right). Terracotta figurine of a horse (Lilimbaki-Akamati 1996, Pl. 26d).

Drinking and storing vessels, clay tablets, miniature and cooking vessels were also found (Lilimbaki-Akamati 1996, pp. 80-93 Pls. 30-39). It is noteworthy that no lamps are to be found among the spectrum of the finds.

The figurines were produced locally (Lilimbaki-Akamati 1996, pp. 77-80) and vary widely in their forms (Lilimbaki-Akamati 1996, pp. 27-77 Pls. 7-28; Gelou 2012,

Figure 10. Reconstruction drawing of the quadriga assembled by the terracotta figurines (Lilimbaki-Akamati 1996, p. 73 Fig. L).

pp. 112-120 Figs. 236-255). *Hydriaphoroi* are especially numerous, also kneeling women with covered heads holding a *thymiaterion* or other cultic objects, or with their arms downwards. These have been interpreted as worshippers. The so-called *hierodoules*, children, and pigs are rare. As usual, many female figurines cannot be identified with certainty: they could be worshippers or goddesses *e.g.* Kore or Demeter (Fig. 4). As far as a denomination is possible, figurines showing deities are more frequent than human figurines, among them strongly moving Nikes (Fig. 5), figurines of Athena (Fig. 6), Artemis (Fig. 7), and Aphrodite. Among the male figurines, Pan, maybe Hermes, Heracles and Hades (Fig. 8) were identified. Furthermore, galloping horses were found. Holes were pierced through the sides of the animals to insert a thin wooden stick and connect the horses in groups of four, thus assembling a *quadriga* (Figs. 9 and 10).

Dating

The 59 coin finds provide evidence for the sanctuary's dating. The oldest ones are bronze coins by Philipp II (359-336 BCE), while the majority are bronze coins by Kassander (316-297 BCE) and Demetrios II (239-229 BCE). The edification of the complex can thus be dated into the third quarter of the 4th century BCE, its heyday into the 3rd century; the sanctuary was gradually abandoned after the Roman conquest after the middle of the 2nd century BCE (Lilimbaki-Akamati 1996, pp. 95-102 Pls. 42-43; Gelou 2012, p. 121 Figs. 256-258).

Religious context and assessment of the sanctuary in Pella

Thesmophoria

The identification of the sanctuary by the excavator as a Thesmophorion is based above all on the *megara* containing animal bones and the terracotta figurines of the deities. The sanctuaries of Demeter and Kore called Thesmophoria were connected mainly with the fertility of earth and men. Attested are the epithet Thesmophoria for Demeter, the denomination Thesmophorion for sanctuaries of the goddess, and the festival of the Thesmophoria dedicated to her. A strict typology is not apparent for either the sanctuaries or the procedure of the festivals (Lilimbaki-Akamati 1996, p. 20 no. 6; Parker 2005, pp. 270-283; Schipporeit 2013). Nevertheless, the testimony of Aristophanes is very often cited to suggest such an identification. In his *Thesmophoriazousae* (693) – performed in 411 BCE – he describes a peculiar custom: at some point before the festival of the goddess, the Athenian women threw piglets into pits dug for this purpose in Demeter's sanctuary; the animals decomposed to a certain degree until the Thesmophoria; in this condition they were taken out of the pits, mixed with crop seeds on the altar and spread on the fields. Pausanias (9, 8, 1) also mentions, in the context of the Thesmophoria in Boeotia, that piglets were thrown into the *megara*, though in contrast to the Athenian ones these are believed to reappear in the sanctuary of Dodona in the subsequent year and don't end up being used on the land.

The procedure described by Aristophanes can be seen as a ritual manuring of the land in order to optimize the harvest earnings. The close connection between this custom and Demeter, goddess of agriculture and fertility, is obvious thus the existence of pits in a sanctuary – especially with remains of animals in them – provides sufficient evidence to identify a cult place for her. The exclusivity of this ritual for the Thesmophoria is, on the contrary, not testified by either Aristophanes or Pausanias. This is why I dispute the identification of the sanctuary in Pella as a Thesmophorion. To support these doubts, I will discuss my considerations on the worshipped deities in the following sections.

Worshipped deities

The evidence for the interpretation of the complex as a place for worship in the sphere of Demeter is still strong. The *hydriaphorai, hierodoules,* piglet, and child figurines are frequently found in her sanctuaries. The female figurines performing rituals can be seen in connection with acts common for the worship of Demeter. The goddess herself could not be firmly identified among the figurines, though some of them could be depictions of Demeter or Kore. I assume that both are to be found among the figurines and that both were worshipped in Pella, but in my opinion the importance of Kore in this context has been rather disregarded to date.

The central myth concerning Kore is well-known and most extensively recounted in the Homeric hymn to Demeter. In short, the divine king of the underworld Hades fell in love with Kore, the daughter of Zeus and Demeter, approached his brother and asked for Kore's hand in marriage. Neither the mother of the bride nor the bride herself were aware of the agreement between both Cronides, so what came next was a huge surprise for both women. While Kore was gathering flowers in a meadow – in some variations of the myth, she was in the company of Athena, Artemis and Aphrodite – the earth opened up, Hades emerged from the opening riding on his chariot, grabbed the maiden, and disappeared with her into the earth to return back to the underworld. Demeter shocked by the disappearance of her child searched for her all over the world and let nature decay. When the goddess found her daughter, an arrangement was made that explains the cycle of the seasons: Kore would henceforth spend half (or more) of the year in this world with her mother and the other half (or less) in the underworld with her husband.

Now, what do we find in Pella? Among the goddesses identified in the terracotta figurines are Nike, Athena, Artemis, and Aphrodite. All of them are frequently present at the abduction of Persephone by Hades: Nike as the charioteer, the other three with Persephone in the meadow (Lindner 1984). More iconographic elements of this episode appear among the terracotta figurines found in the sanctuary; the galloping horses can be reconstructed as part of a *quadriga* due to their technical features (Figs. 9 and 10). Hades appears bearded, with hair flowing in the wind, while even Hermes, who leads the carriage back to the underworld, is possibly identified. Only Persephone cannot be recognized beyond doubt in the spectrum of the figurines, but since her iconography is not distinctive enough, her identification is always problematic; many of the fragmented female figurines could be parts of her depiction. In my opinion, the mentioned indications are so meaningful that the dedication of terracotta figurine groups showing the abduction of Persephone by Hades in Pella can be taken for granted. Consequently, the sanctuary's cultic identity gains a further facet beyond its Demeter-centred orientation to agriculture.

The dedication of terracotta figurine groups showing the abduction of Persephone by Hades suggests that, as in Locri Epizephyrioi or Thasos, in Pella too their marriage – which followed the abduction – and thus their role as a paragon married couple was essential for the sanctuary. Similar to Locri and Thasos, marriageable maidens also addressed the divine couple here and devoted the figurine groups ahead of and for the sake of their own wedding (Rolley 1965, pp. 468-483; Redfield 2003, pp. 346-385; Gelou 2012, pp. 97-98 Figs. 200-204).[5] As a result, the group of deities adored here can be extended to Persephone and Hades. This insight does not support the identification of the sanctuary as a Thesmophorion – although it certainly doesn't disprove it either.

Practice

After elaborating on the cult recipients, I approach the main question considering the common subject of this volume about the agency of this unique architecture. What does the location and design of this installation disclose about the cultic practice? Analytically speaking, two phases can be reconstructed based on the location and disposition of the sanctuary: the walk to the cult place and the subsequent operations in its interior.

The sanctuary is located on a hill at the north-eastern edge of the city – whether still inside or right outside is unclear, as mentioned above. The walk to the sanctuary on the occasion of the festivals was usually performed as a procession of the worshippers. The starting point of the pageant is unknown, but it is very probable that the crowd gathered at some central point in the city and then solemnly strode towards the cult place. If we set this point hypothetically at the agora, the centre of the regularly laid-out city,[6] the distance to the sanctuary would be 1.150 km as the crow flies. The actual way – initially through the rectangularly laid out streets of the city, later on

5 The interpretation of the terracotta figurines depicting the abduction of Persephone by Hades found in the Thesmophorion of Thasos will be extensively discussed in the monograph by the author on the Greek god Hades, in preparation.

6 Processions often started at city gates, but in this case the gate would be a rather unsuitable place for the cortege to begin since its destination lay directly by the city walls and thus too close to the gate to allow for a proper procession to be formed. Concerning the starting points of processions, cf. Agelidis forthcoming.

less regular lanes on the outskirts – was longer. Anyway, the worshippers strode with the required cultic equipment from the urban area to the edge of the city, into more rural realms, and then climbed higher and higher on their way until they approached the sanctuary. Due to its construction, the complex was not visible from the distance, except for the top of the circuit wall, until they reached the stair head.

Now the second phase of the procedure began. After the ascent to the sanctuary, the worshippers began their descent into the enclosure. By using the stairs, they accessed the interior of the round, about 1.50 m beneath the upper surface of the circuit wall.[7] Standing down there one could only partially see the environs of the enclosure: sky, maybe parts of the city wall, and some trees. Sondages in the surroundings did not reveal any traces of other buildings (Lilimbaki-Akamati 1996, p. 25).

Inside the sanctuary actions were concentrated on the altar and the pits. The finding of bones suggests that animals were thrown into the *megara* at some point and were probably removed later – for the pits were not filled with bones when they were excavated but contained only few remains. Presumably, the subsequent treatment of the animals took place on the altar since no other suitable installations like a bench are retraced in the sanctuary. The lack of animal bones at the altar or on the floor suggests that they were handled according to the Aristophanean testimony and tossed on the fields. Evidence suggests the final practice was the deposition of votives at the altar which were then sealed inside the altar itself when it was renewed with the next layer of clay plaster and stones.

To sum up: the location of the sanctuary in relation to the city and its architecture decisively formed the ritual practice and, moreover, influenced the psychological condition of the worshippers prior to and during their encounter with the divine. The agency of the sanctuary building, however, affected the individuals even more strongly through its location, design, and materiality, and effected their appropriate predisposition for the cult as we will see next.

Agency of the architecture

The edification of the sanctuary on a hill above the city could result from a conscious desire to make the experience of approaching the cultic place more impressive for each individual through their physical effort. The more difficult the way to the deities, the more deliberate the encounter with the divine.[8] On the other hand, the descent into the interior of the enclosure was undoubtedly staged. The discrepancy between the surface level inside and outside the circuit wall was man-made – either by deepening the inside by cutting the bedrock or by raising the surrounding area by filling it with earth. Thus, the location and form of the structure were crucial elements for the agency of the architecture erected here.

In my opinion, the same holds true for how it was built and the materials used for the enclosure and its furnishing. The circuit wall was constructed very carefully out of ashlars of considerable size. The expenditure was even increased by plastering the walls with clay in two layers and inserting the fragments of roof tiles on the inner surface, as well as covering them with stone grit on the outer surface. The stairs were built in a similar manner. The floor was furnished with stone grit even though openings had to be created to dig and use the *megara* inside the bedrock. The altar was made of the same materials as the covering of walls and floor, that is to say, clay plaster

---

7 Whether both staircases were used for descending into the round and later ascending outside the sanctuary or one for the descent and the other for the subsequent (immediate?) ascent cannot be decided based on the available evidence.

8 On the psychological effect of processions on their participants, cf. Agelidis 2019; Agelidis forthcoming. On the effect (or 'experiential potential') of landscape and architecture for sanctuary visitors and worshippers, cf. also Westcoat et al. in this volume, on the 'experience of the divine', cf. Christina Williamson in this volume.

and stones. At first it was a narrow installation, but it grew higher over the course of time. With regards to the whole venture we thus notice a remarkable effort made in the choice and combination of materials as well as in every step of the construction.

The sanctuary has been occasionally characterised as 'simple' (Lilimbaki-Akamati 1996, pp. 19. 24). The described expenditure though does not confirm this appellation at all. Certainly, the building's appearance was neither prestigious nor luxurious: the walls were not finely plastered with marble stucco or was the interior embellished with colourful painting or mosaics as in other private and public buildings of Pella.[9] However, the whole workmanship of the edifice documents a careful planning and realisation with a conscious choice of materials and forms. The guise of the sanctuary can be perceived as close to nature, meaning the pristine environment beyond the man-shaped ambience of cities and settlements, given that the intensively-used bedrock, clay, and earth are crude materials provided by nature that keep their rough character even when used for building.[10] Hence the sanctuary is rather more accurately characterised as 'raw textured' than 'simple'. The visibility of the single construction elements that evoke rather basic material than representative design in connection with such a sophisticated building is still intriguing and has to be a semantic component.

The combination of clay and earth in a sanctuary of deities associated with agriculture and fertility is in fact quite obvious, but as far as I am aware has never been applied in a similar way to Pella or as a visual marker to associate a sanctuary with these chthonic deities. This connection was further forged by the architecture's form, which again determined the action and perception of the worshippers: a circuit wall surrounds an area on a narrower level; from the outside, the enclosure appears to be of stone, but resembles an earth pit from the inside. In order to enter the complex, one must descent into this pit and loses visual contact with the everyday world outside; inside the enclosure cultic rites are performed, including the deposition of votives. The entire ambience suggests that the worshippers went down towards the inner earth, which is simultaneously the medium for the communication between humans and the divine. Worshippers and offerings physically descended down into their sphere.

In my opinion this unique, striking feature combined with the unusual and expensive use of ashlar masonry for the walls of the enclosure strongly suggests that the initiators of this building project belonged to the elite of the Macedonian capital, or could even be members of the royal family itself.

Conclusion

Whether the interpretation above is correct or not, the so-called Thesmophorion in Pella is still an exception within the practice of the Macedonians, who usually worshipped their deities in places other than built sanctuaries. The large number of finds, especially terracotta figurines, and the life span of the enclosure testify that the cult at this place was intensive and thus widely accepted, regardless of its founder. Finally, concerning the characteristics of its Hellenistic architecture, the building was innovative in design, materiality, and function and can thus be regarded as

---

9 Buildings in Pella show a common construction method: above a stone pedestal – made of rough or roughly straightened stones – mudbrick walls rise while the roof framework was made of wood and the roof itself consisted of Laconian roof tiles (Makaronas and Giouri 1989, pp. 23-24. 88-123; Akamatis 1999, p. 25; Lilimbaki-Akamati 2000, pp. 31-32). Due to the evidence for plaster covering the walls of the houses giving the appeal of marble (Makaronas and Giouri 1989, p. 29), the excavators assume that this was common practice for all buildings in Pella even when the concrete evidence is missing (Lilimbaki-Akamati 2000, p. 32).

10 Similar to the Sanctuary of the Great Gods in Samothrace, the materials used evoked 'visual resonances' and the architecture merged to a certain degree with the surrounding landscape – cf. Westcoat et al. in this volume.

ground-breaking for the sophisticated style of architecture to follow in the increasingly cross-linked world around the Mediterranean (e.g. Gehrke 2008, pp. 102-103). The large complex staged like a humble installation close to nature meets the Hellenistic *zeitgeist*. The interest in nature is growing, relevant cults flourish, sanctuaries are edified in inaccessible pristine places, and natural formations are modified for cultic use.[11] The construction of a sanctuary for deities connected with the earth is anything but surprising. If my interpretation is correct, however, the disposition of the sanctuary potentially had considerable effect on the cultic practice and individual perceptions of the worshippers, but also set a keen visual mark for the presence of the worshipped deities in the Macedonian capital.

Acknowledgements

I thank Asja Müller and Annette Haug for the invitation to participate in the conference and contribute to this volume, as well as the anonymous reviewers and participants of the conference for their comments and suggestions, especially Katja Sporn and Bonna Wescoat. Moreover, I am deeply grateful to Maria Lilimbaki-Akamati who gave me permission to reproduce photographs and drawings of her research in the Thesmophorion of Pella published in 1996. Finally, I thank Mitja Musberg and Diane Shugart for improving my English text. All mistakes are nevertheless certainly my own.

References

Agelidis, S. 2019. Individuals and polis in cult: the procession from Athens to Eleusis in Classical Times, in: Friese, W., Handberg, S., Kristensen, T.M. (eds.). *Ascending and descending the Acropolis: movement in Athenian religion*, Monographs of the Danish Institute at Athens 21. Aarhus: Aarhus University Press, 179-190.

Agelidis, S. forthcoming. Connecting routes within a polis: religious processions as a reflexion of identity and self-perception in Classical Athens, in: Williamson, C. (ed.). *Sacred landscapes and connecting routes.* Groningen.

Akamatis, I.M. 1999. Αγορά Πέλλας: 15 χρόνια αρχαιολογικής έρευνας, in: Laourdas, B. and Makaronas, C. (eds.). *Ancient Macedonia VI*, Papers held at the fifth international symposium held in Thessaloniki, 15-19 October 1996, Institute for Balkan Studies 272 vol. 1. Thessaloniki: Idryma Meletōn Chersonēsu tu Haimu, 23-43.

Christesen, P. and Murray, S.C. 2010. Macedonian religion, in: Roismann, J. and Worthington, I. (eds.). *A companion to Ancient Macedonia*. Malden, MA: Blackwell Publishing, 428-445.

Chrysostomou, P. 1998. Μακεδονικοί τάφοι Πέλλας Ι. Τάφος *Β', ο ασύλητος. Macedonian tombs at Pella I. Tomb B', undesecrated.* Thessaloniki.

Drougou, S. 1992. Ανασκαφή Πέλλας 1957-1964. Οι *πήλινοι* λύχνοι, Bibliothēkē tēs en Athenais Archaiologikēs Hetaireias 128. Athens: En Athenais Archailogikē Hetaireia.

Gehrke, H.-J. 2008. *Geschichte des Hellenismus*, 4th ed. Oldenburg: Wissenschaftsverlag.

Gelou, L. 2012. Το Θεσμοφόριο της Πέλλας. Μελέτη – Πρόταση Συντήρησης, Αποκατάστασης και Ανάδειξης. Thessaloniki. Available at: http://ikee.lib.auth.gr/record/131467/files/ΤΟ%20ΘΕΣΜΟΦΟΡΙΟ%20ΤΗΣ%20ΠΕΛΛΑΣ.pdf (Accessed 20th August 2019)

Lauter, H. 1986. *Die Architektur des Hellenismus.* Darmstadt: Wissenschaftliche Buchgesellschaft.

11 For another handling with natural elements in Hellenistic times, cf. Sporn in this volume. This inclination towards nature though is not exclusive, neither *for* nor *in* the Hellenistic age; Asja Müller (in this volume) focuses on a different approach to landscape by human actors in the context of sanctuary architecture. On the various ways of this encounter, cf. Mylonopoulos 2008.

Lilimbaki-Akamati, M. 1994. Λαξευτοί θαλαμωτοί τάφοι της Πέλλας, Demosieumata tou Archaiologikkou deltiou 53. Athens: Tameio Archaiologikōn Porōn kai Apollotriōseōn.

Lilimbaki-Akamati, M. 1996. Το Θεσμοφόριο της Πέλλας, Demosieumata tou Archaiologikkou deltiou 55. Athens: Tameio Archaiologikōn Porōn kai Apollotriōseōn.

Lilimbaki-Akamati, M. 1999. Το ιερό της μητέρας των θεών και της Αφροδίτης στην Πέλλα, in: Laourdas, B. and Makaronas, C. (eds.). *Ancient Makedonia VI*, Papers held at the sixt international symposium held in Thessaloniki, 15-19 October 1996, Institute for Balkan Studies 272 vol. 1. Thessaloniki: Idryma Meletōn Chersonēsu tu Haimu, 691-704.

Lilimbaki-Akamati, M. 2000. Το ιερό της μητέρας των θεών και της Αφροδίτης στην Πέλλα. Thessaloniki: Idryma Meletōn Chersonēsu tu Haimu.

Lilimbaki-Akamati, M. 2007a. Στοιχεία για την Πέλλα του πρώτου μισού του 4[ου] αι. π. Χ, in: Laourdas, B. and Makaronas, C. (eds.). *Ancient Makedonia VII*, Papers held at the seventh international symposium held in Thessaloniki, 14-18 October 2002, Institute for Balkan Studies 280. Thessaloniki: Idryma Meletōn Chersonēsu tu Haimu, 585-604.

Lilimbaki-Akamati, M. 2007b. Πέλλης *1*. Κιβωτιόσχημος τάφος με ζωγραφική διακόσμηση από την Πέλλα. Thessaloniki: Υπουργείο Πολιτισμού, ΙΖ' Εφορεία Προϊστορικών και Κλασικών Αρχαιοτήτων.

Lilimbaki-Akamati, M. 2008. Πέλλης *2. Ο πολυθάλαμος τάφος της Πέλλας*. Thessaloniki: Υπουργείο Πολιτισμού, ΙΖ' Εφορεία Προϊστορικών και Κλασικών Αρχαιοτήτων.

Lilimbaki-Akamati, M. and Akamatis, I. (eds.) 2003. Πέλλα και η περιοχή της - *Pella and its environs*. Athens: Υπουργείο Πολιτισμού, 11η Εφορεία Βυζαντινών Αρχαιοτήτων.

Lilimbaki-Akamati, M. and Akamatis, N. 2014. Ανατολικό νεκροταφείο Πέλλας: Ανασκαφικές περίοδοι *1991-2007*. Thessaloniki: Υπουργείο Πολιτισμού και Αθλητισμού.

Lilimbaki-Akamati, M. and Akamatis, I. (eds.) 2015. Συντήρηση-ανάδειξη αρχαιολογικού χώρου Πέλλας και περιοχής της *(2002-2015). Conservation-enhancement of the archaeological site of Pella and its environs (2002-2015)*. Thessaloniki: Εφορεία Αρχαιοτήτων Πέλλας.

Lindner, R. 1984. *Der Raub der Persephone in der antiken Kunst*. Würzburg: Triltsch.

Makaronas, C. and Giouri, E. 1989. Οι οικίες αρπαγής της Ελένης και Διονύσου της Πέλλας, Bibliothēkē tēs en Athenais Archaiologikēs Hetaireias 109. Athens: En Athenais Archailogikē Hetaireia.

Mylonopoulos, J. 2008. Natur als Heiligtum – Natur im Heiligtum. *Archiv für Religionsgeschichte* 10, 51-83.

Papakonstantinou-Diamantourou, D. 1971. Πέλλα Ι. Ιστορική επισκόπησις και μαρτυρίαι, Bibliothēkē tēs en Athenais Archaiologikēs Hetaireias 70. Athen: En Athenais Archailogikē Hetaireia.

Parker, R. 2005. *Polytheism and society at Athens*. Oxford: Oxford University Press.

Pingiatoglou, S. 1999. Η λατρεία της θεάς Δήμητρας στην αρχαία Μακεδονία, in: Laourdas, B. and Makaronas, C. (eds.). *Ancient Makedonia VI*, Papers held at the sixth international symposium held in Thessaloniki, 15-19 October 1996, Institute for Balkan Studies 272 (2). Thessaloniki: Idryma Meletōn Chersonēsu tu Haimu, 911-919.

Redfield, J.H. 2003. *The Locrian Maidens: love and death in Greek Italy*. Princeton: Princeton University Press.

Robert, F. 1939. *Thymélè: Recherches sur la signification et la destination des monuments circulaires dans l'architecture religieuse de la Grèce*. Paris: Éditions De Boccard.

Rolley, C. 1965. Le sanctuaire des dieux Patrôoi et le Thesmophorion de Thasos. *Bulletin de Correspondance Hellénique* 89, 441-483.
Schipporeit, S.T. 2013. *Kulte und Heiligtümer der Demeter und Kore in Ionien*, Byzas 16. Istanbul: Ege Yayınları.

Notes on contributor

Soi Agelidis - Institute of Archaeological Studies, Ruhr-Universität Bochum (present). Studies of Classical Archaeology, Art History and Classical Philology (Greek) in Bonn; PhD Bonn 2004; Independent Researcher at the Staatliche Skulpturensammlung, Kunstsammlungen Dresden 2005-2006; Research Fellow at the Deutsches Archäologisches Institut Abteilung Istanbul 2006-2008; Assistant Researcher at the Antikensammlung, Staatliche Museen Berlin 2008-2010; Research Associate at the Deutsches Archäologisches Institut Abteilung Athen 2010-2015; Lecturer at the Institute of Classical Studies Albert-Ludwigs-Universität Freiburg 2015-2016; Assistant Professor at the Institute of Archaeological Studies, Ruhr-Universität Bochum 2016-2019; Scientific Director of the Kunstsammlungen Antike at the Ruhr-Universität Bochum 2020-.

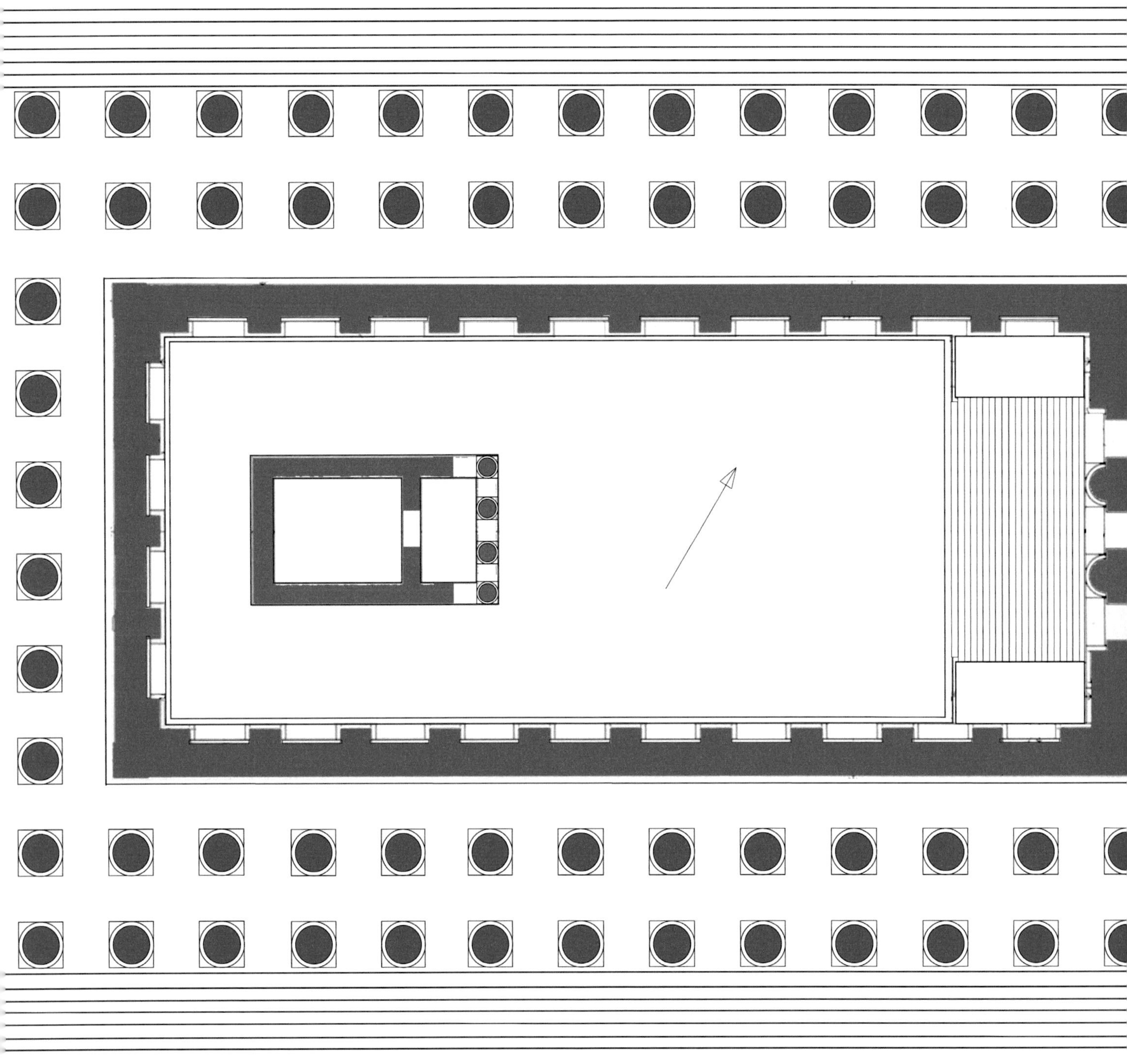

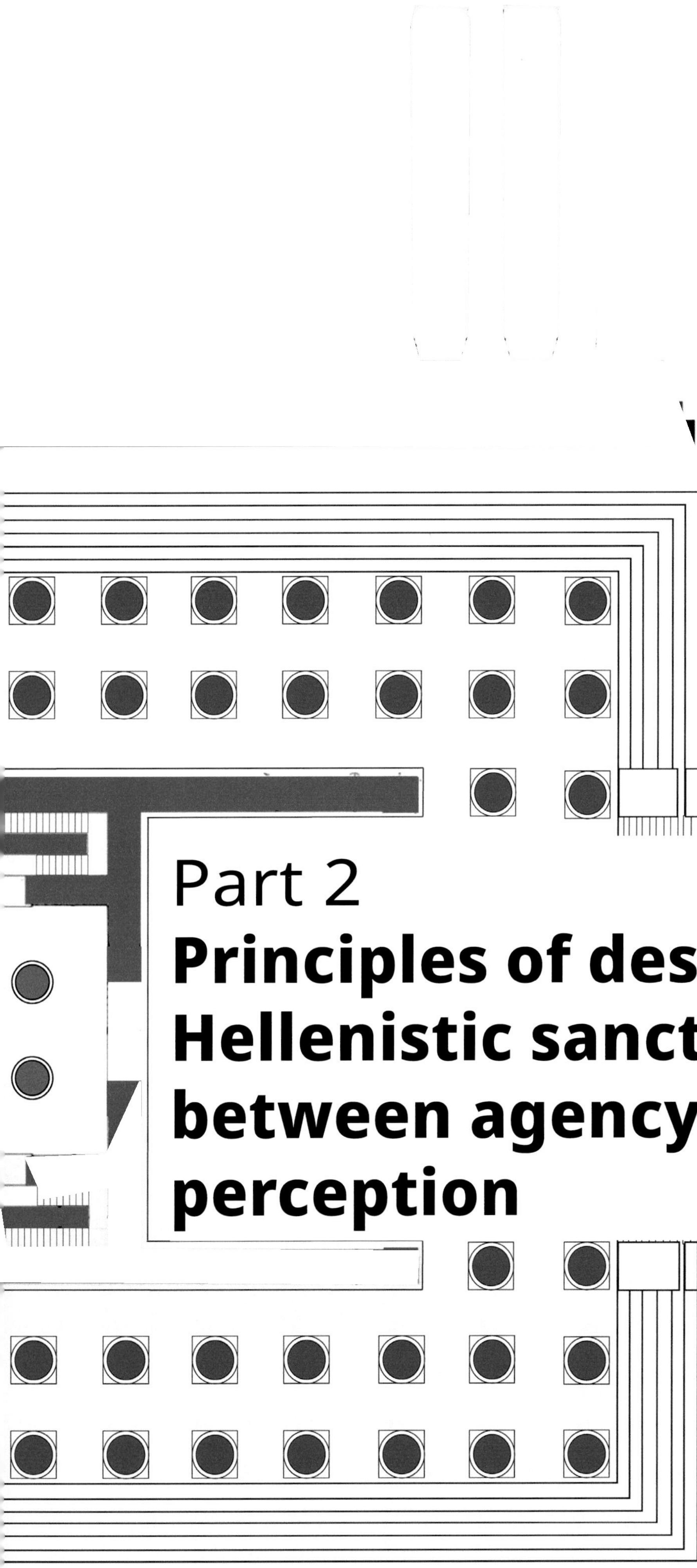

Part 2
Principles of design: Hellenistic sanctuaries between agency and perception

The Usage of the Pronaos of Hellenistic Temples

Philipp Kobusch

Abstract

The article deals with the pronaos of Hellenistic temples as a space for action. The aim is to explore its characterization and usage in antiquity. On the basis of an analysis of the architectural disposition on the one hand and the equipment on the other, it can be shown, that different pronaoi show a broad spectrum of different usages. Although pronaoi are a relatively uniform architectural room, they could be partly staged as open public space, partly they were used as treasury, as waiting room and as a place for cultic activities. Thus the building type 'pronaos' could be used multifunctional. However, the individual pronaos is not a multifunctional room per se but could sometimes be subject to specific concepts of usage.

Keywords: temple, pronaos, ritual, agency, public and sacral space

Introduction

> *'συμπροθυμουμένων δὲ καὶ τῶν Συρακοσίων τῇ τοῦ Διονυσίου προαιρέσει, πολλὴν συνέβαινε γίνεσθαι τὴν φιλοτιμίαν περὶ τὴν τῶν ὅπλων κατασκευήν. οὐ μόνον γὰρ ἐν τοῖς προνάοις καὶ τοῖς ὀπισθοδόμοις τῶν ἱερῶν, ἔτι δὲ τοῖς γυμνασίοις καὶ ταῖς κατὰ τὴν ἀγορὰν στοαῖς, ἔγεμε πᾶς τόπος τῶν ἐργαζομένων, ἀλλὰ καὶ χωρὶς τῶν δημοσίων τόπων ἐν ταῖς ἐπιφανεστάταις οἰκίαις ὅπλα παμπληθῆ κατεσκευάζετο.'*

> *'And since the Syracusans enthusiastically supported the policy of Dionysius, it came to pass that rivalry rose high to manufacture the arms. For not only was every space, such as porticoes [i.e.* pronaoi*] and back rooms of the temples [i.e.* opisthodomoi*] as well as the gymnasia and colonnades of the market place, crowded with workers, but the making of great quantities of arms went on, apart from such public spaces, in the most distinguished homes.'* (Diod. 14, 41, 6; transl. Oldfather 1954).

Christian-Albrechts-Universität zu Kiel
Johanna-Mestorf-Str. 5
24118 Kiel
Germany
kobusch@klassarch.uni-kiel.de

In his report on the preparations for war by the Syracusans in the 4th century BCE, the Greek historian Diodor (1st century BCE) described the production of weapons in the *pronaoi*[1] and *opisthodomoi* of urban temples as a matter of course. The situation only becomes extraordinary by the fact that the Syracusans used even rich private houses as workshops.

Regardless of the question about the historical truth of this report, two central statements about the Greek *pronaos* can be derived from it, which Diodor expected to be familiar to his readers. Firstly, the *pronaos*, and with it the *opisthodomos*, were together with the colonnaded halls and the *gymnasia* considered as public spaces (*δημόσιος τόπος*), so that it could not surprise the reader that they were used for public purposes if necessary, even if these concerns had no obvious relation to the cult.

At the same time, it can also be deduced that both rooms were understood as clearly defined compartments of the Greek temple. Although they were part of the entire temple, their use differed fundamentally from that of the *cella*, which was not counted among the public spaces.

In modern research, on the contrary, without reference to Diodor, the *pronaos* is generally understood merely as the antechamber of the *cella* and, accordingly, evaluated only in its dependence on the *cella*.[2] Mattern (2015, pp. 118-127), for example, analysed the effects of his design on the illumination of the *cella*, while von Hesberg (1994, p. 71; 2007, pp. 447-449) thematised the *pronaos* as part of a staggered spatial staging of the entire temple. If, however, according to Diodor, the *pronaos* could also be understood as part of the public space, it seems worthwhile to consider the *pronaos* not only in its relationship to the *cella*, but also in its larger topographical context, *i.e.* in relation to the outside space. Of particular interest are its openness and accessibility, which can be regarded as a basic prerequisite for public use. On the other hand, it is also possible to ask about specific forms of use which have found their expression in an archaeologically comprehensible furnishing of *pronaoi* and which might give hints for the characterization of the room in general. In this way, the interpretation of Diodor can be checked and, if necessary, corrected or extended.

With the *pronaos*, a space is taken into focus that is architecturally clearly defined. Despite a certain typological diversity, it is always a semi-open space directly in front of the *cella*. As such, it is an essential part of the Greek temple, which is missing only in exceptional cases. In contrast to the *cella*, however, its use is not marked by a cult image that is always present in the inner temple, at least in Hellenistic times. Therefore, the question arises how such a space between inside and outside was used and perceived. Answers to this question can contribute to the understanding of architecture and its impact on human action and perception.

Peripteral temples and their topographical integration

Already the earliest Doric *peripteroi* in Greece (for a general outline of the development of Greek temples, cf. in the following: Gruben 2001; Knell 1988), such as the temple of Hera in Olympia (Fig. 1.1; Dörpfeld 1892, pp. 32-33 Pl. 18; Mallwitz 1966) or the temple of Artemis on Corfu (Schleif 1940, pp. 48-50 Fig. 39), have a fully developed *pronaos* as an essential element. This compartment preserves some basic typological characteristics until the Hellenistic period. In almost all cases the room is completely closed at the sides by the far

1 Diodor uses the rarely applied noun πρόναος/πρόναον. More commonly used in antiquity was the term ὁ πρόδομος: von Gerkan 1946, pp. 46-47.

2 The only exception is the investigation of Steuernagel 2014a, pp. 62-63, which discusses individual examples. See as well Williamson 2018, p. 316, with a focus on the *cella* door and the threshold.

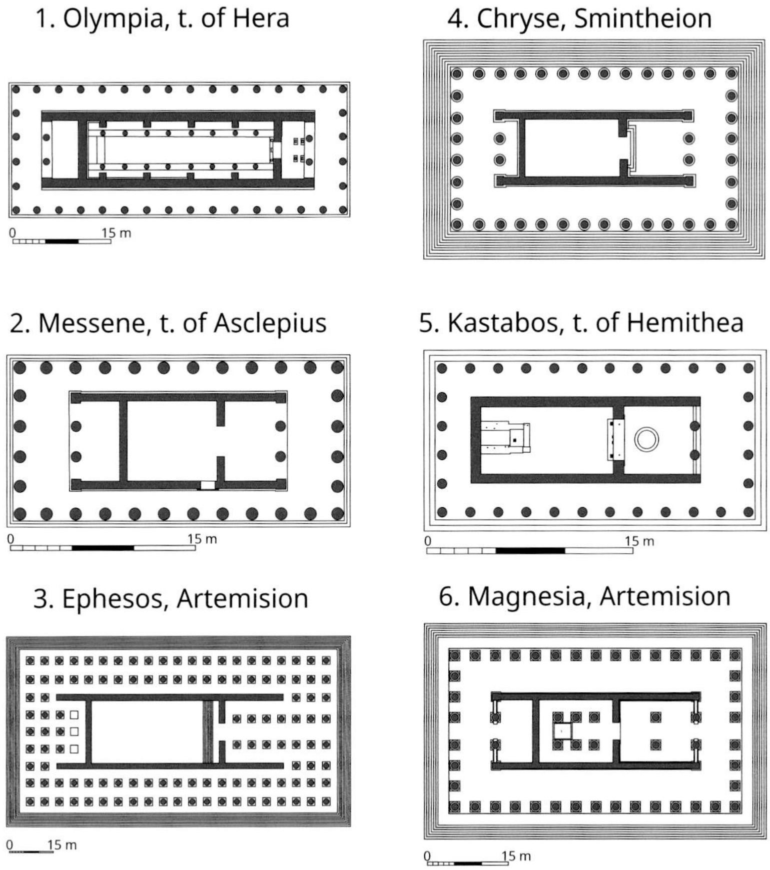

Figure 1. Peripteral temples. 1 Olympia, temple of Hera (plan: Philipp Kobusch after Mallwitz 1966, Fig. 17); 2 Messene, temple of Asclepius (plan: Philipp Kobusch after Sioumpara 2011, Pl. 15); 3 Ephesos, Artemision (plan: Philipp Kobusch after Bammer and Muss 1995, Fig. 62); 4 Chryse, Smintheion (plan: Philipp Kobusch after Newton and Pullan 1881, Pl. 26); 5 Kastabos, temple of Hemithea (plan: Philipp Kobusch after Cook and Plommer 1966, Fig. 78); 6 Magnesia, Artemision (plan: Philipp Kobusch after Kohte 1904, Fig. 30).

advancing antae, while it opens to the *pteron* via two columns at the front. Only in Magna Graecia do *pronaoi* exist, which are also open at the sides with *prostyle* columns, for example the temple of Athena in Paestum or temple G in Selinunt (Mertens 2006, pp. 224-225. 231-232. 234 Figs. 389. 390. 401). In Greece and Asia Minor, the depth of the *pronaoi* at this time is often oriented on the dimensions of the porch of the *peristasis* or even somewhat smaller compared to it.

Through this and through the usual axial relationship of the columns in antis with the columns of the *peristasis*, the *pronaos* is on the one hand staged as an extension of the *pteron*, but at the same time distinguished by the closed *antae* as an independent interior and separated from the *pteron*. In Archaic and especially in Classical times, however, due to its small size, it usually remains a subordinate room to the deep *cella*. In Doric buildings, the inner columns of the *cella* are usually not continuing into the *pronaos*, which clearly distinguishes the design of both rooms from each other.

This is particularly clear in cases where the inner columns are close to the *cella* walls, as in the Heraion of Olympia, or later in Bassae (Cooper 1996, pp. 283-292 Pl. 10) and Tegea (Østby 2014, Pl. 1). The *pronaos* of these buildings can certainly be described as an independent space, but it does not take on any special importance in the overall ensemble, and stands and mediates between *pteron* and *cella*.

Exceptions can be observed above all in outstanding Archaic Ionic buildings, such as the *dipteroi* of Heraion on Samos (Kienast 2012, Fig. 1.6) or the Archaic Artemision of Ephesus (Ohnesorg 2007, Pls. 36. 37), where the *pronaos* is not only significantly extended, but also contains two rows of inner columns as a continuation of the *peristasis*. The same can be observed in some Late Classical and Hellenistic buildings in Asia Minor, partly because they adopt an Archaic ground plan, as it was the case in the Artemision of Ephesus (Fig. 1.3).

But in comparison to the Archaic and Classical times, in the Late Classical and Hellenistic period, the *pronaos* is often clearly accentuated compared to the porch and the *cella*, by enlarging it and at the same time reducing the size of the *cella*, for instance in the so-called Smintheion (Fig. 1.4; Newton and Pullan 1881, pp. 40-48 Pl. 26), the temple of Hemithea at Kastabos (Fig. 1.5; Cook and Plommer 1966, passim) or in the temple of Asclepius in Messene (Fig. 1.2; Sioumpara 2011, passim Pl. 15) up to the point, where *pronaos* and *cella* are of the same size (Fig. 1.6). Even if the balance of the individual parts of the room changes in a few cases in the Archaic, and in many cases in the Hellenistic period, the *pronaos* nevertheless remains a component of the temple that can be characterized as an interior room due to its three-sided closure – the general typological characteristica didn't change. Through the *peristasis* it is in any case separated from the open spaces of the sanctuary, specifically the temple forecourt with the altar as the most important sacrificial site. In addition, the *pronaoi* of *peripteral* temples were regularly fenced off, at the latest since the Late Archaic period.[3] For the Late Classical and Hellenistic periods, barriers can indeed be found in every temple whose state of preservation permits a statement, *i.e.* in which the *stylobate* or the columns are preserved *in antis*,[4] while the *ptera* as a rule remained freely accessible.[5]

Most of these barriers were permanently installed and are considered to be part of the first phase. This is proven for the temple of Asclepius in Epidauros, where such doors between the columns (τὰ διὰ στύλων θυρώματα) are attested in the construction accounts (Prignitz 2014, text I, line 44-45. 61-62. 259; 54. 260-261). In all cases it will be lattice constructions, probably made of wood, as Vitruvius demands for a *peripteros*.

> '*et si aedes erit latitudine maior quam pedes XX, duae columnae inter duas antas interponantur, quae disiungant pteromatos et pronai spatium. item intercolumnia tria, quae erunt inter antas et columnas, pluteis marmoreis sive ex intestino opere factis intercludantur, ita uti fores habeant, per quas itinera pronao fiant.*'
>
> '*The three intercolumniations between the antae and the columns should be blocked off by parapets of marble or cabinetry, but in such a way that they have doors to provide access to the front portico.*'(Vitr. 4, 4, 1; transl. Rowland 1999).

The *pronaos* was clearly separated from the *pteron* by these barriers and the accessibility of the *pronaoi* could be controlled situatively. Temple inventories also repeatedly record large quantities of small-format valuable votive offerings, which were stored and exhibited not only in the *cella*, but also in the *pronaos* (Hamilton 2000). The latticework provided protection for the objects and made it possible to perceive them from the outside, without entering the room itself. With the door of the *cella* open at the same time, the innermost part of the temple with the central cult image could additionally be made visible from the *pteron*, without neglecting the protection of the votive offerings. In this case, the viewer thus perceived the *pronaos* and the *cella* at one glance as a joint ensemble and as equally isolated and thus exclusive interiors with presumably rich furnishings. However, the use of the *pronaos* as a lockable treasure house is completely contrary to Diodor's characterization of a public, multifunctional space.

---

3 *E.g.* Aegina, temple of Aphaia: Fiechter 1906, pp. 34-35.

4 *E.g.* Cos, temple A (Schazmann 1932, p. 5); Kastabos, temple of Hemithea (Fig. 1.5; Held and Wilkening Aumann 2015, p. 83); Labraunda, temple of Zeus (Hellström and Thieme 1982, p. 24 Pls. 7.2-3. 29.3. 40); Magnesia, temple of Artemis Leukophryene (Fig. 1.6; Kohte 1904, pp. 77-79 Figs. 74-78); Priene, temple of Athena Polias (Koenigs 2015, pp. 22-23 Fig. 23).

5 The only exceptions where barriers between the columns of the peristasis are detectable can be found in Aegina (Fiechter 1906, p. 34; Bankel 1993, pp. 8. 85 Pl. 54) and in Kalapodi (Hellner 2014, pp. 298-299 Fig. 10.14).

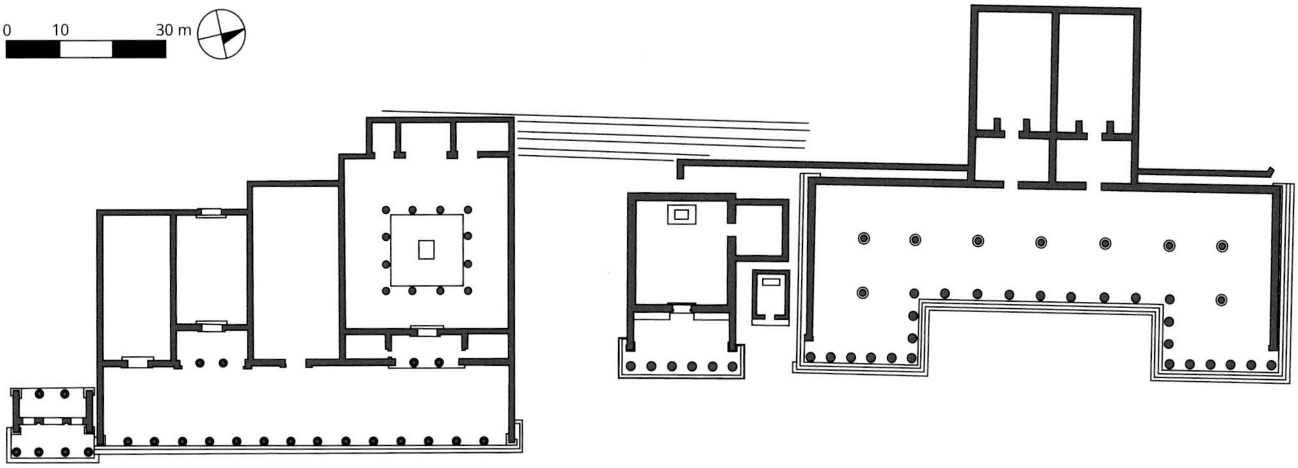

Non-peripteral temples and their topographical integration

Figure 2. Athens, western part of the agora. Temple of Apollon Patroos (plan: Philipp Kobusch after Knell 1994, p. 223 Fig. 4; Thompson 1937, p. 219 Fig. 126).

While the *pronaos* of *peripteral* temples had to be perceived as an interior space simply because a colonnade is located in front of it, the *pronaos* of temples without *peristasis* is always directly part of the outer facade. Accordingly, the room immediately adjoins the free space in front of the temple. With the decline of *peripteral* buildings towards the end of the Classical period, smaller *antae* temples and *prostyloi* are known to represent the majority of the newly erected temples (Knell 1983; Lauter 1986, pp. 180. 189).

Parallel to the development of the *peripteral* temples, an increased interest in the *pronaos* can also be noticed in smaller temple buildings. This is reflected both in the fact that the *pronaoi* could be deeper in comparison to many Archaic or Classical buildings and thus have a completely new importance compared to the *cellae*. (Fig. 9; Mattern 2015, pp. 107-115). On the other hand, the use of different floors, for example, made it possible to create a staggered space (von Hesberg 1994, p. 71; 2007, pp. 447-449).

In the Late Classical period, however, the topographical embedding of the temples also changed fundamentally, as has been pointed out on various occasions (Knell 1983, pp. 226-228; Lauter 1986, pp. 106-110. 193; for the archaic time, s. esp. Bergquist 1967, pp. 96-100). Until the 5th century, temples were primarily staged as three-dimensional bodies in space – for example by a path leading to a corner of the building. In this way, the depths of both the long and narrow sides could be perceived at a glance. Since the 4th century, however, temple buildings have been increasingly related to a frontal view and the front façade has become the defining design element – *i.e.* the *pronaos* behind it came into special focus.

This evolution also includes the fact that temples were increasingly used for the architectural bordering of public squares and were integrated into overarching architectural prospectuses (Lauter 1986, pp. 106-111. 113; Gruben 2001, pp. 440-468).

A good example is the temple of Apollo Patroos (second half of 4th century BCE) on the west side of the Athenian *agora* (Fig. 2; Thompson 1937, pp. 77-115). It adjoins the open square of the *agora* and due to its *prostyle* design fits in with the halls bordering the agora. Its *hexastyle* front (Knell 1994, pp. 220-221 Fig. 5) especially mirrors even in its dimensions the shape of the *risalite* of the neighbouring *stoa* of Zeus from the 5th century. Although the latter fulfilled a religious function as well, it has explicitly been recorded that it was used for informal purposes, for example for philosophical lectures (Wycherley 1957, nos. 25. 33-34. 36).

Due to its comparable architectural structure, the *pronaos* of Apollo Patroos offered more or less the same options for usage. The fact that this room was open

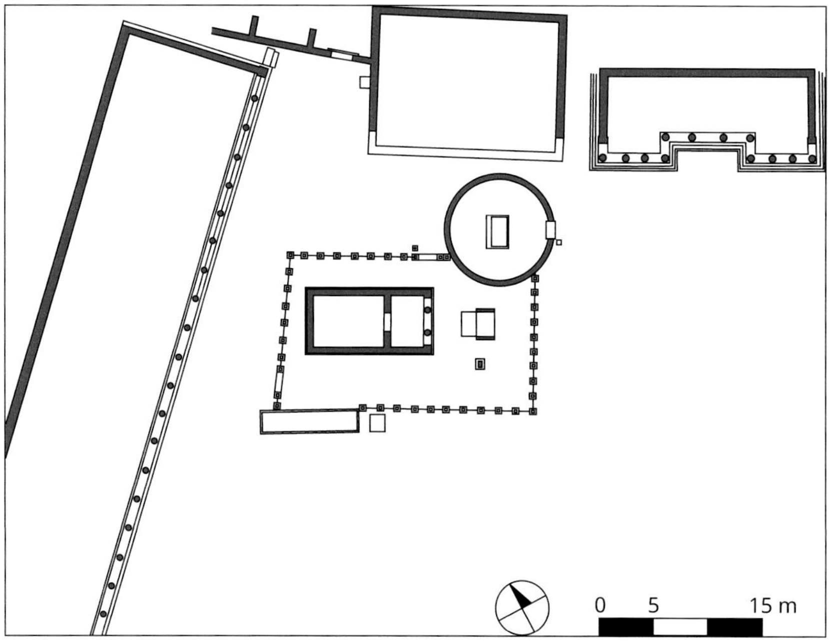

Figure 3. Thasos. Temple of Zeus Agoraios in the north-western part of the agora (plan: Philipp Kobusch after Grandjean and Salviat 2000, p. 74 Fig. 31).

to a wider public is also suggested by a lattice door on the threshold to the *cella* (Thompson 1937, p. 100 Fig. 53). Similar to the barriers of the *pronaoi* in *peripteral* temples, this lattice allowed a glimpse into the interior and onto the cult image without entering the *cella* itself. However, the access control had now moved to the *cella* threshold and thus further into the interior of the entire building.

The temple of Zeus Agoraios on Thasos (Fig. 3) shows a similar topographical situation but a fundamentally different solution (beginning of 4th century BCE: Grandjean and Salviat 2000, p. 76 Figs. 31. 32). The temple was positioned in the open space of the *agora* and therefore played an extraordinarily prominent role in the entire ensemble. It too was in close proximity to a pi-shaped *stoa* with gable-crowned *risalites* (Grandjean and Salviat 2000, pp. 66-67 Figs. 26-28). But in contrast to the situation in Athens, the temple was neither in its dimensions nor in its design oriented on this hall. Rather, the builders chose the form of an *antae* temple. Moreover, the small *temenos* around the temple was separated from the *agora* square by barriers, and so the temple as a whole and the *pronaos* in particular remained largely excluded from the public life in the *agora*. Although both examples were cults with a clear political function, their relation to public space was interpreted in different ways.

A third alternative of the relationship to public space can be observed in Magnesia. The temple of Zeus Sosipolis was likewise erected on the open space of the *agora*. Its *pronaos* showed a certain openness with *prostyle* columns but was probably barred already in the first phase (Kohte 1904, p. 157). This *pronaos* was therefore intended to be easily visible, but not accessible to the public.

In some sanctuaries, temple fronts were set in direct dependence to column halls, *i.e.* to multifunctional buildings. Especially impressive is the situation in the sanctuary of Despoina in Lykosoura (Leonardos 1896, pp. 95-120 Pls. 1-4; Billot 2008). Here a long *stoa* has been placed directly adjacent to the temple so that the fronts of the *stoa* and the temple together formed almost a joint column

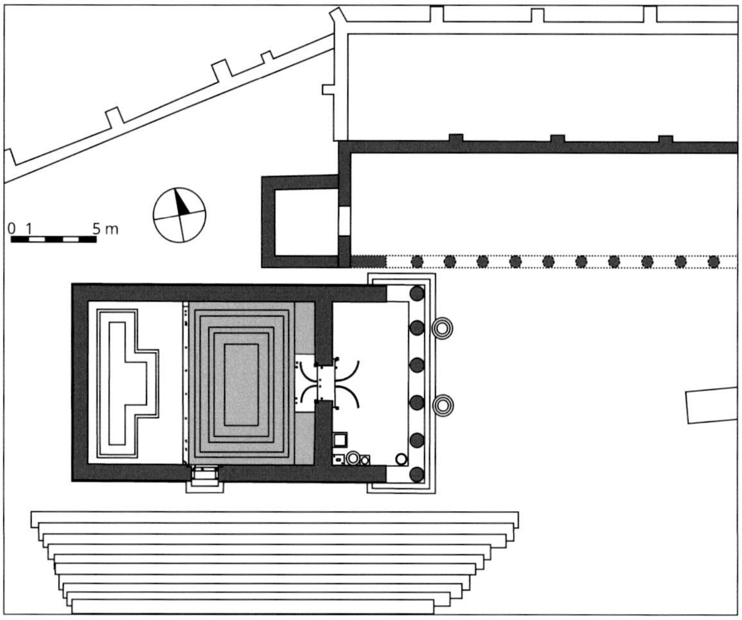

Figure 4. Lykosoura. The sanctuary of Despoina (plan: Philipp Kobusch after Leonardos 1896, Pls. 1. 2).

façade (Fig. 4).[6] Via the passage between the northern temple, and the northern column, the *pronaos* was directly connected to the columned hall, so that it will have looked almost like a continuation of the hall with only a slightly smaller depth. A barrier between the front columns can certainly be excluded, because there are no visible signs for it at the *stylobate* or the columns.

But what has been recorded in this example, too, was a grille in front of the main door, probably already in Hellenistic times. In fact, two different grilles can be distinguished. One latticed door can be reconstructed on the basis of holes in the pavement in front of the threshold (Billot 2008, p. 146; von Hesberg 2007, p. 446; Steuernagel 2014b, p. 80). This one might have undergone a later restoration, as there is an additional hinge hole at the north. A second latticed door is indicated by several holes on the tread of the threshold itself.[7] Although there is evidence that the temple underwent two major repairs in the Early Imperial period (*IG* V2, 515. 520), at least this complex situation with possibly three phases of grilles suggests that one of these constructions may have been part of the original plan and later had to be replaced by a second construction.

The whole situation was based on an understanding of the *pronaos* as a space accessible to the public while the access to the *cella* was restricted.

Significantly, there are several comparisons (Lauter 1986, p. 102) for the disposition of temple and *stoa*, but in none of them is the connection between the two architectures as close as in Lykosoura. Rather, a greater distance between the two buildings and the use of the type *antae* temple emphasise the closeness of the *pronaos* in comparison to the *stoa*, for example in the Asclepieion of Athens, (Travlos 1971, pp. 127-128 Figs. 171-175) or in the sanctuary of Demeter in Pergamon (Bohtz 1981, pp. 40-41 Pl. 42.2). Moreover, in Athens the *stoa* is also partially fenced off so that the direct transition from hall to *pronaos* was explic-

6 However, the proportions of the columns were different. While the temple columns had a lower diameter of about 0.81 m (Leonardos 1896, p. 105), the columns of the hall were much smaller at about 0.68 m (Coulton 1976, p. 253). The chronological relationship between *stoa* and temple is not known. Leonardos (1896, p. 118) assumed due to the levels that the hall could not be younger than the temple. Coulton (1976, p. 253) on the other hand thought that the hall must be later than the temple because of the equipment. But this can also be added secondary and therefore only gives a terminus *ante quem* for the *stoa* in Hellenistic times.

7 Leonardos 1896, Pl. 2. There is no description published yet.

itly prevented in both buildings. Thus, although the sanctuaries follow a very similar basic concept, the *pronaos* was included in very different ways.

The same can be observed in examples in which *pronaoi* are directly integrated into surrounding columned halls, as is the case at the so-called northern market of Miletus, (Fig. 5; von Gerkan 1922, pp. 30-33. 92-93 Figs. 46-48 Pl. 4.1-2. 16) or in the sanctuary of Zeus Soter in Megalopolis (Fig. 6; Lauter-Bufe 2009, esp. pp. 53-55). In both instances columned halls enclose the *pronaos* so that in the front view only the slightly protruding temple front with the pediment emphasized the temple.

In Miletus, the back wall of the Pronaos was aligned with the back wall of the *stoa*. The transition from the hall to the *pronaos* was possibly accentuated only by a narrowing of the passage via two *antae*. A door between these two *antae* cannot be reconstructed safely because there is no continuous foundation between the *antae* that could indicate the existence of a threshold.[8]

In other words, the *pronaos* and the halls were staged as part of the same ensemble, the transition from one to the other was possibly without restriction, but nevertheless they were conceived and staged as two different rooms. In Megalopolis, on the other hand, the narrow antechamber in front of the *cella* was preceded by a second hall with protruding *antae* and *prostyle* columns, which formed the outer façade of the temple – a similar situation to that of a *peripteral* temple. The outer porch opened onto the court, while the inner antechamber was separated from the surrounding halls by a closed wall after the recent reconstruction by Heide Lauter-Bufe. Although the temple and the surrounding colonnaded halls formed a closed building complex here as well, they were structurally clearly differentiated from each other. It was not possible to cross directly from the portico into the *pronaos*.

The situation in Dodona (Charises 2010, pp. 163-166 Fig. 19) is very comparable. In the last phase, an open colonnade was also placed in front of the temple of Zeus, which in this case exactly took up the depth of the surrounding halls, but was not connected to them. The real anteroom of the *cella* was only accessible via this porch, but not from the surrounding halls.

Further examples can be added, which show that a similar topographical situation could nevertheless lead to very different solutions, depending on the interpretation of the *pronaos*. For example, in both the Asclepieia of Cos and Epidauros, smaller temples have been used bordering the main road within the sanctuary. But while in Epidauros the temple Lambda (Roux 1961, pp. 241-246 Fig. 59) had a *prostyle* and therefore very open porch, the *pronaos* of the small temple B on Cos (Fig. 7; Schazmann 1932, pp. 34-39 Figs. 24-27 Pls. 16-21. 49. 51. 53) was closed off by protruding *antae*. Moreover, in the latter case the *intercolumnia* were blocked by barriers (Fig. 7.2; unpublished) and the *pronaos* was thus closed for uncontrolled use. The threshold has been replaced in a secondary phase. The new threshold has two small latching holes on the tread (Fig. 7.3), which could speak in favour of a latticed gate in front of the *cella* door.

A particularly striking staging of a public *pronaos* can finally be observed at the temple of Hera Basileia in Pergamon (Fig. 8; Schazmann 1923, pp. 102-110 Pls. 4-8. 32; Dörpfeld 1912, pp. 256-269 Fig. 3 Pls. 17. 18. 22-22A). The sanctuary, above the gymnasium, consists of two long narrow terraces on a slope. Centrally on the upper terrace, the *prostyle* temple faces south towards the altar, which can be located on the lower terrace. To the west and east of the temple there are other buildings on the upper terrace: an exedra and a large rectangular building. The sanctuary was accessible from the west. The path first led to the lower terrace. From there a central staircase led to

8 Emme (2013, p. 51) on the other hand, assumes a closed wall, analogous to the sanctuary of Zeus in Megalopolis. In fact, it cannot be completely ruled out that the foundations were looted at this point, but the fact that the foundations are missing on both sides in a similar way suggests an opening.

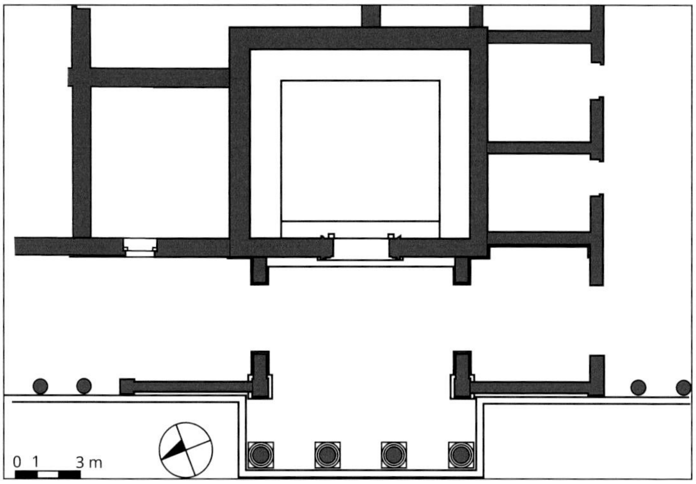

Figure 5. Miletus. Northern market (plan: Philipp Kobusch after von Gerkan 1922, Fig. 47 Pl. 12).

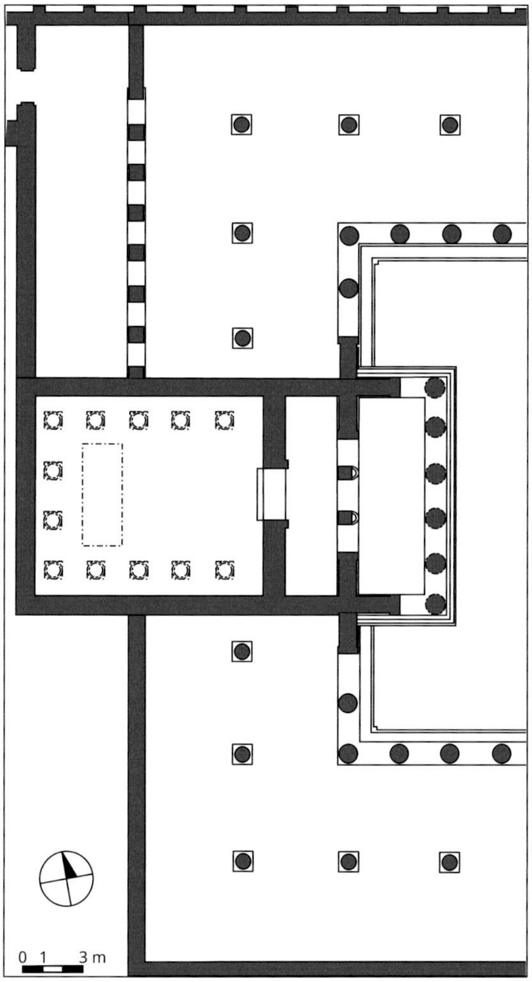

Figure 6. Megalopolis. Temple of Zeus Soter (plan: Philipp Kobusch after Lauter-Bufe 2009, Beil. 5).

the temple front, ending directly in the *pronaos* of the temple. Possibly there was also a small rock staircase in the west, but because of its size it was certainly not part of the main route. In order to reach the buildings to the west, and especially the ones to the east of the temple via the main staircase, a visitor had to necessarily enter the *pronaos*, which here functioned as a central distribution room of the sanctuary. Again, in this example, a lattice door on the threshold to the *cella* (Schazmann 1923, p. 107 Pl. 34.26)

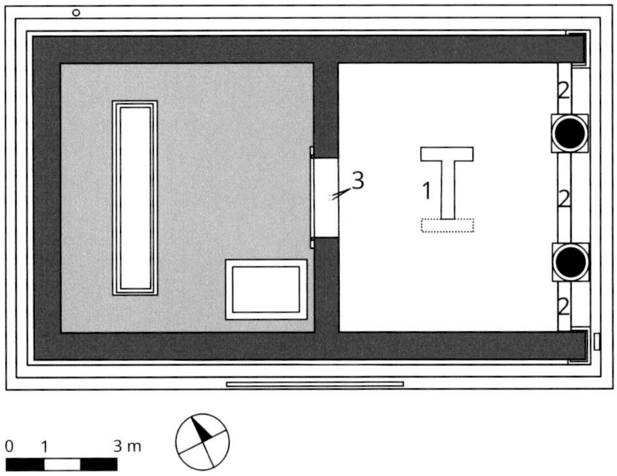

Figure 7. Cos. Temple B (plan: Philipp Kobusch after Schazmann 1932, Pl. 17).

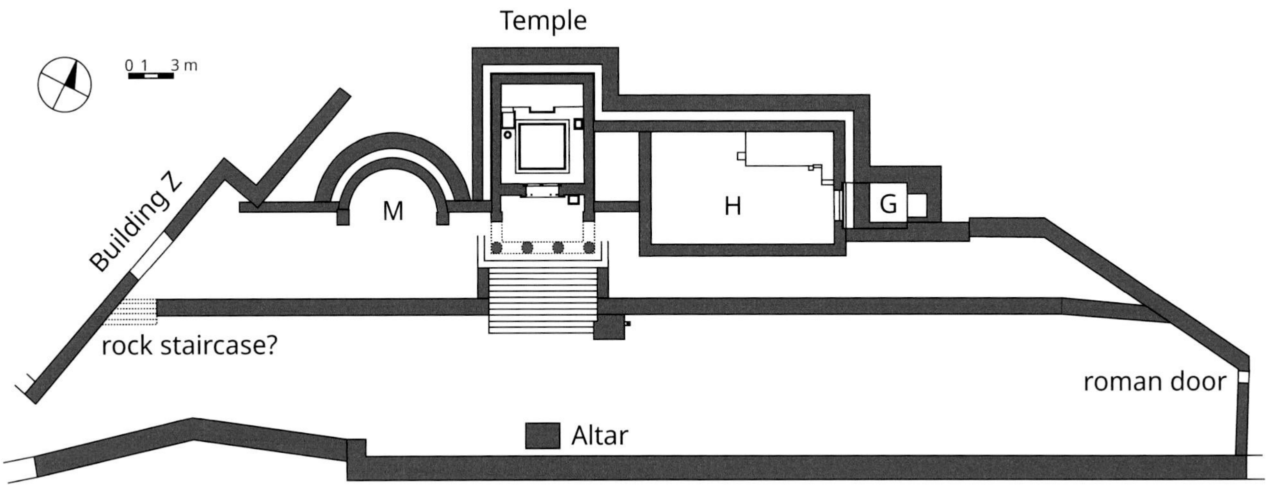

Figure 8. Pergamon. Sanctuary of Hera Basileia (plan: Philipp Kobusch after Dörpfeld 1912, Pl. 18).

closed the *cella*, but enabled the visitors to view the cult group from inside the *pronaos*, possibly as they passed by.

At the other extreme, however, there were also *pronaoi*, which had no column front, but could only be entered at the front through a lockable door.[9] They were basically excluded from public life and not only were there restrictions for entering, but even for viewing. Inscriptions nevertheless use the term *prodomos* for such rooms as well, for example in the case of the temple of Aphrodite on Delos (ID 1417, A, II, 1).

Preliminary conclusion

Especially the last-mentioned examples show the broad spectrum of different concepts that could stand behind the design of a *pronaos*. A flexible combination of topographical situations inside the *temenos*, the typology of the *pronaos* and additional access restrictions in the form of barriers and grilles made it possible to assign a very different character to structurally very similar rooms.

9 For example: temple of Aphrodite on Delos (Durvye 2006, pp. 92-96. 102-104 Figs. 2-5; 2009, pp. 198-202 Figs. 1-4); temple of Zeus and Athena Soter in Phigaleia (Arapogianni 2002; 1996, pp. 129-137 Figs. 1. 2 Pl. 46-52); temple of Athena Polias in Stymphalos (Schaus 2014).

For the use of the *pronaos*, such installations mean that it did not only function as a passageway to the *cella*, *i.e.* it was not only perceived while passing through.

In fact, it could represent a space that remained inaccessible to many visitors and, together with the *cella*, functioned as a showroom for valuable dedications. But it could also be a publicly accessible space that could be used independently of the *cella*. In addition, the threshold lattices[10] point out that it could also be a place where one could stay to admire the cult image, even if it was not allowed to enter the *cella* itself. In a certain sense, the *pronaoi* of non-*peripteral* temples, equipped with such lattices at the threshold, took over the functions of the front *ptera* of *peripteral* temples. All these possibilities are verifiable during the Hellenistic period. Thus they do not refer to chronological trends, but were in existence at the same time.

It is well documented from many ancient texts that the preoccupation with the cult image does not only include the artistic contemplation of a Pausanias, but of course also prayer, supplication, possibly also the throwing of kisses of the hands as greetings *etc.* (Scheer 2000, pp. 54-77; Bettinetti 2001, pp. 137-231; Nick 2002, pp. 30-76). These forms of religious communication with the deity will, according to the lattices, probably not only have been carried out in the *cella* itself, but also out of the *pronaos* in front of the threshold.

The furnishings of the *pronaoi*

The image obtained by observing the topographical incorporation of temples can be enlarged by adding an analysis of the very sporadically preserved furnishings of the *pronaoi*.

Written sources, both literary and epigraphic, testify that the placement of portrait statues in the *pronaoi* was a widespread phenomenon. However, this can hardly be verified archaeologically, since the dating and interpretation of the few preserved bases is problematic in all cases.[11] Stefanos Paliompeis (1996, passim, esp. pp. 244-248) and Katja Sporn (2014 passim, esp. pp. 119-127), who collected the relevant sources comprehensively, were able to ascertain that portrait statues of mainly private individuals were erected in the *pronaos*. Hellenistic rulers and other important statues of gods, on the other hand, found their place more frequently in the *cella*, and were often worshipped there as *synnaoi theoi*. Nevertheless, as they could show, these are not fixed rules.

Pronaoi could thus be used as a place of social representation through one of the most widespread media of the time for this purpose – namely portrait statues. The corresponding inscriptions usually not only reproduced the names of the depicted persons, but could also refer to the occasion of the erection or its initiators. The objects are therefore closely linked to the social or political life of the society and its protagonists. Thus, the *pronaoi* do not differ from the public space or the rest of the sanctuary, but also only gradually from the *cella* itself. Unfortunately, the bad preservation does not allow us to judge whether this phenomenon was particularly strong in *pronaoi* that were open to the public.

In Asia Minor, mainly Ionia and Caria, the regular publication of official decrees at the *Pronaos* is well documented (Sherwin-White 1985; Detienne 1992, pp. 41-46;

---

10 Such lattices in front of the *cella* door itself are a widespread phenomenon that can be detected in a large number of Late Classical and Hellenistic temples. A comprehensive collection and evaluation cannot be carried out within this scope and will be presented as part of the habilitation thesis.

11 For example, in Lykosoura several bases have been preserved in the *pronaos* (Fig. 4). These, however, as far as they are datable, mainly originate from Roman times (IG V2, 516. 517. 533. 536. 538. 539. 544; Leonardos 1896, pp. 107-108 Pl. 2). This, in connection with the extensive Roman repairs, shows that the location of the only surviving Hellenistic base in the south-west corner (*IG* V2, 534) does not necessarily indicate its original location in the Hellenistic phase.

von Hesberg 2009; Roels 2018). However, their placement was mainly restricted to the outer walls of the temple.[12] If the *pronaos* had two columns *in antis*, the front side of the *antae* must also be included. In fact, there are no inscriptions on the front sides of *antae* that were part of a *prostyle pronaos*. Thus, the texts usually affected less the *pronaos* interior than the place in front of the *pronaos*, respectively the *pteron* in *peripteral* temples.

Only three examples are known in which official texts were explicitly attached to the inner walls of the *pronaos*. In Sardeis (Buckler and Robinson 1932, pp. 1-7 no. 1) a deed of pledge was attached, which specified the properties a certain Mnesimachos had to cede after he could not repay the money borrowed from the temple treasure. In Delphi (Hansen 2010, pp. 258-266 Fig. 8.3; Plassart 1970, pp. 5-24 nos. 276-285) – the only example of official decrees being affixed to the temple wall on the Greek mainland before the Imperial era – the solution of a major corruption scandal was recorded, in the course of which the ownership structure between the city of Delphi and the sanctuary were redefined. Finally, in the Temple of Zeus of Magnesia (Kern 1900, no. 98) there was a cult decree which regulated the course of festivities in honour of Zeus Sosipolis and other deities.

What is striking is that these three texts each deal with matters that specifically concerned the sanctuary,[13] while on the outer walls of the temple, urban or state matters were frequently negotiated as well.

The publication of decrees is not a unique feature of the temple front or the *pronaos*. It is well known that the sanctuary area as a whole served as a publication site for the most important state decrees. In Attica even the placement of inscription steles in the *cella* next to the cult image is ensured (*IG* II^2 1322, l. 13; *IG* II^2 2501, l. 22). Accordingly, the publication at the temple will only be distinguished from it in so far as the attachment to the temple or the placement in the front of the temple provided a better visibility or accentuation of the inscriptions.

If, nevertheless, the decrees inside tend to differ in their content from those on the outer facade, as the three examples mentioned suggest, this indicates at least a gradual difference in the characterization between the outer area and the *pronaos*. But the extent to which legal factors played a role here, or merely if certain groups of addressees were taken into consideration, the few examples can seldomly tell. However, it can be assumed for certain that there were no cult restrictions since only one of the three texts dealt specifically with ritual concerns, while the other texts recorded the processes of the administration of the sanctuary.

Both these objects, the statues and the inscriptions, are part of practices that are implemented by priests, benefactors, and the urban public on or in the temple building that has already been erected. The central position, the often high-quality architecture, and the significance of the building attracted private and public representation and provoked a desire for divine legitimacy. The temple in general, and with it the temple's anteroom, became the venue for social negotiation processes with at most a gradual distinction between the exterior, the *pronaos*, and the *cella*.

---

12 Inscriptions on the front of the *antae*: Aigai (Bohn and Schuchhardt 1889, p. 42 Fig. 50); Amyzon (Hellström 2009, pp. 284-290 Fig. 16); inscriptions on the front of the *antae*, which turn over to the outer walls: Herakleia (Wörrle 1990); Lagina (van Bremen 2010, pp. 488-493 Fig. 5); Priene (Sherwin-White 1985, Fig. 1). Inscriptions which are only attached to the outer walls: Magnesia, temple of Artemis Leukophryene (Kern 1900, no. 95); Pergamon, temple on the middle terrace of the *gymnasion* (von Prott and Kolbe 1902, pp. 106-132 nos. 113- 158); Pergamon, temple R (Jacobsthal 1908, pp. 384-400 nos. 6-23; Hepding 1910, pp. 418-432 nos. 9-18).

13 A fourth example may be added. An honorary decree from Cos has been preserved that states that it should be attached to an ante: *IG* XII 4, 1, 96. The formulation ἐς τὰν / προστάδα τοῦ ναοῦ probably refers specifically to the *pronaos* since the term προστάς usually means the space between the *antae* respectively the porch: Liddell – Scott – Jones, s. v. Προστάς. But here also the costs for the stele were paid by the treasurers of the god, so that in this case too the sanctuary was directly involved as an institution.

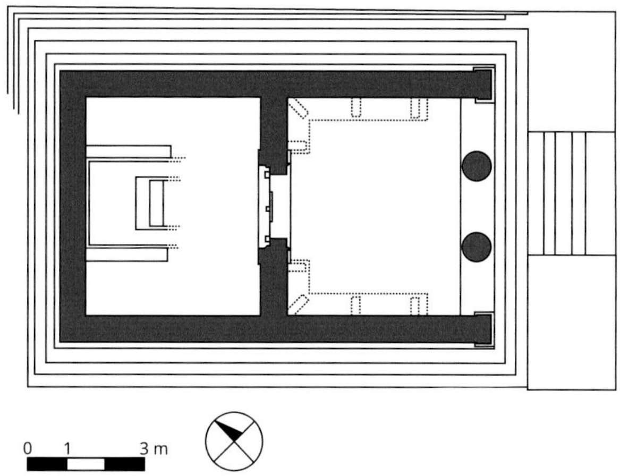

Figure 9. Mamurt Kaleh. Temple of Meter (plan: Philipp Kobusch after Conze and Schazmann 1911, Pl. 2. 4).

A much more specific feature is the presence of stone benches in some *pronaoi*. Such benches can be verified archaeologically in the temple of Apollo in Delphi (Hansen 2010, pp. 280-284 Figs. 9.4. 10.1-2), in the temple of Meter at Mamurt Kaleh near Pergamon (Fig. 9; Conze and Schazmann 1911, p. 19 Fig. 5.10), in the sanctuary of Demeter and Kore in Priene (Wiegand and Schrader 1904, p. 152 Fig. 119), and in the temple of Aphrodite on Delos (Durvye 2006, p. 95). For the temple of Agathe Tyche on Delos, benches are epigraphically documented inside the *pronaos* (ID 1403, Bb II, 24; Hamilton 2000, GF 16 suggests a translation with *piedestal*). The fact that such benches had a certain tradition on Delos is further documented by the temple of Hera (Plassart 1928, pp. 188. 204 Fig. 154. 156) from Archaic times.

The fact that there are always several symmetrically arranged and, as far as can be ascertained, uniformly designed specimens speaks for the fact that they are not successively donated possessions of the deity, but that they were a functional component of the temples. Their design, which is typical for seating furniture, indicates that they were indeed used for sitting. This is underlined by traces of abrasion on the floor in front of the benches in the temple of Aphrodite on Delos (Durvye 2009, p. 200 Fig. 3). Comparable objects are not documented for the *cella*. It is therefore a unique feature of some *pronaoi*.

The benches in the *pronaoi* are always arranged in such a way that the cult image was not or only partially visible. Contemplation in front of the deity was therefore not intended. Nevertheless, sometimes an integration into the ritual may be imaginable, for example as a waiting room in Delphi before invoking the oracle. But in any case, the benches point out that *pronaoi* could function as a room to spend time in.

The list of benches in *pronaoi* may be extended by another example. In the *pronaos* of the temple of Apollo Patroos, which has already been examined in detail (Fig. 2), two narrow pedestals are placed in a similar position on both sides of the *cella* door. They are often hypothetically associated with the statues of Apollo recorded by Pausanias (Paus. 1, 3, 4; Thompson 1937, pp. 97-99. 109; doubtly Knell 1994, p. 231 no. 89). However, the proportions of the constructions with a very shallow depth and a large width speak against such a solution. Rather, an interpretation as seating furniture in analogy with the verifiable benches is very obvious. In this case, therefore, an opportunity to sit was offered in a particularly open *pronaos*, which can be regarded as part of the public space.

A second possible functional element are tables, which, however, are much less detectable than benches. This is for example the case in the temple B of the Asclepieion of Cos (Fig. 7.1). The excavator Herzog documented a foundation in the middle of the unusually deep *pronaos* and thus frontally in front of the cult image. In addition, he reports the discovery of a table foot made of reddish marble, which he associated with this foundation (Herzog 1903, pp. 7-8; 1907, p. 204).

Another cult table was set up with some certainty in the temple of Zeus at Labraunda. In the pavement directly behind the *intercolumnium* between the *pronaos* columns a typical long rectangular cutting has been preserved (Hellström and Thieme 1982, Pls. 6.2. 7.3. 30. 31. 39. 40, without reference in the text). This situation can certainly be associated with a cult decree that restricted access for visitors to the temple: it stipulates that entry was only permitted up to the barrier next to a cult table and an incense altar (Crampa 1972, pp. 119-123 no. 60).[14]

The use of such tables can be well reconstructed from sacral decrees – one of them even stems from the sanctuary of Cos, but its assignment to the cult of Asclepius cannot be conclusively proven. It determined which parts of the sacrifice are to be laid down on the table.[15] The sacrifice at the table in the antechamber is thus an integral part of the entire sacrificial ritual, which is to be carried out parallel, in other cases also isolated from the main sacrifice at the altar. By the positioning of the table, the *pronaos* at Cos and Labraunda thus becomes one of the central sites of sacrifice in the sanctuary.

Elsewhere, however, cult tables have also been found in other locations, *e.g.* in the *cella* itself, but also outside the temple near the altar (Miller 2001; Gill 1991, Figs. 1. 2; Deonna 1938, p. 16). Since as a rule only one cult table per cult is to be expected, a cult table certainly did not belong to the standard equipment of the antechamber.

As shown, in Labraunda, besides the cult table, there is also an incense altar and thus another subordinate sacrificial installation in the *pronaos*. Otherwise, the existence of altars cannot be proved with certainty, even if individual findings might be associated with such installations – as an example, the round base in the temple of Hemithea in Kastabos (Fig. 1.5) is cited here.[16] It is possible that this altar was also used for the performance of incense offerings, as was suggested for many Hellenistic round altars (Kossatz-Deissmann 2005, p. 383).

Other findings, such as the masonry pit in the *pronaos* of the small *naiskos* of Keryneia (Kanellopoulos and Kolia 2011, pp. 159-161 Figs. 25. 28), are difficult to interpret, but even for such objects a ritual function is repeatedly assumed, for example as a sacrificial pit.

These few and disparate findings prove that *pronaoi* could presumably be very closely integrated into the ritual activities. It is important, however, that this integration was not uniform, but that it took place to different degrees and with different objects, which accordingly also included integration into different steps of the ritual.

Conclusion

The observations discussed here refer to a broad spectrum of different uses of the *pronaos*. Although the *pronaos* was an architecturally clearly defined, typologically relatively uniform, and in principle existential component of a Greek temple, there existed no fixed concept of use for this space. Rather, architects and those responsi-

---

14 In a very similar position a table in the Heraion of Olympia can be reconstructed as well (Fig. 1.1; Dörpfeld 1892, p. 32), but it is not possible to date it.

15 *IG* XII 4, 1, 346: '[...] τῶν δ]ẹ̀ ἄλ[λ]ων σκέλος· λαμβανέτω δὲ καὶ [. .] [. . το]ῦ̣ πυρὸς τὸ τρίτον μέρος· τιθέντω δὲ τοὶ θύοντε[ς] ἐπὶ τὰν τράπεζαντᾶι θεῶι πθόϊν καὶ σπλάγχνα· λαμβανείτω δὲ ἁ ἱέρεια καὶ ἀπὸ τῶν ἐπιτιθεμένων ἐπὶ vac. τὴν τράπεζαν τᾶι θεῶι τὰ τέταρτα μέρηι·' '[...] from the other (sacrificial animals): thighs. But it shall take ... of the fire the third part. Those who sacrifice should put on the offering table for the goddess offering pastries and *splanchna*. The priestess should also take the fourth part of what is placed on the offering table for the goddess. Cf. the German translation by K. Hallofs: http://telota.bbaw.de/ig/*IG* XII 4, 1, 346.' On the use of tables, see in detail: Mischkowski 1917; Gill 1974; 1991, pp. 2-28.

16 Cook and Plommer 1966, pp. 45-46 nos. 12-16; 60. 125-127 Figs. 61. 62 Pl. 8.12-16. 10.5. 20.1. They are thinking of a function as a *puteal*. But there is no reference to a cistern or a well. The existence of a figural relief also suggests the reconstruction as altar.

ble for the sanctuary, as well as donors, were able to interpret the room in different ways and assign it a different character through individual functional elements – doors, grilles, benches, or sacrificial installations, *etc.*

The characterization of the *pronaos* as a public, multifunctional space, as Diodor puts it, is only one possible form of utilization, namely when the *pronaos* was in direct proximity to the public space and was unrestrictedly accessible. At the same time, however, there are also *pronaoi* which are excluded from public life by various means and to varying degrees, or which are directly integrated into the ritual activities of the sanctuary through cult installations.

Accordingly, the building type *pronaos* could be multifunctional, as it is also known for *stoai* and similar buildings. That means that the type of architecture did not generally determine specific practices. Nevertheless, the individual *pronaos* is not per se a multifunctional space, but could be subjected to very distinct concepts of use.

Because of the big problems when it comes to the dating of the individual objects and locking systems and the general problem of conservation chance, it is very difficult to decide whether this flexible handling of the *pronaos* is a Late Classical or Hellenistic phenomenon – here the presented analysis naturally reaches its limits. But it can at least be observed that in the Late Classical and Hellenistic period, a greater value was placed on the *pronaos* in general and on its design, as shown by the fact that the size of the *pronaoi* grew significantly in relation to the *cella*. Also, the architectural variability seems to have increased during this period, as does the variety of the furnishings, so that the responsible persons had considerably expanded possibilities of differentiation at their disposal. Diodor's contribution remains the only direct literary source that provides an interpretation of the *pronaos*. But on the basis of the observations made here, it can at least be assumed very plausibly that this great diversity in the setting and use of space also led to a differing and multifaceted perception of the individual *pronaos*.

In a culture in which the individual cults were very heterogeneous, and in which there was no universally applicable liturgy, only the architectural form of the temple's anteroom was standardised in order to mark the temple as the most important cult building externally. However, the specific characterization and usage, and with these its perception, were obviously the result of local traditions and social negotiation processes.

Acknowledgements

The present considerations are part of my habilitation project, which deals in detail with the accessibility and use of Late Classical and Hellenistic temples. The project was generously funded by a DFG research fellowship (KO 5734/1-1). A comprehensive publication of the results is planned for 2020.

References

Arapogianni, X. 1996. Ανασκαφή στη Φιγάλεια. *Πρακτικά της εν Αθήναις Αρχαιολογικής Εταιρείας* 151, 129-137.

Arapogianni, X. 2002. Neue archäologische Entdeckungen in der weiteren Umgebung von Olympia, in: Kyrieleis, H. (ed.). *Olympia 1875-2000: 125 Jahre Deutsche Ausgrabungen*, Internationales Symposion, 9.-11. November 2000 Berlin. Mainz: Zabern, 317-329.

Bammer, A. and Muss, U. 1996. *Das Artemision von Ephesos: Das Weltwunder Ioniens in archaischer und klassischer Zeit*. Mainz: Zabern.

Bankel, H. 1993. *Der spätarchaische Tempel der Aphaia auf Aegina*. Berlin: De Gruyter.

Bergquist, B. 1967. *The archaic Greek temenos: a study of structure and function.* Lund: Gleerup.

Bettinetti, S. 2001. *La statua di culto nella pratica rituale greca.* Bari: Levante.

Billot, M.F. 2008. Le temple de Despoina. *Ktema* 33, 135-180.

Bohn, R. and Schuchhardt, C. 1889. *Altertümer von Aegae.* Berlin: Reimer.

Bohtz, C.H. 1981. *Das Demeter-Heiligtum,* Altertümer von Pergamon 13. Berlin: De Gruyter.

van Bremen, R. 2010. The inscribed documents on the temple of Hekate at Lagina and the date and meaning of the temple frieze, in: van Bremen, R. and Carbon, J.-M. (eds.). *Hellenistic Karia,* Proceedings of the First International Conference on Hellenistic Karia, 29 June-2 July 2006 Oxford. Paris: De Boccard, 483-503.

Buckler, W.H. and Robinson, D.M. 1932. *Greek and Latin inscriptions,* Sardis 7 (1). Leiden: Brill.

Charises, V.A. 2010. *Δωδωνη: αρχιτεκτονικα μελετηματα.* Ioannina: Ekdoseis E.Ē.M.

Conze, A. and Schazmann, P. 1911. *Mamurt-Kaleh: Ein Tempel der Göttermutter unweit Pergamon.* Berlin: Reimer.

Cook, J.M. and Plommer, W.H. 1966. *The sanctuary of Hemithea at Kastabos.* London: Cambridge University Press.

Cooper, F.A. 1996. *The temple of Apollo Bassitas.* Princeton: The American School of Classical Studies at Athens.

Coulton, J.J. 1976. *The architectural development of the Greek stoa.* Oxford: Clarendon.

Crampa, J. 1972. *The Greek inscriptions,* Labraunda: Swedish excavations and researches 3 (2). Stockholm: Gleerup.

Deonna, W. 1938. *Le mobilier délien.* Paris: De Boccard.

Detienne, M. 1992. L'espace de la publicité: ses opérateurs intellectuels dans la cite, in: Detienne, M. (ed.). *Les savoirs de l'écriture.* Paris: Presses Université de Lille, 29-81.

Dörpfeld, W. 1892. Das Heraion, in: Adler F. and Curtius, E. (eds.). *Die Baudenkmäler von Olympia.* Berlin: Asher, 27-36.

Dörpfeld, W. 1912. Die Arbeiten zu Pergamon 1910-1911. *Mitteilungen des Deutschen Archäologischen Instituts: Athenische Abteilung* 37, 233-276.

Durvye, C. 2006. Aphrodite à Délos: culte privé et public à l'époque hellénistique. *Revue des études grecques* 119, 83-113.

Durvye, C. 2009. Recherches récentes à Délos: l'Aphrodision de Stèsiléôs. *Revue archéologique* 1, 198-207.

Emme, B. 2013. *Peristyl und Polis: Entwicklung und Funktionen öffentlicher griechischer Hofanlagen.* Berlin: De Gruyter.

Fiechter, E.R. 1906. Der Tempel, in: Furtwängler, A. (ed.). *Aegina: Das Heiligtum der Aphaia.* München: Verl. der K. B. Akad. der Wiss., 10-68.

von Gerkan, A. 1922. *Der Nordmarkt und der Hafen an der Löwenbucht.* Berlin: De Gruyter.

von Gerkan, A. 1946. Pronaon, Metope und Proskenion. *Jahreshefte des Österreichischen Archäologischen Institutes in Wien* 36, 46-53.

Gill, D.R. 1974. Trapezomata: a neglected aspect of Greek sacrifice. *Harvard Theological Review* 67, 117-137.

Gill, D.H. 1991. *Greek cult tables.* New York: Garland.

Grandjean, Y. and Salviat, F. 2000. *Guide de Thasos.* Athens: Ecole française d'Athènes.

Gruben, G. 2001. *Griechische Tempel und Heiligtümer.* München: Hirmer.

Hamilton, R. 2000. *Treasure map: a guide to the Delian inventories.* Ann Arbor: University of Michigan Press.

Hansen, E. 2010. *Le temple d'Apollon du IVe siècle,* Fouilles de Delphes 14. Athens: De Boccard.

Held, W. and Wilkening-Aumann, C. 2015. Vom karischen Bund zur griechischen Polis: Archäologischer Survey in Bybassos und Kastabos auf der karischen Chersonesos, in: Matthaei, A. and Zimmermann, M. (eds.). *Urbane Strukturen und bürgerliche Identität im Hellenismus*, Die hellenistische Polis als Lebensform 5. Mainz: Verlag Antike, 74-98.

Hellner, N. 2014. Räumliche Führung am Beispiel der spätgeometrischen und archaischen Süd-Tempel von Abai/Kalapodi, in: Kurapkat, D., P.I. Schneider, P.I., Wulf-Rheidt, U. (eds.). *Die Architektur des Weges. Gestaltete Bewegung im gebauten Raum*, Internationales Kolloquium in Berlin, 8.-11. Februar 2012. Regensburg: Schnell & Steiner, 289-307.

Hellström, P. 2009. Sacred architecture and Karian identity, in: Rumscheid, F. (ed.). *Die Karer und die Anderen*, Internationales Kolloquium an der Freien Universität Berlin, 13.-15. Oktober 2005. Bonn: Habelt, 267-290.

Hellström, P. and Thieme, T. 1982. *The temple of Zeus*, Labraunda: Swedish excavations and researches 1 (3). Stockholm: Gleerup.

Hepding, H. 1910. Die Arbeiten zu Pergamon 1908-1909: Die Inschriften. *Mitteilungen des Deutschen Archäologischen Instituts: Athenische Abteilung* 35, 401-493.

Herzog, R. 1903. Vorläufiger Bericht über die archäologische Expedition auf der Insel Kos im Jahre 1902. *Archäologischer Anzeiger*, 1-13. 186-199.

Herzog, R. 1907. Aus dem Asklepieion von Kos 1: Schlangenopfer. *Archiv für Religionsgeschichte* 10, 201-228.

von Hesberg, H. 1994. *Formen privater Repräsentation in der Baukunst des 2. und 1. Jahrhunderts v. Chr.* Köln: Böhlau.

von Hesberg, H. 2007. Die Statuengruppe im Tempel der Dioskuren von Cori. Bemerkungen zum Aufstellungskontext von Kultbildern in spätrepublikanischer Zeit. *Mitteilungen des Deutschen Archäologischen Instituts: Römische Abteilung* 113, 443-460.

von Hesberg, H. 2009. Archäologische Charakteristika der Inschriftenträger staatlicher Urkunden: Einige Beispiele, in: Haensch, R. (ed.). *Selbstdarstellung und Kommunikation: Die Veröffentlichung staatlicher Urkunden auf Stein und Bronze in der Römischen Welt.* Internationales Kolloquium an der Kommission für Alte Geschichte und Epigraphik, 1.-3. Juli 2006 München. München: C.H. Beck, 19-56.

Jacobsthal, P. 1908. Die Arbeiten zu Pergamon 1906-1907: Die Inschriften. *Mitteilungen des Deutschen Archäologischen Instituts: Athenische Abteilung* 33, 375-420.

Kanellopoulos, C. and Kolia, E. 2011. Ancient Keryneia of Aigaleia: excavations and architecture in the sanctuary of Profitis Elias. *Mitteilungen des Deutschen Archäologischen Instituts: Athenische Abteilung* 126, 138-176.

Kern, O. 1900. *Die Inschriften von Magnesia am Maeander*. Berlin: W. Spemann.

Kienast, H.J. 2012. Die Dipteroi im Heraion von Samos, in: Schulz, T. (ed.). *Dipteros und Pseudodipteros: Bauhistorische und archäologische Forschungen*, Internationale Tagung, 13.-15. November 2009 Regensburg. Istanbul: Ege Yayınları, 5-17.

Knell, H. 1983. Dorische Ringhallentempel in spät- und nachklassischer Zeit. *Jahrbuch des Deutschen Archäologischen Instituts* 98, 203-233.

Knell, H. 1988. *Architektur der Griechen*. Darmstadt: Wissenschaftliche Buchgesellschaft.

Knell, H. 1994. Der jüngere Tempel des Apollon Patroos auf der Athener Agora. *Jahrbuch des Deutschen Archäologischen Instituts* 109, 217-237.

Koenigs, W. 2015. *Der Athenatempel von Priene*. Wiesbaden: Reichert.

Kohte, J. 1904. Die Bauwerke, in: Humann C., Kohte, J., Watzinger, C. (eds.). *Magnesia am Maeander: Bericht über die Ergebnisse der Ausgrabungen der Jahre 1891-1893*. Berlin: Reimer, 9-172.

Kossatz-Deissmann, A. 2005. Darstellungen von Kultorten, in: Lambrinoudakis, V. and Balty, J.C. (eds.). *Thesaurus cultus et rituum antiquorum 4*. Los Angeles: Getty Publications, 363-408.

Lauter, H. 1986. *Die Architektur des Hellenismus*. Darmstadt: Wissenschaftliche Buchgesellschaft.

Lauter-Bufe, H. 2009. *Das Heiligtum des Zeus Soter in Megalopolis*. Mainz: Zabern.

Leonardos, V. 1896. Ανασκαφαί του εν Λυκοσούρα Ιερού της Δεσποίνης. *Πρακτικά της εν Αθήναις Αρχαιολογικής Εταιρείας*, 95-116.

Mallwitz, A. 1966. Das Heraion von Olympia und seine Vorgänger. *Jahrbuch des Deutschen Archäologischen Instituts* 81, 310-376.

Mattern, T. 2015. *Das Herakles-Heiligtum von Kleonai: Architektur und Kult im Kontext*. Wiesbaden: Reichert.

Mertens, D. 2006. *Städte und Bauten der Westgriechen: Von der Kolonisationszeit bis zur Krise um 400 vor Christus*. München: Hirmer.

Miller, S. 2001. Cult tables from Nemea, in: *Καλλιστευμα. Μελέτες προς τιμήν της Όλγας Τζάχου-Αλεξανδρή*. Athens: Hypourgeio Politismou, 461-468.

Mischkowski, H. 1917. *Die heiligen Tische im Götterkultus der Griechen und Römer*. Königsberg: Kümmel.

Newton, C.T. and Pullan, R.P. 1881. The Sminthium, in: Society of Dilettanti (ed.). *Antiquities of Ionia 4*. London: Macmillan & Co, 40-48.

Nick, G. 2002. *Die Athena Parthenos: Studien zum griechischen Kultbild und seiner Rezeption*. Mainz: Zabern.

Ohnesorg, A. 2007. *Der Kroisos-Tempel: Neue Forschungen zum archaischen Dipteros der Artemis von Ephesos*. Wien: Verlag der Österreichischen Akademie der Wissenschaften.

Østby, E. 2014. The Classical temple of Athena Alea at Tegea, in: Østby, E. (ed.). *Investigations in the sanctuary of Athena Alea 1990-94 and 2004 [in italics]*, Tegea 2. Athens: Norwegian Institute at Athens, 317-351.

Paliompeis, S. 1996. *Studien zur Innenausstattung griechischer Tempel: Skulptur und Malerei*. Thesis (PhD): Universität Mainz.

Plassart, A. 1928. *Les sanctuaires et les cultes du Mont Cynthe*. Paris: De Boccard.

Plassart, A. 1970. *Les inscriptions de la terrasse du temple et de la région nord du sanctuaire: les inscriptions du temple du IVe siècle: Nos 276 à 350*, Fouilles de Delphes 3 (4). Paris: De Boccard.

Prignitz, S. 2014. *Bauurkunden und Bauprogramm von Epidauros (400-350): Asklepiostempel, Tholos, Kultbild, Brunnenhaus*. München: C.H. Beck.

von Prott, H. and Kolbe, W. 1902, Die Arbeiten zu Pergamon 1900-1901: Die Inschriften. *Mitteilungen des Deutschen Archäologischen Instituts, Athenische Abteilung* 27, 44-151.

Roels, E.J.J. 2018. The queen of inscriptions contextualized: the presence of civic inscriptions in the pronaos of ancient temples in Hellenistic and Roman Asia Minor (fourth century BCE-second century CE), in: van Opstall, E.M. (ed.). *Sacred thresholds: the door to the sanctuary in Late Antiquity*. Leiden: Brill, 221-253.

Roux, G. 1961. *L'architecture de l'Argolide aux IVe et IIIe siècles avant J.-C*. Paris: De Boccard.

Schaus, G.P. 2014. The sanctuary: site description, in: Schaus, G.P. (ed.). *Stymphalos: the acropolis sanctuary 1*. Toronto: University of Toronto Press, 12-35.

Schazmann, P. 1923. *Das Gymnasion: Der Tempelbezirk der Hera Basilea*, Altertümer von Pergamon 6. Berlin: De Gruyter.

Schazmann, P. 1932. *Asklepieion: Baubeschreibung und Baugeschichte*. Berlin: Keller.

Scheer, T.S. 2000. *Die Gottheit und ihr Bild: Untersuchungen zur Funktion griechischer Kultbilder in Religion und Politik*. München: C.H. Beck.

Schleif, H. 1940. *Der Artemistempel: Architektur, Dachterrakotten, Inschriften*. Berlin: Gebr. Mann.

Sherwin-White, S. 1985. Ancient archives: the edict of Alexander to Priene: a reappraisal. *Journal of Hellenic Studies* 105, 69-89.

Sioumpara, E.P. 2011. *Der Asklepios-Tempel von Messene auf der Peloponnes: Untersuchungen zur hellenistischen Tempelarchitektur*. München: Hirmer.

Sporn, K. 2014. Individuum und Gott: Privatbildnisse in griechischen Tempeln, in: Griesbach, J. (ed.). *Polis und Porträt: Standbilder als Medien der öffentlichen Repräsentation im hellenistischen Osten*. Wiesbaden: Reichert, 117-129.

Steuernagel, D. 2014a. Individuelle Bedürfnisse und kollektive Normen: Zur baulichen Gliederung und zur Nutzung griechischer Tempelräume in hellenistischer Zeit, in: Matthaei, A. and Zimmermann, M. (eds.). *Stadtkultur im Hellenismus*. Mainz: Verlag Antike, 52-75.

Steuernagel, D. 2014b. Rules of the game: individual donations in relation to the cult image during the Hellenistic Period, in: Estienne, S., Huet, V., Lissarrague, F., Prost, F. (eds.). *Figures de dieux: Construire le divin en images*. Rennes: Presses Universitaires de Rennes, 77-97.

Thompson, H.A. 1937. Buildings on the west side of the agora. *Hesperia,* 6, 1-226.

Travlos, I.N. 1971. *Bildlexikon zur Topographie des antiken Athen*. Tübingen: Wasmuth.

Wiegand, T. and Schrader, H. 1904. *Priene: Ergebnisse der Ausgrabungen und Untersuchungen in den Jahren 1895-1898*. Berlin: Reimer.

Williamson, C.G. 2018. Filters of light: Greek temple doors as portals of epiphany, in: van Opstall, E.M. (ed.). *Sacred thresholds: the door to the sanctuary in Late Antiquity*. Leiden: Brill, 311-340.

Wörrle, M. 1990, Inschriften von Herakleia am Latmos II: Das Priestertum der Athena Latmia. *Chiron* 20, 19-58.

Wycherley, R.E. 1957. *Literary and epigraphical testimonia*. Princeton: American School of Classical Studies at Athens.

Translations of ancient authors

Oldfather, C.H. 1954. *Diodorus of Sicily, 6: Books XIV-XV*, Loeb Classical Library 399. London: Harvard University Press.

Rowland, I.D., 1999. *Vitruvius: ten books on architecture*. Cambridge: Cambridge University Press.

Notes on contributor

Philipp Kobusch - Institute of Classical Studies / Classical Archaeology, CAU Kiel (present). Studies of Classical Archaeology and History in Gießen; PhD Gießen 2011; Travel Scholarship of the German Archaeological Institute 2011-2012; Assistant Professor at the Institute of Classical Studies/Classical Archaeology, CAU Kiel 2012-.

Constructing the Sublime: Landscape, Architecture and Human Encounter in Hellenistic Sanctuaries

Christina G. Williamson

Abstract

Sanctuaries of the Hellenistic period have at times been characterized as being rationally designed to produce spectacular effects through their architecture, such as the sequential spaces at the temple of Apollo in Didyma or the climactic ascent of the terraced shrine of Athena at Lindos. More rarely addressed, however, is the balance of nature and human design in shrines that exploit the landscape, those that focus on epiphanies, or the many that accommodate spectacles and the thrill of the crowd. Such sanctuaries were clearly designed to evoke a sense of awe. This paper explores the sublime and the importance of artifice as a lens through which the coordination of landscape, architecture, memory, and human encounter so characteristic of sacred architecture of this era might be better understood.

Keywords: sublime, landscape, epiphany, festivals, Greek temple architecture, Hellenistic sanctuaries

Whether Heron of Alexandria (Automata, 37) was in fact contemplating the sublime or simply tackling another engineering challenge when he designed his *automata* is unclear. But his temple doors that automatically opened were surely a source of spine-tingling wonder, as if the god himself welcomed you into his temple. On the same foot, the long curtains hung in the temple of Artemis of Ephesos, or of Zeus at Olympia, must have heightened the suspense of epiphany, as the splendour of the cult image was gradually revealed (Paus. 5, 12, 4; also Apul. Met. 11, 20). Such enhancements were clearly meant to evoke an emotional response, yet have been dismissed as gimmickry, or more seriously as a sign of the thrill-seeking superstition that religion had become by the late Hellenistic age. Richard Gordon (1979, p. 13) emphasized that the gods themselves were seen as the master tricksters. Temple design in the Hellenistic period is often considered as a reflection of the overall decline of the *polis*, and *polis* religion, and the rise of individualism (for a full discussion

University of Groningen
P.O. Box 716,
9700AS Groningen
The Netherlands
c.g.williamson@rug.nl

see Deshours 2011, pp. 23-24; Melfi 2016). But another approach is to consider such phenomena within the larger pursuit of the sublime. The concept is best known from (Pseudo-) Longinus's treatise 'Peri hypsous' (On the Sublime) from the imperial period. Primarily concerned with the generation of the sublime in rhetoric, the author of this work does not actually give a definition, yet his focus on the role of human artifice is clear:

> *'The Sublime leads the listeners not to persuasion, but to ecstasy: for what is wonderful always goes together with a sense of dismay and prevails over what is only convincing or delightful, since persuasion, as a rule, is within everyone's grasp: whereas, the Sublime, giving to speech an invincible power and* [an invincible] *strength, rises above every listener.'* (Longinus, On the Sublime 1, 4, transl. Roberts 1899).

Longinus's assessment of the experience of the sublime involves ecstasy, astonishment, wonder and, as pointed out by Robert Doran (2015, pp. 40-48), is essentially dualistic: a combined sense of being overwhelmed and elevated at the same. An awareness of human failings, but also the human ability to frame superhuman power, is key to triggering a sense of transcendence in the mind. Since its translation by Boileau in the 17th century, 'Peri hypsous' has largely been considered an anomaly in the ancient world. Edmund Thomas (2014), however, believes it to demonstrate a contemporary resonance between rhetoric and architecture, as emphasis is increasingly laid on the aesthetic appreciation of harmony between art and nature. James Porter (2016a; 2016b) goes much further in arguing that 'Peri hypsous' should be seen as an echo of a much longer conversation on the role of nature and art that looks back as much as it looks forward, noting that Longinus himself finds the sublime in Homer, Sappho, Plato, and Demosthenes (Porter 2016b, p. 74). This conversation further includes Aristotle on *ekstasis* (Arist. Rh. 1361a37), and culminates in what Porter describes as the '*hypsos* bubble' in late Hellenistic and early imperial sources (2016b, pp. 94-102).[1] The sublime is a 'fascinating and fearful' combination of the impossible with a material objectivity that dislocates the mind and 'produces profound mental or spiritual disruption, be this momentary or lasting – it is like a shock of the real', while at the same time challenging perceptions of reality (Porter 2016b, p. 77). The experience of the sublime, therefore, is relational and entirely dependent upon one's mental sense of order and understanding of the structure of reality. This is what makes artifice so important. Besides being a central part of the experience, human framing creates an archive of palimpsests for understanding the larger mindset, whether this is through rhetoric or architecture.

Generally relegated to philosophy as a strand of aesthetics, several studies have recently reconsidered conceptualizations of the sublime, from Longinus to Edmund Burke and Immanuel Kant (Constelloe 2012; Doran 2015), and the impact on architecture (Nesbitt 1995; Etlin 2012). My aim is not to recapitulate these, nor to assess the relevance of 'Longinus' to the architecture of his day (Thomas 2014) or the larger context in which his work appeared; for this see Porter (2016a; 2016b). My focus is instead on the wider potential of the sublime as a lens through which developments in sacred spaces of the Hellenistic period might be better understood, starting with those that might be considered as places of disorientation, whether due to the location of cult, complexity of ritual, or the overall scale.

Sanctuaries in the Hellenistic era seem caught between general principles of design and theatrical architecture (*e.g.* Pollitt 1986) but also local idiosyncrasies of cult. In an age of scientific discoveries, the application by architects of new and awe-inspiring innovations in sacred monuments almost seems paradoxical. Artifice is a domain of engineering, but is also elemental to the experience of the divine. State-of-the art technology has almost always been applied first and foremost

1 Porter gives a critical discussion of whether this 'bubble' – that includes Cicero, Virgil, and Lucan among several others – represents a true peak in this period or is due to the hazards of survival, 101.

to sacred architecture in the ancient world, especially when this is imbued with political power. As the sublime revolves around the extraordinary *de facto*, it should come as no surprise that temples were constructed to mediate interaction between otherwise incompatible beings, a transitional space that reconciled divine power with human necessity. The main difference in the Hellenistic era was an increase in architectural, ritual, and religious repertoire, with more means and varieties to work with and new ways of interpreting these dynamic encounters. Emotional responses were clearly a central element in the organization of ritual (Chaniotis 2012), and we should expect to see this reflected in ritual space as well. The degree to which ecstasy was incorporated in the design of sacred structures is difficult to measure, but interpreting its effect, through architecture or literary testimony, can yield important insights into conceptualizations of the divine in this era.

This paper represents an initial probe in which I explore human interaction in a small selection of Hellenistic sanctuaries, first through the incorporation of the sublime through landscape and ritual at two extreme examples, Mount Lykaion in Arkadia and the underground oracle of the Trophonion in Boiotia. The transcendence of these places is best conveyed by Pausanias who, although from a few centuries later, nonetheless provides an impression of the ritual experience that such heights and depths could provoke. The next section examines ways that the sublime could be activated through architecture to create spectacular experiences at sanctuaries in less extreme locations, assessing how temple architecture facilitated encounters with the divine. Human encounter at these sanctuaries further shaped the experience of the divine and the last section explores the aspect of spectacles and games, rituals that became more and more common but were no less sublime, and the responses they evoked. Landscape, architecture, memory, and human engagement is thus shown to be a critical combination in triggering an overwhelming sense of place and divine presence that these sacred spaces could provide.

Transcendent places of cult

In his assessment of the sublime in the ancient world, Porter (2016b, pp. 118-121) points out no less than 21 different situations that provoke a sense of the sublime. Some common threads include rapid change, or a disruption of the senses, as the regular world falls away and makes room for one in which other rules apply. Another key signal of the sublime is the element of immeasurability, especially regarding the sense of being confronted with, or transported over, unfathomable heights. As Porter (2016a, pp. 533-536) points out, this is equally true of depths, such as abysses. Profundity may be found with both extremes simultaneously and is physically integral to specific landscape features such as mountains, and their seeming inverse, caves. Both are ready magnets for locating the gods in the Graeco-Roman world, *e.g.* Mount Olympus, or Mount Ida, or the cave of Pan in Athens, or of Hades in Eleusis, the gateway to the Underworld. Clearly these extreme types of landscape could elicit responses of sublimity, albeit in different ways (*e.g.* Scully 1962; Miles 2016). But in certain cases their settings were framed primarily through ritual so as to elicit extreme human responses as well; this section examines two such opposite cases, at Mount Lykaion in Arkadia and the cave oracle of Trophonios in Boiotia.

Incredible heights – the Lykaion

Mountains hold a degree of fascination for virtually every culture in every period (Hooley 2012). Their solidness, their ruggedness and remoteness, the spectacular views they afford, the myths and stories associated with them, set them in a class of their own. The inherent capacity of mountains for the sublime is perhaps best

Figure 1. View from Mount Lykaion, looking west. The temple of Apollo at Bassai is barely visible on the horizon to the right (photo: Christina Williamson).

assessed by Veronica della Dora (2008), who observes their ontological timelessness and simultaneous mediation of past and present. In part this is derived through the difficulty of the ascent, but also the 'view from above' that they afford from the peak. The panorama of the landscape below provides a sense of immediacy, with individual locations visibly existing within the larger whole. Despite the tremendous distance, the tiny places can almost be touched in mid-air by the pointing finger, following the eye. The vastness, the difficulty, the simultaneous exhaustion and ecstasy of reaching the peak, places the viewer on the mountain in a completely different frame of time and space, a world very different from the one in the valley or plain below. Little wonder that such heights are considered sacred.

Mount Lykaion in Arkadia is a perfect example of this (see also Romano and Voyatzis 2014, and http://lykaionexcavation.org/ [accessed 14 August 2019]). Writing in the 2nd century AD, Pausanias (8, 38, 2-7) informs us that this peak was known by the Arcadians as Olympus, or the Sacred Peak, or the birthplace of Zeus. He further observes that most of the Peloponnese could be seen from there, and the panorama is indeed extensive (Fig. 1). Sites such as Bassai, Lycosoura, Alipheira, Gortys, the mountains near Mantineia to the east, the area of Megalopolis to the south, and the sea to the west, may in fact readily be identified from its peak.

More than a mountain with a splendid view, however, the precinct of Zeus on this mountain was a different universe with a logic of its own. Pausanias (8, 2, 6) tells us that no one was allowed to enter the *temenos*, and that if they did they would die within a year. Moreover, nothing within the *temenos* cast a shadow, all year round. Finally, this is one of the rare places in the Greek world where human sacrifices and cannibalism allegedly took place, the 'secret sacrifices' that Pausanias is reluctant to mention, and the source of werewolf stories since those who unwittingly ate of human flesh during the sacrifice were turned into a wolf (*e.g.* Pl. Resp. 565d-e; Eidinow 2019, with references). As with all mountains, but for other reasons than most, this was a place of beauty and terror. One detects the sublime through the words of Pausanias, intimating both wonder and dismay in this world within a world at the top of Arkadia. This was a world not to be trodden nor inquired after, best to leave things as they are. Mount Lykaion and its ritual space was clearly perceived as a place beyond human comprehension.

Sensory deprivation – the Trophonion

At the opposite end of the spectrum was the equally terrifying oracular shrine of Trophonion, located in a chasm in the earth, near Lebadeia in Boiotia. According to Herodotos the shrine was consulted by Croesus's messengers (1, 46) and Mys (8, 134), but our most extensive source is again Pausanias (9, 39, 6-14). Rather than being beyond human comprehension, this oracular shrine, linked to the hero Trophonios, was aimed at producing or revealing knowledge – people visited it to learn the future, as Pausanias did himself. Nonetheless, one could not just walk in, but had to go through days of rituals, as we are informed in 9, 39, 6-14. Sacrifices were performed until a positive response was delivered, after which the inquirer was led by two adolescents, called Herms, to the river Herkyna to purify himself. Next he was brought by the priests to drink first from the spring of Forgetfulness (Lethe) and then from Memory (Mnemosyne). The lengthy period of preparation surely put the inquirer in the right mental state for the new encounter, intentionally clearing his mind and opening it up for the new experience. He was then shown the cult image of Trophonius, made by Daidalus, which he had to worship. After this the inquirer was given special clothing for entering into the chasm. The descent was via a ladder, with a narrow opening at the bottom through which the inquirer entered feet first, holding barley cakes for the snakes. Halfway through, he was rapidly sucked or pulled in, presumably in darkness, to a place where he could learn the future, through what he (believes he) would hear or see himself – the inquirer is thus his own medium and it is significant that the oracle is entirely based upon individual experience, rather than being transmitted via a prophet or priest, as Raymond Clark points out (1968, p. 72). Following an undefined period of time (days?) the inquirer left the chasm by the same way, was taken by the hand and set down in the 'chair of Memory' by the priests who interrogated him as to what he learned. After they were finished with him, the inquirer, still paralyzed with terror and detached from the world, was entrusted to his relatives and brought to a place to recuperate. Pausanias ensures us that, after this very sobering experience, the inquirer does regain his senses and 'the power to laugh' (9, 39, 13), as he himself discovered. Finally, the inquirer dedicated a tablet recording his experiences for others, much like the *iamata* at healing shrines. Niches found near a grotto were thought to have once held these tablets (Fig. 2).

The many phases of the ritual are significant, and Pierre Bonnechère (2003) considers this as something between an oracle and mystery cult, as a kind of shamanism. The rituals themselves, as much as the chasm and spatial setting, would have induced the cataleptic trance, which Clark (1968) believed was part of a psychedelic experience. Like a Near Death Experience, the sensory deprivation would have led to an extremely heightened acuity of the senses, producing something like a total recall. The role of memory in the ritual, both before and after the descent, is key to the overall experience.

The subterranean setting of the Trophonion represents on the one hand the opposite type of cult place from that of Zeus on Mount Lykaion. Yet a sense of unfathomable heights or depths played an important role in both cults, as did rapid transitions in light and dark. In this regard it is interesting to note that the chasm of the

Figure 2. Edward Daniel Clarke and Elizabeth Byrne 'Cave of Trophonius in Lebadia, with the cavities cut in the rock for votive tablets, &c.', 15.6 x 21.6 cm, London (Strand): T. Cadell & W. Davies, 31 January 1813 (picture: Creative Commons: Wellcome Collection, https://wellcomecollection.org/works/yk7x6dht [accessed 14 August 2019]).

Trophonion was situated on a mountain. In fact, based on a 3rd century inscription that connects this cult with that of Zeus Basileus (IG VII.4136), Albert Schachter (1984) believes the oracle to even have been relocated at a later stage to a more prominent place in the precinct of Zeus near the top of the mountain and highly visible from the road to Delphi. The portability of such a chthonic cult seems improbable, yet as Pausanias notes, the shrine, and chasm, were 'not natural, but artificially constructed after the most accurate masonry' (9, 39, 9-12). Not only was it man-made, it was apparently also a wonder to behold. Here, also, it is human framing that articulates the sense of the sublime, as architecture served to amplify the ritual experience.

The Trophonion has not been identified with any certainty, but a somewhat similar configuration may be found in southern Pisidia, at Arpalık Tepe near Perge. In 1997, rescue excavations revealed a small Doric temple built over a chasm of 12-15 m deep (Işın 2005). The chasm widened underground to about 9 meters and contained finds from the Archaic to Late Roman phases, with no less than 714 coins from the Hellenistic period (most were from Selge). The finds appeared to have been placed, rather than tossed from above. A tunnel leading from the north seems to have provided access, although this was not excavated beyond a few meters. Among the finds was a Roman statuette bearing a dedication to the 'Great God Mamblasenos/Apollo' but also some Late Classical *terracottas* representing women, as pregnant, before or after pregnancy, and *kourotrophos* statuettes carrying a child, with other dedications to the 'Mother Goddess'. Especially of interest is the votive ear from the Hellenistic era – dedicated to a listening god. Nothing is known of the rituals or cult, but the finds point towards fecundity, motherhood, and life-giving aspects in life-threatening situations, as childbirth surely was.

The actual nature of the cult of Trophonios remains unknown, except for Pausanias's descriptions of the rituals of the oracle. The underground passage might also represent a kind of rebirth, although the Trophonion is generally considered as one of the *nekyomanteia*, or 'death-oracles' (Friese 2010; Boutsikas 2017). These however are typically situated in natural caves, rather than artificial chasms (see also Sporn, this volume). Although the function of the complex at Ephyra, designated as the Nekyomanteion of Acheron, is disputed, Lauter nonetheless considers this as 'das erstaunlichste Beispiel für rationalistische Inszenierung des Übersinnlichen' (1986, pp. 230-23). Vapours may have been the source of the oracle at the Trophonion, as the author (Pseudo-Aristotle) of 'Peri kosmou' (On the Cosmos, or De Mundo) seems to believe. Chasms emitting vapours were generally regarded as a profound source of cosmic knowledge, and he counts the Trophonion among Delphi and the Ploutonion in Hierapolis in his observation:

> '*...in the same way many outlets for wind* [pneumata] *are opened in many places of the earth. Some of these have the effect that those who come near them are inspired by god, some that they waste away, others that they prophesy, as those at Delphi and Lebadeia, and still other outlets destroy them completely, like the one in Phrygia.*' (Ps.-Aristot. De Mundo 395b26, transl. Thom 2014).

The emphasis on ecstasy, and out-of-body experience that the inquirer clearly had, indicates the sublime experience evoked by the combination of ritual and physical setting, but also sudden changes in light. A passage often cited from Longinus concerns his appreciation for the sublime effect of the first words of Genesis:

> '*A similar effect was achieved by the lawgiver of the Jews—no mean genius, for he both understood and gave expression to the power of the divinity as it deserved—when he wrote at the very beginning of his laws, and I quote his words: "God said,"—what was it?— "Let there be light, and there was. Let there be earth, and there was"*' (Longinus, On the Sublime 9, 9, transl. Roberts 1899).

Night and the appearance of light are presumed to be at the centre of the Eleusinian mysteries (Clinton 2004; Patera 2010), as new avenues of research are now demonstrating (*e.g.* Seaford 2010; Boutsikas 2017; Chaniotis and Derron 2018).

Mount Lykaion and the Trophonion both exemplify some of the complexities that we must address in reviewing places of cult as part of a sacred and sublime but also political landscape. They touch exactly on the same aspect of the sublime as Longinus's treatise – the need of artifice to enhance the power of nature. This is the same theme that we observe in developments in several sanctuaries in the Hellenistic world, especially in outlying, remote areas, where landscape was clearly activated through architecture.

Architectural activation

As remarkable as the Lykaion and the Trophonion are, they are not widely considered in assessments of Hellenistic sanctuaries as their innovations lie principally in the peculiar combination of legend, ritual, and setting, rather than their architectural configuration. Temples that are generally discussed include the shrine of Apollo at Didyma with its architectonic eccentricities, and sanctuary complexes such as that of Asclepios at Cos, or Athena at Lindos on Rhodes. While the design of these will briefly be reviewed in this section in the cadre of the sublime, it will also be demonstrated that they were not isolated cases.

Figure 3. Reconstruction of the entrance to the temple of Apollo at Didyma, showing the great 'Erscheinungstür', Apollontempel in Didyma bei Milet, print by Georg Niemann (1841-1912), 1912 (photo: Johannes Laurentius, Antikensammlung, Staatliche Museen zu Berlin-Preussischer Kulturbesitz).

Light and epiphany

Light plays a strong role in both the Trophonion and Mount Lykaion through their setting but also through ritual. As noted above, sudden changes in light and dark can usher in a profound sense of the sublime. Temple architecture is generally presumed to take lighting effects into account, whether on sunrise on feast days as William Bell Dinsmoor (1939) believed, or night-time constellations as Efrosyni Boutsikas (2009) argues. An extreme case, however, is provided by the younger temple of Apollo at Didyma, with its mixture of openings that are not entrances, entrances that are tunnels, and inversion of interior and exterior space (*e.g.* Gruben 1986, pp. 359-375; Pollit 1986, pp. 236-238; Clarke 2012). Added to this is the sheer scale, comparable to the shrine of Artemis in Ephesos: it took the goddess herself to lift the monolithic lintel of the Archaic temple in place, or so the story goes (Plin. HN 36, 21). The Hellenistic version of the Artemision (also designed by Paionios, and Daphnis from Miletus) was at least as grand. Like its Ephesian counterpart, the Didymaion was constructed on an immense *stylobate*, over 100 m long, with a dipteral Ionic peristyle, each column soaring nearly 20 m high (Fig. 3), at what Jerome Pollitt (1986, p. 237) calls the 'shock scale'. The columns, however, were much closer together, creating a thick *Säulenwald* (Berve and Gruben 1961, p. 251). Their density would have occluded the view of the *cella*, but as one ascended the 14 steps to the *pronaos*, passing from the brightness of the *temenos* (at daytime) through to the deep shade of the peristyle, the colossal doorway – 14 m high – would appear to rise.

Lucian (Syr. D. 30) compares Assyrian Hera's temple to such great temples of Ionia: 'as you mount [the stairs], even the great hall exhibits a wonderful spectacle and it is ornamented with golden doors' (transl. Strong and Garstang 1913). An important difference, however, is that the great doorway in Didyma had no leaves but was entirely open and would have been backlit from the unroofed *cella* within. The sudden switches in light and dark is visible in Jan Köster's 3D models (*e.g.* Köster 2017; Fig. 4).

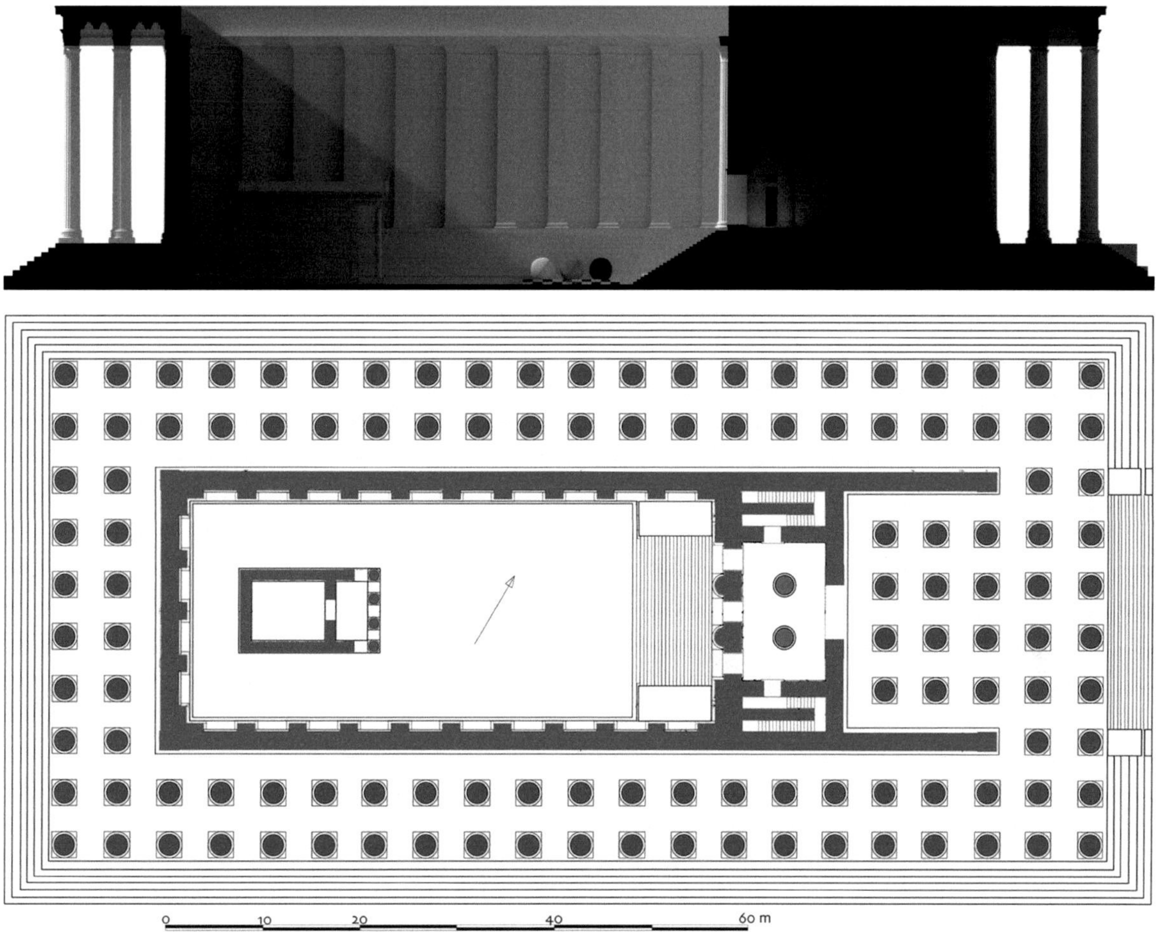

Figure 4. Plan and cross-section of the temple of Apollo at Didyma, showing the sunlight from the west at an elevation of 36° (summer), illuminating the adyton and mid-chamber (elevation: Jan Köster, DAI Istanbul; plan: Christina Williamson, after Knackfuß and Wiegand 1941, p. 8).

Moreover, access was blocked by the high threshold, 1.46 m above the *pronaos*, that may have served as a podium for the transmission of the oracle (Günther 1971). This *Erscheinungstür* clearly had a ritual purpose (a parallel may be found in Naxos, see Büsing-Kolbe 1978; Gruben 1986, p. 347). The portal certainly symbolized passage, but not for humans. Instead it linked the inner and outer spaces of the sanctuary as the great eye, ear, and mouth of Apollo. The mortal inquirers, standing in the obscurity of the *pronaos*, must have been overwhelmed by the scale and luminosity, underscoring the transience of their own existence in the presence of the god. Whether actual access to the *cella* was open to everyone, the priests, or perhaps initiates is unclear, but to enter one had to descend through the dark vaulted passages, called labyrinths, that opened onto the interior, over three meters below the *pronaos* and open to the sky. The cult image of Apollo was housed in a *naiskos*, near the sacred well at the back of the *cella*. In this way a new inner world had been created, again one in which other rules apply – instead of going up, one goes down and inside becomes outside again. Creating this fantastic setting for the reception of the oracle is a vivid portrayal of what Burkhard Gladigow calls 'guided perception' (1990, p. 103), inducing the right state of mind to receive divine revelation.

The Didymaion is an acute example of the kind of architectural alchemy that precipitated a sense of epiphany in Hellenistic sanctuaries. Epiphanies are often linked to viewing the cult image and are reflected in ritual and architecture by framing the approach (Burkert 1997; Clarke 2012; Williamson 2018). Doorways of temples long served to heighten this effect through their scale and fine carvings

Figure 5. Reverse of a Hadrianic silver tetradrachm showing the temple of Artemis in Ephesos, with the cult image visible in the temple and the door-like aperture in the pediment, SNG UK Vol. VI .2 1310 (photo: © The Fitzwilliam Museum, Cambridge).

on doorposts and lintels, initially exclusive to temple architecture (Büsing-Kolbe 1978, p. 82). Certain temples, especially in Hellenistic Asia Minor, received an additional opening in the pediment looking out over the altar. The most famous of these is Paionios's westward-facing temple of Ephesian Artemis; the aperture is shown in imperial coinage (Fig. 5).

As the altar would have blocked a direct view from the *cella*, Anton Bammer (1972, pp. 10. 41) reconstructed a sightline to the aperture above, which may have held the cult image, or priestess appearing as the goddess to watch the sacrifices. In 1904, Julius Kohte had already suggested a similar ritual function for the aperture in the 2nd century BCE temple of Artemis Leukophryene, constructed by Hermogenes of Priene (Humann *et al.* 1904, p. 64 no.1). Under the right conditions, such performances surely brought about a real sense of the presence of the divine.

Figure 6. The view from the upper terrace of the Asclepieion, looking across the middle and lower terrace, and to the polis of Cos, with the peninsula of Halicarnassus (Bodrum) beyond. (photo: Christina Williamson).

Framing the view

Temple architecture was but one part of this activation. Shrines in this era were often designed as an ensemble of spaces that engaged the wider landscape in a ritualized composition of space, timing, and experience. Significant changes in spatial configuration in this period were identified by Phyllis Lehmann (1954) and became textbook cases in Helmut Berve and Gottfried Gruben's *Griechische Tempel und Heiligtümer* (1961). The year 1986 was bountiful for Hellenistic architecture with the appearance of Hans Lauter's *Die Architektur des Hellenismus*, Pollitt's *Art in the Hellenistic Age*, and the fourth edition of Gruben's *Die Tempel der Griechen*. Besides Didyma, the terraced complexes of the Asclepieion on Cos and Athena Lindos on Rhodes are their archetypes of sensational architectural space with staged views. Pollitt especially goes into the theatrical use of space at these terraced complexes. Regarding Cos, he discerns a dramatic development in the three terraces that ascend the hillside, each affording different views, leading up to the climactic Temple A on the upper terrace with its panorama (1986, pp. 231-232). The visitor would certainly have had changing perspectives of space as he or she moved from the large yet enclosed lower terrace to the sacrificial space on the open middle terrace and finally to the framed panorama from the upper terrace (Fig. 6). The effect would have been greater given the directionality of the gaze enforced by the staircase (see also Hollinshead 2015, pp. 72-77). The focus is on the immediate staircase and only at intervals, or upon arrival, would the panorama become apparent as one turned around. Meanwhile, Temple A would appear to rise before the ascending visitor.

Although we have no literary references, this effect could hardly have been accidental. Gruben linked the developments at Cos, and the general conceptualization of the *Gesamtanlagen*, as part of the growing focus of religion in the Hellenistic era on the individual, demonstrated by the rising popularity of healing cults and cults of salvation (1986, pp. 401-402). At the shrine of Athena at Lindos, on Rhodes,

Figure 7. Lindos. The propylaia of the Athena sanctuary with the monumental staircase (photo: Creative Commons: Bernard Gagnon, https://commons.wikimedia.org/wiki/File:Staircase_of_the_Propylaea (Lindos).jpg [accessed 14 August 2019]).

he observes how landscape is incorporated into the design as part of the dramatic setting, with the scenery radically changing upon ascent from the armature of the enclosed terrace below, up the monumental stairs (Fig. 7) and onto the windswept plateau where the temple of Athena stands (Gruben 1986, p. 419; also Pollitt 1986, pp. 230-231; Hollinshead 2015, pp. 62-64).

Both island sanctuaries offer a breath-taking panorama of the surrounding landscape and sea, giving at least the modern visitor a sense of standing on top of the world. Whether this was the equivalent of a cathartic experience in antiquity is difficult to say, yet the vastness, the potential force of weather, and especially the sudden transitions in light with rapidly shifting perspectives surely contributed to an ecstatic experience. These were effects that could be orchestrated via architecture in combination with landscape and ritual. Bonna Wescoat's discussion of the interstitial spaces at Samothrace (this volume) significantly demonstrates the importance of considering such complexes as part of an entire religious experience rather than as isolated features on their own.

Terraced sanctuaries did not suddenly appear but are part of a longer development. Poul Pedersen (2004) traces this development via the Attalids of Pergamon, who found their inspiration in the 4th century architecture of Hekatomnid Karia, especially the sanctuary of Zeus at Labraunda. The shrine is located on a hillside overlooking Mylasa and southwest Karia on an outlier of the heavily eroded Latmos mountains. The dominant feature of the cult is a split boulder, surely interpreted as the work of Zeus with his characteristic *labrys*, or double-axe. A temple was built in the Late Archaic period, and in the 5th century the shrine was a place of refuge for Karian troops fleeing from the Persians during the Ionian revolt (Hdt. 5, 119, 1-2). In the 4th century, the Hekatomnids, satraps under the Achaemenids, developed Labraunda into their ideological and political centre. Mixing Persian, Greek, and Karian traditions, they radically expanded the site with a multi-terraced complex articulated by *stoas* and additional facilities. Their dedicatory inscriptions on the architraves displayed to all their tight bond with Zeus Labraundos. Among their key additions are the *andrones*, great *prostyle* banqueting halls near (and overshadowing) the temple of Zeus. These halls were sumptuously decorated, and Anne-Marie Carstens (2009, p. 88) has likened the setting to dining in paradise, Achaemenid-style; Labraunda is interpreted as a residence-sanctuary by Olivier Henry (2017). The view from the shrine extends across the plain of Mylasa to the hills behind Halikarnassos, incorporating a good deal of Hekatomnid territory. As Labraunda passed from the satraps to Mylasa in the Hellenistic era, few modifications at the shrine were made, although there are several signs of repair and perhaps even some 'fake' structures from this period. This led Pontus Hellström (2009) to ask whether Labraunda did not serve as some kind of memory theatre. The many material references – in coinage, inscriptions, and even the onomastics of Mylasa – to the by-then historical dynasty answer in the affirmative (Williamson 2013). The shrine served as an important echo chamber of the power from the past in the turbulent times of the present.

Sanctuaries are by nature keepers of memory and, besides commanding heights and theatrical architecture, we should not underestimate the role that memory played in imbuing a sense of the sublime. The Athenaion in Ilion shows how architecture was intentionally shaped to convey a connection between the present and the heroic past. Brian Rose (2012) believes that new rituals, such as the Lokrian maidens in the Archaic period, were developed as ways of establishing political connections but were also etched into the sanctuary through the construction of a well with an underground access for the maidens, who were not allowed within sight of the cult image. He further argues that during the reconstruction of the *temenos*, in the 3rd or 2nd centuries BCE, the north side was intentionally left open, framing the view across the most famous (albeit less spectacular) landscape known to the Greek world – the Dardanelles and the plain of Troy – and incorporating this into the 'coordinated visual network designed to exploit the Homeric associations of the site – in essence to materialize memory' (Rose 2012, p. 159). Rulers like Xerxes, Alexander, and later Julius Caesar, Augustus, and Hadrian are said to have paid homage to Troy – obviously they were after the wonder of the place itself and especially the need to be able to touch the past – and by so doing to become a part of it. Memory sits in places, but it is also activated through them. Architecture can invoke the past, either by being part of it as at Labraunda, or by intentionally showcasing it as with the Athenaion at Ilion.

Human encounters

The visibility of the weight of the past was an increasingly central element at sanctuaries and contributed to a sense of expansion traversing the space and moment of the present. The sanctuary at Lindos had the perfect combination of landscape, elevations, and spectacular vistas, but it also had the 'Lindian chronicle' (*I.Lindos* 2). This carefully composed inscription not only preserved the deep memory of the sanctuary through the votive gifts given by gods, heroes, and kings (Shaya 2005), but also presents no less than four epiphanies of the goddess Athena to the Lindians (Platt 2011, pp. 161-169). The ultimate message is one of incessant divine presence, power, and protection from the beginning of time (for the Lindians) – again at a scale beyond human comprehension. Not all sanctuaries had spectacular views. Most, however, did have some kind of historical record on display through inscriptions. Human encounter with the divine was clearly momentous and the resulting political initiatives and gains, as well as the festivals with games, were a means of broadcasting and commemorating the event, making it last across time, at least according to the epigraphic record.

Epiphanies and security

Temple spaces and *cella* walls were often used as archives of political transactions, but in special cases they spoke directly to the visitor about the divine *enargeia*, or power of the god, in a sacred and historical moment, as at Lindos. Such epiphanies were on the rise in the later Hellenistic period, as cities felt the need to show the world that they mattered and that their gods were actively protecting them (*e.g.* Rostowzew 1920; Platt 2011, pp. 124-169). One of the longest preserved inscriptions, presumably inscribed on the temple walls, is from the shrine of Zeus Panamaros, where the population of Stratonikeia was celebrating the festival of Zeus Panamaros when they were attacked by Labienus's Parthian troops in the mid-1st century BCE (*I.Stratonikeia* 10). This inscription, largely written in the present tense, narrates in vivid and precise detail of the god's intervention as he drove off the enemy through storms, mist, and hallucinations. Although the inscription had a political function (ensuring Stratonikeia's second privilege of *asylia*), it must have nonetheless been a spine-tingling experience to read the story at the very spot where it took place; surely this was meant to invoke both a sense of dismay and ecstasy at the saving power of the god.

Less is known about the exact nature of the epiphany of Artemis Leukophryene in Magnesia on the Maeander, but this was the reason behind the construction of her temple in the 2nd century BCE, discussed in the previous section in connection with the *Erscheinungstür*. The appearance of the goddess led the people of Magnesia to send a delegation to Delphi to inquire as to how they should respond. The oracle was clear: organize a festival in her honour (*I.Magnesia* 16; also Jürgens 2017). They did so in 208 BCE, investing in an enormous diplomatic offensive to invite other cities (via *theoroi*) to recognize the festival, as we learn from the inscriptions listing the cities that responded to the invitation (*I.Magnesia* 16-87 – Fig. 8, center). Several remarkable observations have been made with this inscription on the dating of the games at Magnesia (Slater and Summa 2006; Thonemann 2007), but for our purposes it is important to note the status of 'sacred and inviolable' (*hieros kai asylos*, as restored in lines 9-10) that the Pythian oracle presumably confirmed (Rigsby 1996). This is one of the first in a line of such wide-spread public confirmations of *asylia* by Hellenistic rulers, and later the Senate or Roman emperor. Sanctuaries in the Greek world were presumed to be immune from violence and raids, yet in reality this was not always the case; additional political security was needed, especially in turbulent times. The term 'sacred and inviolable' extended the immunity to a city and its territory, in acknowledgment of the power of its protecting deity (Rigsby 1996, pp. 3-5). The rare occurrence of epiphanies, such as that of Artemis Leukophryene, gave weight to the authority of a sanctuary and the acquisition of this protected status. The irony is that this (probably) led to an increase in this phenomenon, so much so that according to Tacitus (Ann. 3, 60-63), Tiberius later called a special counsel to investigate the validity of the claims of polis and deity.

Spectacles and expanding horizons

Such divine manifestations had ritual and political implications that also led to the organization of festivals that reflected the grandeur of the god while serving as a public and political platform. Spectacles were staged that celebrated the power of the deity, but were carefully orchestrated to engage as wide an audience as possible. At Magnesia the responses mentioned above (*I.Magnesia* 16-87) from the some 100 cities, including rulers, were inscribed in the agora and within view of the *temenos* of Artemis. Such lists put the city on centre-stage, as much as it created a cognitive map of the world that mattered (Ma 2003).

Figure 8 (opposite). Theoric networks of Cos (top), Magnesia on the Maeander (center), and Stratonikeia (bottom) (credit: Christina Williamson, plotted with Palladio from Stanford University).

THEORIC NETWORK OF KOS, c.242 BC

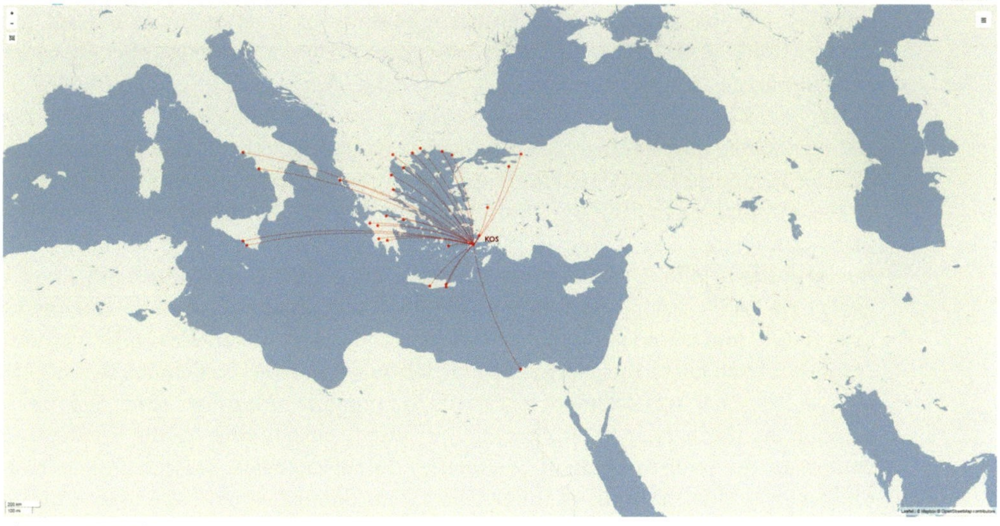

THEORIC NETWORK OF MAGNESIA ON THE MAEANDER, c.208 BC

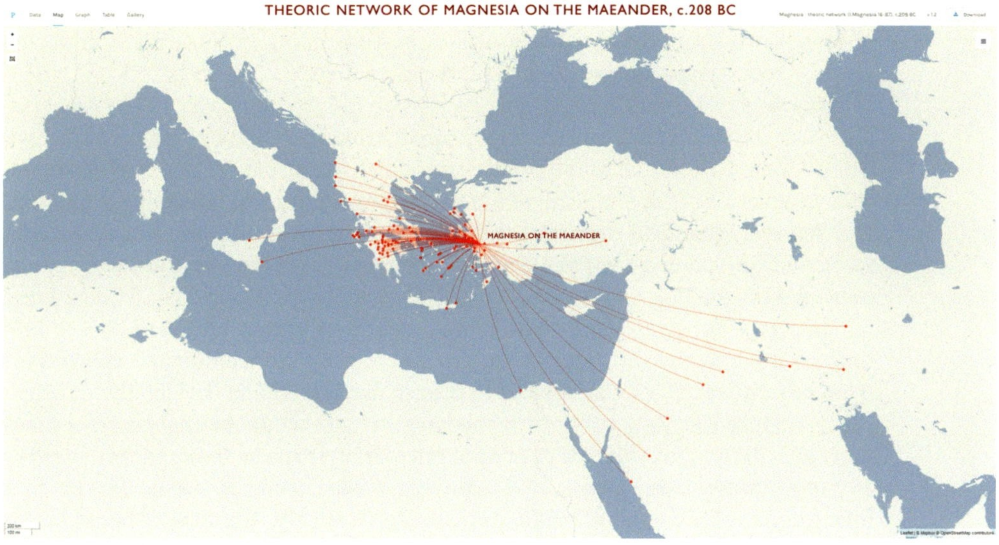

THEORIC NETWORK OF STRATONIKEIA, c.80 BC

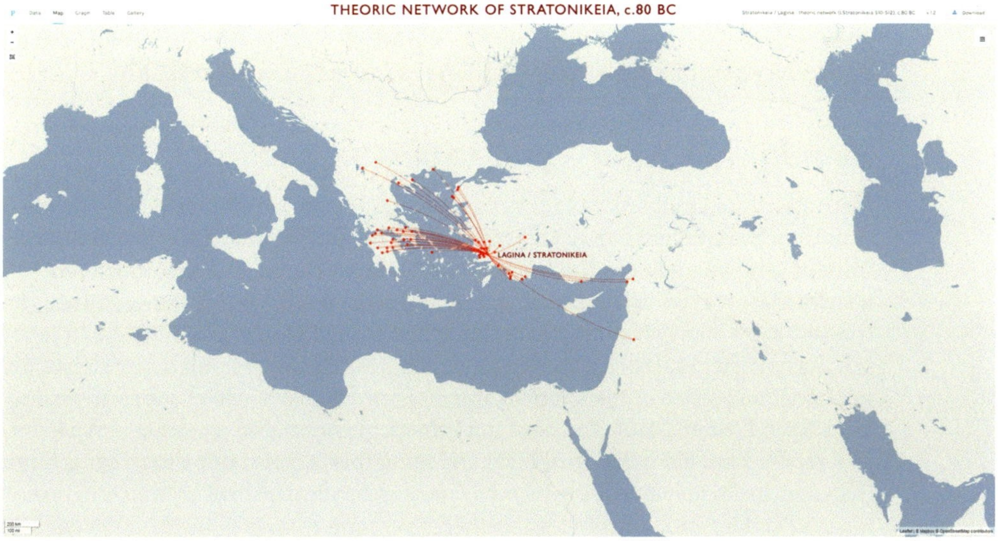

Some two generations earlier, Cos had undertaken a similar endeavour, sending an embassy to Delphi to procure the status of inviolability in 242 BCE for the sanctuary of Asclepios. This does not appear to be the result of a specific event as with Magnesia or Stratonikeia, but rather the widely acclaimed healing power of the god. The oracle was positive, resulting in the establishment of a new Asclepieia, with games that were recognized as panhellenic in 241 BCE (Rigsby 1996, pp. 106-154; Buraselis 2004). In anticipation of the first festival, Cos sent out teams of *theoroi*, diplomats inviting cities and rulers across the Greek world to participate (Rutherford 2013). Kent Rigsby observes the wide variety of formulary in the responding letters, some even expressing surprise; this would also indicate an early date and a premier at this level (1996, p. 110). While the known catchment area (Fig. 8, top) is less spectacular than at Magnesia, it nonetheless also includes responses from kings and shows the wide latitude that cities could have in creating festival ties that transcended territorial boundaries. Although their inscribed location at the shrine is unknown, the letters responding to the invitations comprised the cognitive map of Cos, as they did in Magnesia, and must have been on display within the walls of the *temenos*. This dossier would have placed in the mind's eye of the reader a bird's eye view of the expanded world of the Asclepieion. Besides geopolitical positioning, it created a multi-level ontological experience of being in the sanctuary while at the same time being in the wider connected world, a transcendental experience for those open to it.

This would provide a clear framework for the first terraces of the great Asclepieion, assuming they were being finished around the time of the great festival (Interdonato 2016). A decree stipulating the construction of a treasury, IG XII,4 1:71, calls in lines 19-21 for the festival assembly (*panegyris*) and delegations (*theoroi*) and contests (*gymnikoi agones*) to be conducted as 'beautiful and illustrious and worthy of the god and the people' (*kalos kai epiphanos syntelontai kai axios ton te theon kai tas tou damou proairesios*). The element of civic pride is involved here, but this goes further. The intention was clearly to create an event that would impress not only the god, but also the entire community including the delegations from other (peer?) cities that would witness the production. At Cos this effect is highly nuanced, as visitors entering the lower terrace would be enclosed in a space more or less recognizable as a cosmopolitan, peristyle space, found in nearly every city (*e.g.* Lauter 1986; Emme 2013). Moving up the terraces surely developed a mixed sense of being both inside and outside physically, but also of being in Cos while being connected to the wider world, through the many visitors from across the oecumene, as well as the testimony of the theoric inscriptions. Architecture and the organization of festivals such as the Megala Asklepeia were an orchestrated human effort that mobilized the divinity to evoke a human response.

Human endeavour – games and the sublime

Festivals are generally geared towards creating a common focus, reiterated through ritual, but the emphasis on the splendour and the inclusion of athletic and musical contests with an audience from across the Greek world made it that much more of a spectacle, an event to be remembered and passed on. Besides the sacrifices, the contests were themselves central to this spectacle and surely contributed to a sense of ecstasy. Porter (2016a, pp. 413-414) includes epinician odes in his discussion of the pre-Longinian sense of the sublime, due to their extensive use of superlatives (*e.g.* Lunt 2009; Steiner 2010). The odes put athletic prowess into a cosmic perspective, as it represented a perfection of body and mind that touched upon the divine. More than just the achievement on its own, sport is about the thrill of watching excellence in action, and watching it together. Everyone witnesses the same event and witnesses each others' reactions to it. As Michael Suk-Young Chwe (2001) argues, such situations are the best kinds of coordinating mechanisms, as they produce common knowledge instantaneously (also van Nijf and Williamson 2016). Yet this was also a kind of ritual viewing that, especially with outstanding victories or close calls, surely gave rise to an epiphanic experience. One sees, but also hears, smells, and can even touch excellence, at the same time realizing one's own failure and inability to even come close to such an accomplishment, producing a simultaneous feeling of dismay and exaltation (Roueché 1993; Serres 2011). Civic rivalry surely played its part, yet sport has an exceptional capacity to engage and overwhelm an audience at the individual level as well as the collective, giving a sense of elation while under the approving gaze of the gods.

Victory was engrained in the value system of ancient Greece, and sport, its rules, the training in the gymnasia, was one of its strongest channels besides actual warfare. Cos and Magnesia were among the early poleis to adopt this pan-hellenic perspective of festivals and use it to incorporate their own geo-politics with ritual, spectacle, and architecture before the divine. This was to become more and more widespread in the Hellenistic era and Angelos Chaniotis (1995) counted over a hundred new festivals that took place in both new and existing cities all across the Greek world (also Parker 2004) and would eventually lead to the 'explosion agonistique' in the imperial period, as Louis Robert (1984) identified it (see among many others Newby 2005; van Nijf 2012; Blanco Perez 2018).

Stratonikeia provides one more example. Tacitus shows the city as the only one to have two claims of *asylia* to defend in the tribune under Tiberius: one for Zeus Panamaros (discussed above) and one for her other primary sanctuary, Hekatesion at nearby Lagina (Ann. 3, 62). The cult of Hekate at Lagina seems to have a longer and tighter history with the polis than Panamara, and her cult place became a major civic shrine at least by the end of the 2nd century BCE, if not before. Her temple, famous for its friezes and Corinthian order, is among those with an aperture in the pediment, possibly as an *Erscheinungstür*. Hekate figured on the coins and had acquired the epithet of Soteira Epiphaneia (Manifest Savior) after the Mithradatic wars, although the circumstances are not clear (*I.Stratonikeia* 512). In any event, the Stratonikeians suffered heavy losses during the wars but were rewarded afterwards for their loyalty to Rome. Sulla issued a Senatus Consultum (*I.Stratonikeia* 505) that granted them a massive territorial grant and especially the privileged status of *asylia* for the sanctuary of Hekate, 'the most manifest and greatest goddess' (*epiphanestates kai megistes theas*, line 57). The city responded with a new festival for Hekate together with Thea Rome, with delegations, similar to Cos and Magnesia. At least 57 cities and kingdoms, from Elis to Damascus (Fig. 8, bottom), responded positively. This shows some of the extent of the world that Stratonikeia was able to mobilize through the festival of Hekate, but also through the powerful connections between Stratonikeia and Rome (van Nijf and Williamson 2016). As at Magnesia, we see again how an epiphany is combined with geopolitics in a festival linked with games used to position the city in the larger Greek world. The decree of Rome and the lists of cities that endorsed the festival was inscribed on the temple walls, presumably as Riet van Bremen (2010) has argued on one of the most high-profile lateral sides, across from the tribunes.

Lagina served as a memory theatre for Stratonikeia, and its fame and festivals had a magnetic attraction, making this one of the most apparent places to erect civic monuments, such as the one honouring the sibling benefactors Menekles and Epainetos in the late 1st century BCE, whose long statue, next to the entrance of the sanctuary, occupied a prime spot and would have served to frame the view of the temple (Fig. 9). But besides the official monuments, less formal 'graffiti' or private markings are visible on the *crepidoma* of the temple, and on the sides of the grand-stands. Their chronology poses obvious problems and is likely from the imperial era, but they at least demonstrate that at some point in time people claimed their

Figure 9. Lagina. Monument for Menekles and Epainetos, I.Stratonikeia 1426-1427, seen from the propylon with the temple in the background (photo: Christina Williamson).

place, showing a tight connection with either the deity, the public spectacle, or both. Sometimes they inscribed their personal spots, as did Leon with his *topos Leontos*, inscribed in prime space between the *propylon* and the public monument of Menekles and Epainetos.[2] Others only left traces of their bare footprints, but incised on the temple crepidoma, possibly as a reference to the divine presence (Ziebarth 1909, p. 104; Dunbabin 1990, on the dedication of feet), or more probably as a token of one's own presence and experience in the shrine.

Architecture and the organization of festivals such as the Megala Asklepeia, were a combined effort that was clearly meant to inspire a response.

Conclusion – constructing the sublime

This study began with the question of whether an engineering challenge or a true religious experience was the ultimate motivation of Heron of Alexandria with his *automata*. Although we will never know, the developments in both architecture, religion, and more general conceptualizations indicate that it may have been both. In Longinus's view, the sublime, *hypsos*, is primarily experienced as such through human framing, producing a mixture of dismay and elevation. We may observe this at sanctuaries at many different levels. The Lykaion, with its crowning landscape, is nonetheless regulated by ritual, with the *temenos* of Zeus at the top being forbidden to humans – legends of weird light, human sacrifice and cannibalism, and the

2 This phenomenon has been rigorously documented at Aphrodisias in the Roman period, see Roueché 1993.

perceived reality of turning into a wolf surely heightened the sense of 'otherness' of this world not meant for humans. The same may be said of the inverse situation, in a world of darkness and an underground chasm as with the Trophonion, and the emotional response connected with disorientation and sensory deprivation. Although both clearly have man-made features, the perception of landscape was paramount, but the perception was clearly coloured through the lens of ritual. Ritual certainly shaped the temple at Didyma, designed to disorient the visitor with sudden changes in light and dark, up and down, access and restriction, and inside and outside, and all at an overwhelming scale – the temple was meant to throw you off your guard, not knowing what to expect next. Didyma created an inner world of its own, separated from the landscape, while other shrines exploited enclosed and open spaces more subtly, such as the sanctuary of Athena at Lindos and the Asclepieion at Cos, with terraces that shift from enclosed armature to open panoramas, presumably guiding the visitor up into the world of the divine in stages. Nearby Hekatomnid Karia may well have been a direct source of inspiration for this kind of architecture, especially the shrine of Zeus at Labraunda that was conceived as a sequence of terraced spaces that afforded increasingly spectacular views of their territory. The weight of the past could also play a role in precipitating a sense of the sublime, with the legacy of the architecture itself as at Labraunda, or with views of the epic landscapes and battlefields, as with the Athena sanctuary at Ilion. The presence of the divine, however, is an element common to every sanctuary, but distinguished in different ways. Epiphanies were on the rise in the later Hellenistic period, and were increasingly important to the security and prominence of a city in turbulent times. As important as the epiphany itself was the way that it was commemorated, with inscriptions but also grand festivals, sometimes with a re-enactment of the presence of the divine, as the apertures in the pediments of temples of Ephesus, Magnesia, or Lagina seem to indicate. Finally, games offered a podium for human excellence bordering on the heroic, as testified by the superlatives in epinician poetry. The thrill of victory surely created a collective sense of the sublime among the spectators as well, as discussed above. Cities and federations were increasingly adding contests to their main festivals. Competitions were held at most of the shrines discussed here, even at the Lykaion with contests that were believed by Pliny to predate the Olympic games (HN 7, 57), and the Trophonion, at least in the second century BCE (Rigsby 1996, pp. 81-82; Knoepfler 1992, p. 487).

This research is only an initial probe into possible reasons behind this seeming tendency towards sensationalism and individual experience in sacred architecture, but also in ritual. Others have long ago stressed the concept of 'staging' cult as a key feature of Hellenistic architecture, such as Pollitt's assessment of the theatrical (1986), Lauter's focus on architectonic and spatial arrangement (1986) and also Margaret Lyttelton's emphasis on the baroque (1974). Thomas (2014) makes an important observation when he states that the key point lies in the realization by architects of the effect of their work on the viewers. Although he argues this was the legacy of Longinus in the imperial era, I agree with Porter (2016b) that both Longinus and other expressions of the sublime are part of a much deeper conceptualization, even if not formally articulated as *hypsos*. Many other cult places that were developed or transformed in the Hellenistic era would underscore this, such as the cult complex for the Great Gods at Samothrace, the terraced sanctuaries at Knidos, or Terracina and Praeneste in the west; these have been left out due to time constraints but should also be included a larger assessment.

The problem rises when these new forms are interpreted as signs of a fraying ideal, *i.e. polis* religion, as if that summed up religion in the Greek world prior to the Chaironea (see now Kindt 2012). The view of a growing, deep-seated lack of confidence in the gods hardly does justice to the reality, vibrancy, and plurality of religious experience. The traces of both formal and informal actions at shrines make clear how intimately engaged people, at every level, could be with their gods, even the 'remote Olympians' – and most of the sanctuaries discussed here were also highly politicized cults, even the principle cult of the *polis*. It is more productive to consider innovations in architecture, as well as ritual and myth, as being driven by human desire to touch and be touched by the divine. The sublime was nothing new in the Hellenistic era, even though the concept had yet to be articulated. But just as with our virtual realities today, technology was catching up with human imagination and new ways were being discovered as to how a higher level of awareness could be invoked. Surely the sanctuaries discussed here were a significant part of this, and contributed in turn to a developing discourse and vocabulary of the sublime.

The role of human perspective and participation is paramount and the point is that in order to understand architecture we have to look beyond it. Focusing on the sublime allows a better grasp on the reasoning behind certain architectural choices. The challenge is to access the many layers at which this worked, across several generations and in many different contexts. How these architecturally defined spaces were turned into places by the people who frequented them, who left their traces through generations and even centuries of footsteps and fingerprints, who embedded their own identities into them through the traces they left behind, and what this meant at a political but also social and personal level, is the next step ahead.

Acknowledgments

I would like to thank the editors for inviting me to contribute to this volume, and for their helpful comments, discussions, and insights. I am also grateful to Jan Köster of the DAI in Istanbul, for the use of his 3D model of the Didymaion, and to the Antikensammlung, Staatliche Museen zu Berlin-Preussischer Kulturbesitz and the Fitzwilliam Museum of Cambridge for their assistance with the images in Figures 3 and 5.

References

Bammer, A. 1972. *Die Architectur des jüngeren Artemision von Ephesos.* Wiesbaden: Franz Steiner Verlag.

Berve, H. and Gruben, G. 1961. *Griechische Tempel und Heiligtümer.* Munich: Max Hirmer.

Blanco Perez, A. 2018. EPINIKIA: Celebrating Roman victory in the Eastern provinces of the empire. *Tyche. Beiträge zur Alten Geschichte, Papyrologie und Epigraphik* 33, 9-42.

Bonnechère, P. 2003. *Trophonios de Lèbadèe: cultes et mythes d'une citè béotienne au miroir de la mentalitè antique.* Leiden: Brill.

Boutsikas, E. 2009. Placing Greek temples: an archaeoastronomical study of the orientation of ancient Greek religious structures. *Archaeoastronomy: The Journal of Astronomy in Culture* 21, 4-16.

Boutsikas, E. 2017. The role of darkness in ancient Greek religion and religious practice, in: Papadopoulos C. and Moyes, H. (eds.). *The Oxford Handbook of Light in Archaeology.* Oxford: Oxford University Press: DOI: 10.1093/oxfordhb/9780198788218.013.12.

van Bremen, R. 2010. The inscribed documents on the temple of Hekate at Lagina and the date and meaning of the temple frieze, in: van Bremen, R. and Carbon, J.-M. (eds.). *Hellenistic Karia*, Proceedings of the First International Conference on Hellenistic Karia, 29 June-2 July 2006 Oxford. Bordeaux: Ausonius, 483-503.

Büsing-Kolbe, A. 1978. Frühe griechische Türen. *Jahrbuch des Deutschen Archäologischen Instituts* 93, 66-174.

Buraselis, K. 2004. Some remarks on the Koan *asylia* (242 B.C.) against its international background, in: Höghammar, K. (ed.). *The Hellenistic polis of Kos: state, economy and culture.* Uppsala: Uppsala Universitet, 15-20.

Burkert, W. 1997. From epiphany to cult statue, in: Lloyd, A.B. (ed.) *What is a god? Studies in the nature of Greek divinity.* London: Duckworth, 15-34.

Carstens, A. 2009. *Karia and the Hekatomnids: the creation of a dynasty.* Oxford: Archaeopress.

Chaniotis, A. 1995. Sich selbst feiern? Städtische Feste des Hellenismus im Spannungsfeld von Religion und Politik, in: Wörrle, M. and Zanker, P. (eds.). *Stadtbild und Bürgerbild im Hellenismus.* München: Beck, 147-172.

Chaniotis, A. 2012. Constructing the fear of gods: epigraphic evidence from sanctuaries of Greece and Asia Minor, in: Chaniotis, A. (ed.). *Unveiling emotions: sources and methods for the study of emotions in the Greek World.* Stuttgart: Franz Steiner Verlag, 205-234.

Chaniotis, A. and Derron, P. (eds.) 2018. *La nuit: imaginaire et réalités nocturnes dans le monde gréco-romain.* Vandœuvres: Fondation Hardt.

Chwe, M.S.-Y. 2001. *Rational ritual: culture, coordination, and common knowledge.* Princeton: Princeton University Press.

Clark, R.J. 1968. Trophonios: the manner of his revelation. *Transactions and Proceedings of the American Philological Association* 99, 63-75.

Clarke, J.R. 2012. Constructing the spaces of epiphany in ancient Greek and Roman visual culture, in: Niang,A.C. and Osiek, C. (eds.). *Text, image, and christians in the Graeco-Roman world: a festschrift in honor of David Lee Balch.* Allison Part PA: Pickwick.

Clinton, K. 2004. Epiphany in the Eleusinian mysteries. *Illinois Classical Studies* 29, 85-109.

Costelloe, T.M. 2012. *The sublime: from antiquity to the present.* Cambridge: Cambridge University Press.

Deshours, N. 2011. *L'été indien de la religion civique: études sur les cultes civiques dans le monde* égéen *à l'époque hellénistique tardive.* Bordeaux: Ausonius.

Dinsmoor, W.B. 1939. Archaeology and astronomy. *Proceedings of the American Philosophical Societ*y 80, 95-173.

della Dora, V. 2008. Mountains and memory: embodied visions of ancient peaks in the nineteenth-century Aegean. *TRAN Transactions of the Institute of British Geographers* 33 (2), 217-232.

Doran, R. 2015. *The theory of the sublime from Longinus to Kant.* Cambridge: Cambridge University Press.

Dunbabin, K.M.D. 1990. Ipsa deae vestigia. Footprints divine and human on Graeco-Roman monuments. *Journal of Roman Archaeology* 3, 85-109.

Eidinow, E. 2019. Consuming narratives: the politics of cannibalism on Mt. Lykaion. *Classica et mediaevalia. Revue danoise de philologie et d'histoire (Danish Journal of philology and history)* 67, 63-89.

Emme, B. 2013. *Peristyl und Polis: Entwicklung und Funktionen öffentlicher griechischer Hofanlagen.* Berlin: de Gruyter.

Etlin, R. 2012. Architecture and the sublime, in: Costelloe, T.M. (ed.). *The sublime: from antiquity to the present.* Cambridge: Cambridge University Press, 230-274.

Friese, W. 2010. Facing the dead: landscape and ritual of ancient Greek death oracles. *Time and Mind. The Journal of Archaology, Consciousness and Culture* 3, 29-40.

Gladigow, B. 1990. Epiphanie, Statuette, Kultbild: Griechische Gottesvorstellungen im Wechsel von Kontext und Medium. *Visible Religion* 7, 98-121.

Gordon, R.L. 1979. The real and the imaginary: production and religion in the Graeco-Roman world. *Art History* 2 (1), 5-34.

Gruben, G. 1986[1966]. *Die Tempel der Griechen.* Munich: Hirmer Verlag.

Günther, W. 1971. *Das Orakel von Didyma in hellenistischer Zeit: Eine Interpretation von Steinurkunden.* Tübingen: Wasmuth.

Hellström, P. 2009. Sacred architecture and Karian identity, in: Rumscheid, F. (ed.). *Die Karer und die Anderen,* Internationales Kolloquium an der Freien Universität Berlin, 13.-15. Oktober 2005. Bonn: Habelt, 267-290.

Henry, O. 2017. Sanctuaire et pouvoir: nouvelles pistes de réflexion à partir des recherches archéologiques récentes sur le site de Labraunda en Carie (Turquie). *Comptes rendus de l'Académie des Inscriptions et Belles-Lettres* 1, 545-579.

Hollinshead, M.B. 2015. *Shaping ceremony: monumental steps and Greek architecture.* Madison, WI: University of Wisconsin Press.

Hooley, D. 2012. Prelude. Classical mountain landscapes and the language of ascent, in: Irreton, S. and Schaumann, C. (eds.). *Heights of reflection. Mountains in the German imagination from the Middle Ages to the twenty-first century.* Rochester NY: Boydell & Brewer, Camden House, 20-32.

Humann, C., Kohte, J., Watzinger, C. 1904. *Magnesia am Maeander: Bericht über Ergebnisse der Ausgrabungen der Jahre 1891-1893.* Berlin: G. Reimer.

Interdonato, E. 2016. Architecture and rituals in the Hellenistic age: the case of the Asklepieion in Kos, in: Melfi, M. and Bobou, O. (eds.). *Hellenistic sanctuaries: between Greece and Rome.* Oxford: Oxford University Press, 170-181.

Işın, G.L. 2005. Yumaklar Arpalık Tepe Küçük Buluntuları: Ön Rapor. *Araştırma Sonuçları Toplantısı* 23 (2), 125-134.

Jürgens, K. 2017. Pilgrimage and procession in the Panhellenic festivals: some observations on the Hellenistic Leukophryena in Magnesia-on-the-Meander, in: Kristensen, T.M. and Friese, W. (eds.). *Excavating pilgrimage: archaeological approaches to sacred travel and movement in the Ancient World.* London: Routledge, 87-105.

Kindt, J. 2012. *Rethinking Greek religion.* Cambridge: Cambridge University Press.

Knackfuß, H. and Wiegand, T. 1941. *Die Baubeschreibung*, Didyma 1 Berlin: Mann.

Knoepfler, D. 1992. Sept années de recherches sur l'épigraphie de la Béotie (1985-1991). *Chiron* 22, 401-504.

Köster, J. 2017. Didyma von oben: Beobachtungen zur Orientierung und Architektur des Apollon-Tempels. *Istanbuler Mitteilungen* 67, 373-380.

Lauter, H. 1986. *Die Architektur des Hellenismus.* Darmstadt: Wissenschaftliche Buchgesellschaft.

Lehmann, P.W. 1954. The setting of Hellenistic temples. *The Journal of the Society of Architectural Historians* 13 (4), 15-20.

Lunt, D.J. 2009. The heroic athlete in ancient Greece. *Journal of Sport History* 36, 375-392.

Lyttelton, M. 1974. *Baroque architecture in classical antiquity.* Ithaca, N.Y.: Cornell University Press.

Ma, J. 2003. Peer polity and interaction in the Hellenistic age. *Past and Present* 180, 9-39.

Melfi, M. 2016. Introduction: on sanctuaries and poleis, in: Melfi, M. and Bobou, O. (eds.). *Hellenistic sanctuaries: between Greece and Rome.* Oxford: Oxford University Press, 1-17.

Miles, M.M. 2016. Birds around the temple: constructing a sacred environment, in: McInerney, J. Sluiter, I. (eds.). *Valuing landscape in classical antiquity: natural environment and cultural imagination.* Leiden: Brill, 151-195.

Nesbitt, K. 1995. The sublime and modern architecture: unmasking (an aesthetic of) abstraction. *New Literary History* 26 (1), 95-110.

van Nijf, O.M. 2012. Political games, in: Coleman, K., Ducrey, P., Nelis-Clément, J. (eds.). *L'organisation des spectacles dans le monde romain,* Entretiens sur l'Antiquité classique (Series) 58. Genève: Fondation Hardt, 47-95.

van Nijf, O.M. and Williamson, C.G. 2016. Connecting the Greeks: festival networks in the Hellenistic world, in: Mann, C., Remijsen, S., Scharff, S. (eds.). *Athletics in the Hellenistic world.* Stuttgart: Franz Steiner Verlag, 43-71.

Newby, Z. 2005. *Greek athletics in the Roman world: victory and virtue,* Oxford studies in ancient culture and representation. Oxford: Oxford University Press.

Parker, R. 2004. New 'panhellenic' festivals in Hellenistic Greece, in: Schlesier, R. and Zellmann, U. (eds.). *Mobility and travel in the Mediterranean from Antiquity to the Middle Ages.* Münster: LIT, 9-22.

Patera, I. 2010. Light and lighting equipment in the Eleusinian Mysteries: symbolism and ritual use, in: Christopoulos, M., Karakantza, E.D., Levaniouk, O. (eds.). *Light and darkness in ancient myth and religion.* Lanham, MD: Lexington Books, 261-275.

Pedersen, P. 2004. Pergamon and the Ionian Renaissance. *Istanbuler Mitteilungen* 54, 409-434.

Platt, V. 2011. *Facing the gods: epiphany and representation in Graeco-Roman art, literature and religion.* Cambridge: Cambridge University Press.

Pollitt, J.J. 1986. *Art in the Hellenistic age.* Cambridge: Cambridge University Press.

Porter, J.I. 2016a. *The sublime in antiquity.* Cambridge: Cambridge University Press.

Porter, J.I. 2016b. The sublime without Longinus. *Boundary* 2, 73-129.

Rigsby, K.J. 1996. *Asylia: territorial inviolability in the Hellenistic world.* Berkeley: University of California Press.

Robert, L. 1984. Discours d'ouverture, in: Pelekides, C., Peppa-Delmouzou, D., Petrakos, B.C. (eds.). *Praktika of the eighth international congress of Greek and Latin epigraphy.* Athens: Hypourgeio Politismou kai Epistēmōn, 35-45.

Romano, D.G. and Voyatzis, M.E. 2014. Mt. Lykaion excavation and survey project. Part 1, The Upper Sanctuary: Preliminary Report 2004-2010. *Hesperia* 83, 569-652.

Rose, C.B. 2012. Architecture and ritual in Ilion, Athens, and Rome, in: Wescoat, B.D. and Ousterhout, R.G. (eds.). *Architecture of the sacred: space, ritual, and experience from classical Greece to Byzantium.* Cambridge: Cambridge University Press, 152-174.

Rostowzew, M. 1920. 'Επιφάνειαι. *Klio* 16, 203-206.

Roueché, C. 1993. *Performers and partisans at Aphrodisisas in the Roman and Late Roman periods.* London: Society for the Promotion of Roman Studies.

Rutherford, I. 2013. *State pilgrims and sacred observers in ancient Greece: a study of theōriā and theōroi.* Cambridge: Cambridge University Press.

Schachter, A. 1984. A consultation of Trophonios (*IG* 7.4136). *The American Journal of Philology* 105 (3), 258-270.

Scully, V.J. 1962. *The earth, the temple, and the gods: Greek sacred architecture.* New Haven: Yale University Press.

Seaford, R. 2010. Mystic light and near-death experience, in: Christopoulos, M., Karakantza, E.D., Levaniouk, O. (eds.). *Light and darkness in ancient Greek myth and religion.* Lanham, MD: Lexington Books, 201-205.

Serres, M. 2011. Vertigo, in: Serres, M. and Burks, R. (eds.). *Variations on the body.* Minneapolis MN: University of Minnesota Press, 111-151.

Shaya, J. 2005. The Greek temple as museum: the case of the legendary treasure of Athena from Lindos. *American Journal of Archaeology* 109 (3), 423-442.

Slater, W.J. and Summa, D. 2006. Crowns at Magnesia. *Greek, Roman and Byzantine Studies* 46, 275-299.

Steiner, D.T. 2010. The immeasures of praise: the epinician celebration of Agamemnon's return. *Hermes* 138, 22-37.

Thomas, E. 2014. On the sublime in architecture, in: Elsner, J. and Meyer, M. (eds.). *Art and rhetoric in Roman culture.* Cambridge: Cambridge University Press, 37-88.

Thonemann, P.J. 2007. Magnesia and the Greeks of Asia (*I.Magnesia* 16.16). *Greek, Roman and Byzantine Studies* 47, 151-160.

Williamson, C.G. 2013. Labraunda as memory theatre for Hellenistic Mylasa: code-switching between past and present? *HEROM* 2, 141-165.

Williamson, C.G. 2018. Filters of light: Greek temple doorways as portals of epiphanies, in: de Blaauw, S. and van Opstall, E. (eds.). *Sacred thresholds: the door to the sanctuary in Late Antiquity.* Leiden: Brill, 309-340.

Ziebarth, E. 1909. *Aus dem griechischen Schulwesen.* Leipzig: B.G. Teubner.

Translations of ancient authors

Roberts, W.R. 1899. *Longinus on the sublime*. Cambridge: Cambridge University Press.

Strong, H.A. and Garstang, J. 1913. *The Syrian Goddess, being a translation of Lucian's De dea Syria, with a life of Lucian*. London: Constable.

Thom, J.C. 2014. ΑΡΙΣΤΟΤΕΛΟΥΣ ΠΕΡΙ ΚΟΣΜΟΥ, in: Thom, J.C. (ed.). *Cosmic order and divine power: Pseudo-Aristotle, On the Cosmos*. Tübingen: Mohr Siebeck, 20-57.

Notes on contributor

Christina G. Williamson - Ancient History, University of Groningen (present). Studies of Ancient History, Mediterranean Archaeology in Groningen; PhD Groningen 2012; Lecturer in Ancient History in Leiden, Amsterdam 2012; Postdoctoral Fellow via the Netherlands Organisation for Scientific Research (NWO) at the Joukowsky Institute for Archaeology and the Ancient World, Brown University, 2014-2015; Research Fellow at the Max-Weber-Kolleg in Erfurt, 2019/2021; Co-Director, with O.M. van Nijf, of the project 'Connecting the Greeks: Multi-Scalar Festival Networks in the Hellenistic World' 2019-2022, funded by NWO.

Secluded or Entangled: Two Modes of Architecture-Landscape Design in Hellenistic Sanctuaries

Asja Müller

Abstract

This chapter focuses on Hellenistic sanctuaries with regard to their design, taking into account the contribution of landscape as well as movement and perception. Two general design modes, secluded and entangled sanctuaries, will be discussed, each exemplified by means of two case studies: for the first mode, the Late Classical Asclepieion of Athens and the Hellenistic sanctuary of Demeter in Pergamon; for the second, the Late Classical sanctuary of Zeus in Labraunda and the Hellenistic sanctuary of Hera in Pergamon. Through these case studies, characteristics as well as transformations in the conception of built space are pointed out.

Keywords: Hellenistic sanctuaries, design, landscape, movement, perception

Introduction

There is a long tradition in research of discussing Hellenistic sanctuaries with regard to their formal layout, in particular the interaction between their single building units. This approach to the analysis of sacred space is closely linked to the separation of so-called 'grown' built space, that is to say, complexes whose building units were assembled over a long time span, as well as so-called '*Gesamtanlagen*' – built space designed at a single moment in history, although not necessarily completed in one construction phase (Lauter 1986, p. 65; Gruben 2001, pp. 440-486). Normally, architectural complexes such as the Coan Asclepieion (Greece, see Interdonato 2013 with previous literature) or the sanctuary of Athena in Lindos (Greece, see Lippolis 1988-1989) as well as the sanctuaries of Pergamon (Turkey, see below) are cited as examples for the latter category. As more recent studies showed, however, the founding of these sacred complexes usually went back to much more ancient times than originally thought, and the layout of these early structures had a profound

Freie Universität Berlin
Fabeckstraße 23-25
14195 Berlin
Germany
asja.mueller@fu-berlin.de

Figure 1. Coan Asclepieion, bird's eye view (Schazmann 1932, Pl. 40).

impact on the later organisation of the built space (Ehrhardt 2014; Lippolis 1988-1989; Helm-Rommel 2009). Where do we draw the border, then, between grown sanctuaries and the ones supposedly designed at once? And, as this separation between the two sanctuary types fosters biases, does the additive character of grown sanctuaries really point to a lack of design, if not lack of forethought?

Being aware of these problems, we may take a different approach to sacred space of the Hellenistic age and look onto the design characteristics shared by both architectural complexes referred to as *Gesamtanlagen* and those assembled step by step. Therefore, a closer look at the construction period of each complex under consideration is necessary, whilst the architectural accentuation of entrances and passageways as well as their mutual relationship with human action are emphasised in this chapter.

For a very long time, sanctuary design was mainly analysed as architecture in isolation with regard to two aspects: the ancient actor and the landscape's contribution. Quite often, ancient architecture appears to us more like an architect's draft than a space that was actually bursting with life. This is particularly obvious, when looking onto the reconstructions permeating archaeological literature since the 19th century (Fig. 1):

Architecture is normally shown in its heyday, being it Hellenistic or Roman times, but deserted: nobody is making offerings to the gods, nobody is seeking oracular advice, and nobody is pleading for recovery from illness. This absence of actors matches the lack of an actor's perspective. Reconstructions of sanctuaries often take a viewpoint that displays the three-dimensionality of a sanctuary at once, without consideration of the (human) actor's position. Bird's eye perspectives are thus more comparable to a sketch on a drawing board than to the perception of an actual actor, who rarely had the option of internalizing the whole sacred space (of which he himself is an essential part) at once, but in multiple steps and constantly changing perspectives whilst moving inside.

That this consideration of the actor is, indeed, not just a modern view imposed on the antique remains but also an ancient concern, can be inferred from textual sources. Hellenistic epigrams in particular frequently refer to the actor's response as sought after by the constructors (von Hesberg 1981, p. 68). Furthermore, as Philon indicates in his 'Belopoiika' (Phil. 1, 4), the responsive audience was indeed something the architect of the time, the Early Hellenistic age, considered when designing a building complex: stepping back and arranging the building units according to aesthetic principles (von Hesberg 1981, p. 89). Unfortunately, we have only fragmentary information about the effects of certain buildings on the ancient viewer. Where textual sources speak of the (desired) actor's response in epigrams, the actual building is usually lost. We may cite here, for example, Poseidippos's epigrams dealing with the Pharos of Alexandria and the temple of Aphrodite-Arsinoe Zephyritis (Bing 1998; Obbink 2005, pp. 105-106). By contrast, when the architecture is fairly well preserved, few textual sources help understand the effect. As the actor's response seemed to have been taken into account by the Hellenistic architect, we may, however, assume that this response was inscribed into the design of any building complex and can therefore at least partly recovered by analysing the material remains.

Yet, before doing so, we should also take into account the second of the two above-mentioned shortfalls when looking onto architecture in isolation: the landscape's contribution. Since for a long period of time, built space was considered container-like (Kant 1787, A23-24, B38-39 as one of the earliest researchers). Architecture is set in the landscape and actors are set in architecture forming a sequence of concentric rings with very little contact between each other. An alternative space concept, developed simultaneously, regards built space as an arrangement of its material components, that is to say, landscape, architecture, and (human) bodies in interaction (Ariew 2000, pp. 14-15). According to this relational perspective, space is not seen as a fixed entity but an ever-changing constellation of its physical entities (Löw 2008). The dynamics of these constellations themselves are the result of human practices, notably movement and perception that constantly re-arrange those physical entities (Schatzki 2015).

Therefore, it is not as important if a building complex was the result of continuous addition and remodelling of features or seemingly designed (and realised) in one single act, compared to the more significant question of how it was lived. We should thus take into account all of its physical components, including landscape, and focus on the interaction between those components and human practices.

Four sanctuaries – the Asclepieion of Athens, the sanctuary of Demeter in Pergamon, the sanctuary of Zeus in Labraunda, and the sanctuary of Hera in Pergamon – may shed some light on the design of built space from Late Classical to Hellenistic times. These sanctuaries were selected for several reasons. First, all are situated on similar topographic conditions on hillslopes. Second, they feature a similar choice of building structures, temple, altar, and framing *stoai* (in addition to other features not part of each sanctuary, such as the *theatron* in the sanctuary of Demeter in Pergamon for example). This approximate consistency of primary conditions regarding landscape and architecture makes these case studies quite suitable in order to work out similarities and differences in their architecture-landscape interaction. As will be shown, two basic modes of design can be detected, called secluded and entangled here, which complement each other. Last but not least, these four sanctuaries have the advantage of being datable by means of dedication inscriptions. Such comparatively secure dates are therefore helpful in formulating hypotheses regarding the characteristics and chronological development of architecture-landscape design in Late Classical and Hellenistic architecture.

Figure 2. Asclepieion of Athens – Ephorate of Antiquities of Athens City, seen from the Acropolis hill (picture: Asja Müller, © Hellenic Ministry of Culture and Sports [L. 3028/2002]).

Secluded sanctuaries

The Asclepieion of Athens

The first sanctuary suitable for exemplifying a certain design type of Hellenistic sanctuaries is the Asclepieion of Athens (Greece). Situated at the southern slope of the Acropolis hill (Fig. 2) from the 4th century BCE in direct vicinity to the theatre, the sanctuary of Asclepios takes a prominent position in the topographical landscape of Athens. Additionally, it is well-positioned in terms of the street network since it lays just north of the Peripatos ringing the Acropolis.

Building phases

The pagan sanctuary has a long building history, starting in the 5th century BCE and ending in the 3rd century AD (Fig. 3). Its foundation phase is firmly dated to the end of the 5th century by means of the Telemachos monument preserving an inscription that names Telemachos of Acharnai as the *temenos* founder (Besci 1967-1968; Mitropoulou 1975) and gives dates for some of the most important buildings such as the altar, *peribolos*, *propylon(s)* as well as a holy grove.

There is some discussion whether the first Asclepieion was set up at the western area of the south slope and later moved to the eastern one (Girard 1881, pp. 4-8) or extended on both (Koumanoudis 1877, pp. 14-16), but most researchers now opt for the complex's location at the eastern terrace for the whole duration of its existence (albeit possibly integrating some of the structures at the western part, compare Köhler 1877, pp. 252-253; Travlos 1939-1941, pp. 59-62; Riethmüller 2005, pp. 253-259; Lefantzis and Tae Jensen 2009, pp. 104-111 amongst others).

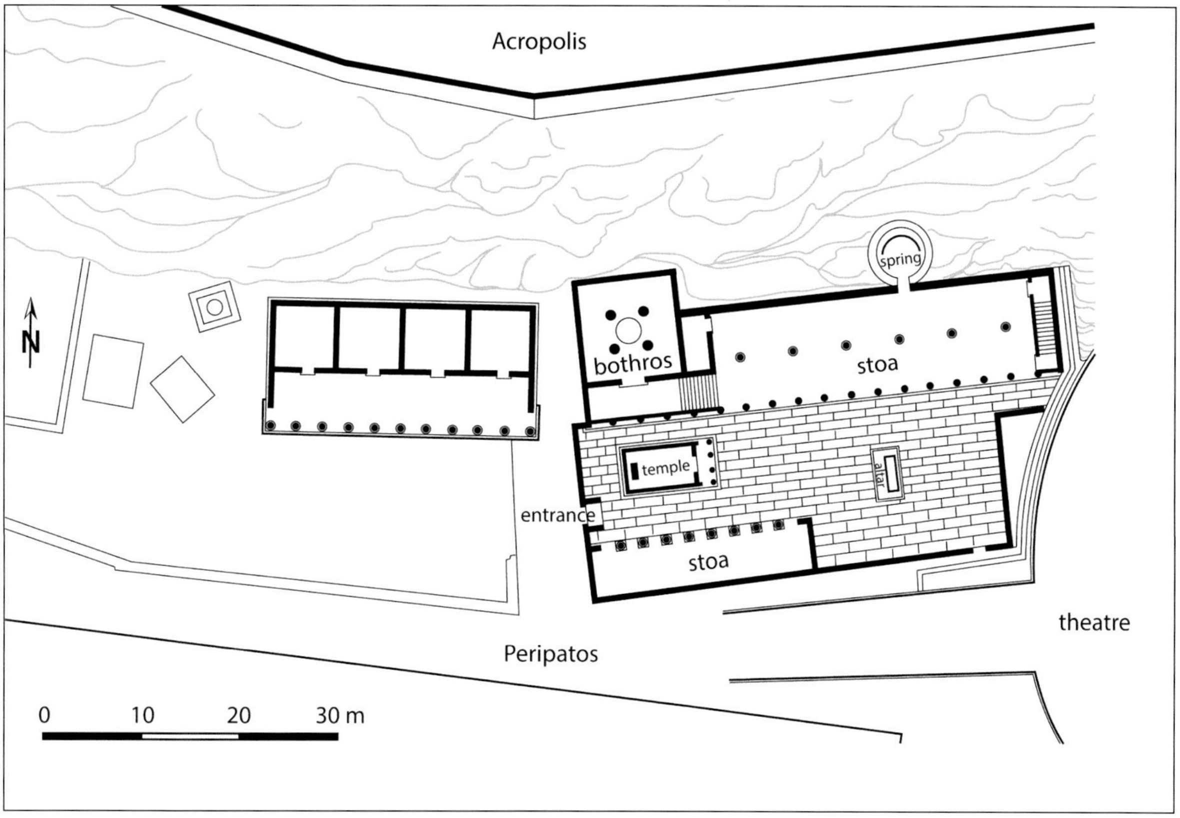

Figure 3. Asclepieion of Athens, situation in the 1st century BCE (plan: Asja Müller after Travlos 1971, p. 129 Fig. 171).

During the earliest phase, the area was equipped with a holy grove, as the Telemachos monument indicates (IG II/III[3] 4, 665). A series of holes was uncovered during the excavation of a Roman structure identified as the altar; those features were subsequently interpreted as planting holes (Papaefthimiou 2009, p. 81; Papaefthymiou 2009, pp. 73-77). If this identification is correct (a different interpretation as a means of fixing the foundation stones of the altar structure was put forward by Lefantzis and Tae Jensen 2009, p. 100), the grove did not, however, survive for long since it was razed in the 4th century in order to make space for the first monumental buildings (Papaefthimiou 2009, p. 82). Furthermore, on the textual basis, the existence of an altar can be assumed, although its position is not known. It is however generally assumed that the altar, if it is one indeed (compare Lefantzis and Tae Jensen 2009, p. 91), did not change its position and can thus be identified with some apparently older stones inside the Roman altar structure (Papaefthimiou 2009, p. 83; Papaefthymiou 2009, p. 80; Lefantzis and Tae Jensen 2009, pp. 100-101). Last but not least, a *bothros* at the far western end as well as a spring's grotto, used from the 5th century onwards, were found (compare Riethmüller 1999; Mantis 2009, pp. 71-72; Papaefthimiou 2009, p. 79).

The Telemachos monument mentions a wooden *propylon* (called *xylopylion* there, possibly even two of them, compare Lefantzis and Tae Jensen 2009, p. 115 note 16) as well as a temple and a *peribolos*. The position of the temple was probably the same as the one of the later cultic building since its *euthynteria* was used for the later *naoi* (Papaefthymiou and Christodoulopoulou 2014, pp. 43-45). The complete *temenos* was encircled by a *peribolos*, whose remains were found at the south-eastern corner (Lefantzis and Tae Jensen 2009, pp. 104-105, compare also pp. 110-111 for the discussion of its western course as well as Riethmüller 2005, pp. 258-259). The position of the original *propylon(s)* is not known, although it has been suggested that the main entrance was either located at the north-eastern corner (Lefantzis and Tae Jensen 2009, p. 108) or at the western limits, where the Roman *peribolos* and entrance exists (Riethmüller 2005, p. 258). However, after the theatre was built in the first half of the 4th century BCE, access via the north-eastern corner was obstructed, which makes the western *peribolos* the most likely site for the location of the *propylon* in Late Classical times.

In the early 3rd century BCE, extensive measurements were undertaken to cut back the Acropolis rock in order to insert a two-storied Doric *stoa* (dated to 300/299 BCE by means of an inscription, compare Aleshire 1991, p. 29), integrating the *bothros* as well as the spring. Presumably, it worked as the *abaton* of the sanctuary (Mantis 2009, pp. 72-73; Papaefthimiou 2009, p. 79).

Much later, in the first half of the 1st century BCE, a new temple was erected (Papaefthimiou 2009, p. 87). It took the shape of a *distyle* Ionic temple *in antis* and was oriented towards the east. By the middle of the 1st century BCE this was followed up by a new altar in front of the temple, although slightly out of the temple's axis (Papaefthimiou 2009, pp. 82-83). The last building project of the pre-Christian era was a second *stoa*, paralleling the *abaton* and flanking the temple (Papefthimiou 2009, p. 79).

The Heruls' attack of the city of Athens in 267 AD caused serious damage to the sanctuary of Asclepios. Afterwards, the temple was re-erected in a new shape as a *tetrastyl* Ionic *prostylos* (Papefthimiou 2009, p. 87). This was the last building project of pagan times until a basilica was set up during the 5th century AD (Mantis 2009, p. 68).

Other than the buildings mentioned above, the area also features an Ionic *stoa* at the western half outside of the area encircled by the *peribolos*, working as a banqueting building (Papefthimiou 2009, p. 79). It is not yet possible, though, to assign an exact date to this building.

Landscape's contribution, movement and perception

Although there are some uncertainties regarding the sanctuary's appearance in the earlier period, we may nevertheless discuss some of its general characteristics.

First, the sanctuary's core, consisting of the temple as well as altar, was always approached in a non-axial (angular) manner, regardless if the first entrance was situated at the north-eastern corner or at the western limits. In Late Classical times, after the erection of the theatre, people would probably approach the sanctuary via the Peripatos, walking along the *peribolos* (compare Friese 2019 for movement on the Peripatos). At the western border, they had to turn right, passing through the passage between western and eastern section and then right again through the proposed wooden *propylon*. They would then move along the southern flank of the temple and turn north to enter either the temple, the *abaton*, or the area between altar structure and temple. The notion of the sanctuary's inner space was therefore dominated by the broad, elongated side of the temple from the first moment before turning to its eastern front. The ancient actors were thus able to perceive the building as a tri-dimensional entity. This angular approach did not change in subsequent centuries but was even carburized when the Roman stone *proplyon* was set.

A second, equally important characteristic of the sanctuary is its interaction with the landscape. From the beginning, a *temenos* wall partially shielded the sanctuary against the view of visitors passing on the street as well as from the broader landscape. Yet, there was a certain number of natural elements integrated in the built space of the 5th century BCE. This holds true for the holy grove as well as the Acropolis rock flanking the northern *temenos* area. However, from the 4th century onwards, there was a tendency to dispel landscape elements from the sanctuary's inner space.

If Vanda Papaefthymiou's interpretation of the plant holes holds true, the holy grove was moved (but might have continued its existence somewhere on the sanctuary's outskirts). Even more important, part of the Acropolis rock was cut away in order to create a broader construction area. Furthermore, the northern side with its spring was hidden behind a huge, two-storied *stoa*, covering the Acropolis

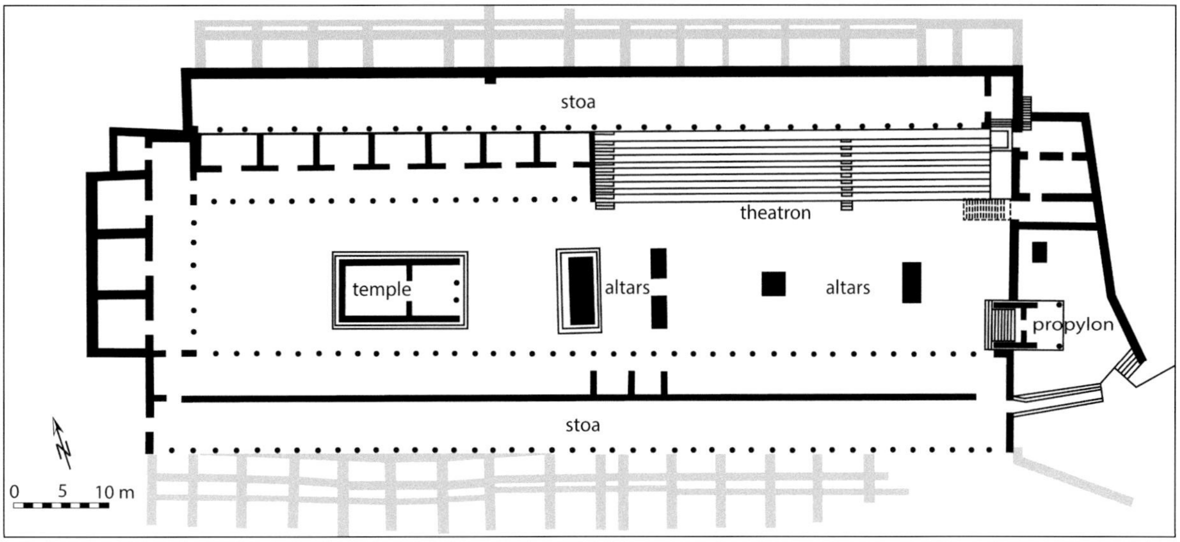

Figure 4. Sanctuary of Demeter, situation under queen Apollonis, 220-186 BCE (plan: Asja Müller after Bohtz 1981, Pl. 43 Fig. 1).

flank. And finally, nearly three centuries later, the sight connection between inner and outer space – that is to say temple and Peripatos – which was supposedly already partially obstructed by the *peribolos* was now completely blocked by a new one-storied *stoa* to the south. The only area not fully encircled by towering buildings, but only by the peribolos, was the sanctuary's eastern part, where the altar structure was set. Only the *abaton's* second storey, in particular its eastern part, might have been visible from outside and provided an outlook. We can thus state a continuous tendency of establishing or enlarging artificial borders between the landscape outside and inside as well as screening natural features (*e.g.* the Acropolis rock and the spring) behind curtains manifested in stone (*e.g. stoai*). Inside the sacred area, landscape and architecture were largely separated.

The Sanctuary of Demeter in Pergamon

We may now compare this sanctuary to another in a similar topographical position at the steep southern flank of the settlement's hill, next to the Upper Gymnasion (Fig. 4). As in the case of the Asclepieion of Athens, the area of the Demeter *temenos* in Pergamon is elongated, following the shape predefined by the slope. Compared to the Asclepieion, it is younger as it was founded in the 4th century BCE.

Building phases

How the sacred area appeared to visitors in the first half of the 4th century BCE is not exactly clear. Some findings may date from that period, but there is no architecture that could be securely assigned to this building phase (Piok-Zanon 2007, p. 325, contrasting opinion by Bohtz 1981, pp. 56-57). Although it has been assumed that the cult of Demeter is as old as the one of Athena in Pergamon (Piok-Zanon 2007, p. 324), there is no solid basis for this assumption until now.

During the second half of the 4th century BCE, a long and narrow terrace was cut into the hill slope. It was later extended further to the east (Bohtz 1981, p. 57). According to Carl Bohtz, there were already several altars arranged along the middle axis as well as a *stoa* at the northern side, whilst the other three sides were delimitated by means of walls. The existence of a temple at this early date is assumed, but cannot be proved yet (Bohtz 1981, p. 57).

Under Philetairos (reigned 283-263 BCE) massive changes in the sanctuary's architecture took place. First, the whole area was extended by means of lowering the

Figure 5. Sanctuary of Demeter, inner space (Bohtz 1981, Pl. 4; picture by Mechau, D-DAI-IST-PERG-541/III/11A).

ground. Then, a *stoa* was erected along the northern border of the *temenos*. Further to the east, a monumental seating area of straight steps was erected. Additionally, the largest altar was increased and a temple *in antis* was built. Both the altar and temple carry inscriptions naming Philetairos and Eumenes as the buildings' constructors. New *temenos* walls encircled the whole area (Bohtz 1981, pp. 57-58).

The next major building phase was initiated by queen Apollonis (reigned 223-159 BCE), as mentioned by an inscription on the new *propylon* (Piok-Zanon 2007, pp. 342-348 narrows this long period down to between the birth of Eumenes II in 222 BCE and the death of Attalos I 197 BCE). Since the ground level of the *propylon* was much higher than the walking area of the inner *temenos*, a staircase was laid out. Having constructed massive retaining walls with buttresses to the north, above the older *stoa*, as well as to the south, it was now possible to surround the terrace with two long *stoai* on either side. The western end, behind the temple, was also supplied with another *stoa* and a small forecourt with a cistern and an ash altar were constructed to the eastern side of the *propylon* (Bohtz 1981, p. 58).

Until the 1st century AD, only minor architectural changes took place, including the foundation of a nymphaeum in the forecourt as well as the erection of new rooms between the *propylon* and some *oikoi* to the east (Bohtz 1981, p. 59).

The last substantial adjustments date to the 2nd and 3rd centuries AD. By means of the financial efforts of Silianus Aesimus, the temple received a new Corinthian porch, changing it to a *prostylos*. The main altar was equipped with a marble coating and a variety of small altars were erected (Bohtz 1981, p. 59).

Figure 6. Sanctuary of Demeter, prospect from the valley (picture: Asja Müller, reproduced by kind permission of the directorate of the Pergamon excavations).

Landscape's contribution, movement and perception

In contrast to the Asclepieion of Athens, access to the *temenos* of Demeter was frontally arranged, along a slightly shifted axis leading from the entrance to the altar and temple (Fig. 5). No angular routes guiding the ancient actor around the building were given, although there was enough space to orbit it. Nevertheless, the architecture with the continuous rows of columns on the halls' front led straight ahead to the altar and temple entrance, presenting its façade *in antis*, increasing in size with every step taken.

Whilst crossing this space visitors discovered themselves as walking in a largely enclosed area, bordered on both sides by towering halls. Only the area at the eastern half was partially opened up by means of the seating area. A visual connection to the landscape at the down-hill side was only established when entering the southern half of the southern *stoa* and perceiving the flicker effect created by the alternating light and dark spaces when passing along the row of columns. However, inside the temenos the architecture did nothing to stimulate such a route since a continuous inner wall obstructed movement and perception between both sides of the *stoa*; the decision to leave the vertical axis and enter the outward-facing part of the *stoa* was completely up to the will of the visitor. There was, however, another area where a spatially restricted outlook to the surrounding was given: the seating area or *theatron* as well as the upper northern *stoa*. Both were high enough to provide a view over the southern *stoa* and into the landscape panorama of the Pergameninan *chora*. In contrast to the southern *stoa*, this area was directed to the process of cultic action since the staircase faced the area just in front of the main altar (see Nilsen 2002 for such *theatra*).

Huge efforts were necessary to draw this partly translucent border between the outer landscape and the sanctuary's inner space, measures that were by no means concealed but highly visible from far distances, as the buttresses confirm. The largely seclusive character of the sanctuary is offset by these two outlook areas. This visual connection between landscape and architecture, perceivable only from certain well-selected sites, has its counterpart in the sanctuary's perspective from the outside, where buttresses, southern *stoa*, and newer northern *stoa* above and behind form a prospect that is discernible from a distance (Fig. 6).

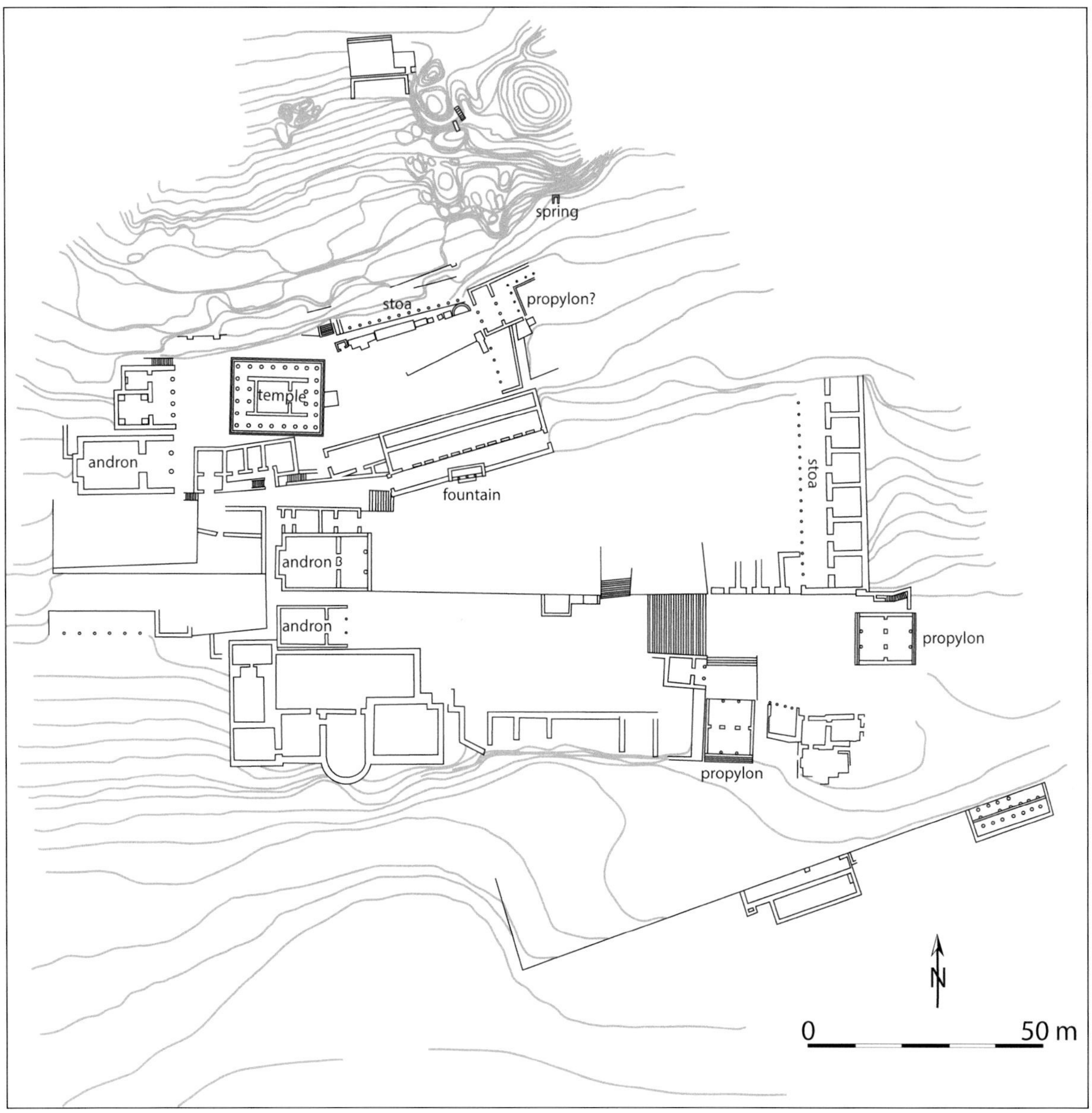

Figure 7. Sanctuary of Zeus, situation in Imperial times (plan: Asja Müller after Henry et al. 2016, p. 344 Fig. 3).

Entangled sanctuaries

The sanctuary of Zeus in Labraunda

A quite different interplay between architecture and landscape can be detected in the second pair of case studies. As in the case of the Asclepieion, the Labraunda sanctuary (Turkey) has a long building history, although its main, pre-Roman phases date between the 6th and 4th centuries BCE (Fig. 7). It is situated on the steep southern slope of the Latmos mountains, just below a huge rocky outcrop with a deep crevice. Several springs flow inside the *temenos* as well as in its direct vicinity. The extra-urban sanctuary was connected to the city of Mylasa by means of an elaborated processional street to the south (Baran 2011) as well as to the cities of Alinda and Alabanda by another way to the east.

Building phases

Ceramic remains found next to a fountain below the rock crevice show that the sanctuary existed already in the 7th century BCE (Hellström 2007, p. 17), whilst its architectural appearance at that time is unknown.

The architectural extension of the *temenos* started during the 6th and 5th centuries at least. During this pre-Hekadomnid period, the sacred area encompassed only one terrace just below the rocky boulder and crevice. It was embellished with an Ionic temple *in antis*, set parallel to the mountain slope and facing to the east (Hellström 2007, p. 111). Probably, an altar was situated just in front of its entrance. There was also a hypostyle (?) propylon, possibly connected to a stoa further to the east (not excavated yet). Furthermore, terrace retaining walls framed the area in direction of the southern valley (Hellström 2007, p. 19; Hellström 2019). Herodotus also mentions a holy grove that must have been part of the sanctuary's layout during the early 5th century BCE (Hdt. 5, 119-121).

This fairly modest architecture was monumentalised during the 4th century BCE under the supervision of the Carian rulers Maussollos and Idrieus. The middle terrace was broadened in order to erect a new Ionic temple, this time a *peripteros* (Hellström 2007, p. 111). A *stoa* defined the northern scopes of the offering place in front of the temple (Hellström 2007, p. 105). An *oikos* building as well as *andron* A defined the border to the west, just behind the temple. Furthermore, four other terraces were erected further down. The second one, just below the temple terrace, was furnished with another *andron* called B (for the dating of the *andrones*: Hellström 2011) and entrance to the sanctuary was given by two *distyle propyla*, one to the south (Hellström 2007, p. 71), oriented to the city of Mylasa, and one to the east, oriented to the cities of Alinda and Alabanda (Hellström 2007, p. 81). The transition from the *propyla* terrace to the terrace above was managed by a monumental staircase (Hellström 2015). A fountain house, the so-called Doric Building, provided water for purification before entering the *temenos* (Hellström 2007, p. 74). The whole area, possibly up to the rock-cut tomb above the crevice but not including the fortress of Classical date (Hellström 2007, p. 139), was encircled by a *peribolos*.

In contrast to this important, Late Classical building phase the architectural embellishing of the Hellenistic age was rather modest, featuring only an exedra on the temple terrace (Hellström 2007, p. 106) and a well-house inside the southern retaining wall of the temple terrace (Hellström 2007, pp. 95-96).

Figure 8. Sanctuary of Zeus, outlook from the boulder above the upper terrace (picture: Asja Müller, reproduced by kind permission of Olivier Henry, director of the Labraunda excavations).

Landscape's contribution, movement, and perception

We can thus conclude that the formal layout set up during the 6th and 5th centuries BCE underwent major transformations during the main building phase of the 4th century and entailed profound consequences for movement and perception (compare also Williamson 2014b).

Originally, the complex spread over one single terrace with the temple, parallel to the hill slope, must have appeared similar to the Asclepieion of Athens and the sanctuary of Demeter at Pergamon. If the interpretation of building Y as the old propylon is correct (Hellström 2019, p. 66), access was angular and the temple was approached from the north-eastern edge of the terrace.

After the remodelling of the 4th century BCE, the temple terrace did not change too much regarding the general layout: the temple was oriented to the east, directing its long southern wall to the valley. Instead of the slope, a newly erected *stoa* now functioned as the background foil. Access was probably given from the east as the propylon survived into Hellenistic-Roman times, albeit reconstructed several times.

There was, however, a major difference in the appropriation of natural space (Fig. 8). Due to the larger *temenos*, huge building efforts were necessary. The sanctuary extended in both directions horizontally as well as vertically by means of massive terracing in order to provide enough space for the desired architecture. Yet the challenges posed by the steeply rising terrain to the architects were not concealed by architectural means but even highlighted: monumental terrace retaining walls, visible from a great distance to visitors approaching from the direction of Mylasa, contour the mountain slopes. At the same time, the differences in altitude were physically detectable to any person moving inside the sacred space.

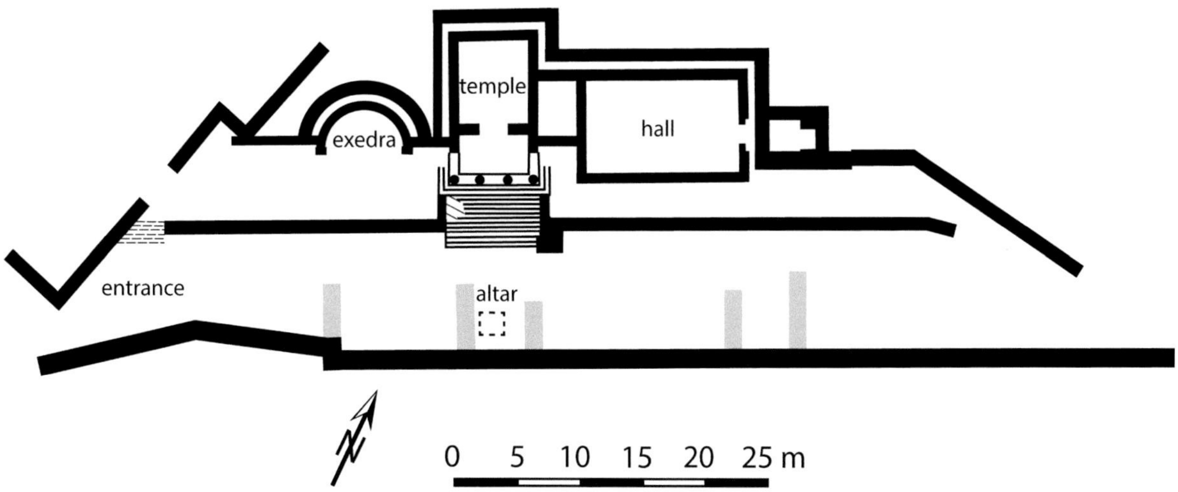

Figure 9. Sanctuary of Hera, situation under Attalos II (plan: Asja Müller after Schazmann 1923, Pl. 32).

Only the last few meters on the temple terrace encouraged angular movement. To reach that area an alternating approach with frequent switchbacks was necessary when entering another terrace. Whilst moving along the different terraces in direct vicinity to the retaining walls, eye contact with the buildings on the higher terraces was broken or only partially enabled. New views of the architecture emerged suddenly after each turning point until finally the temple comes into sight (compare also Williamsons paper in this volume for an idea of the emotions that such a staggering approach might have triggered). Furthermore, there was an unhindered view from each terrace over the architecture on the terraces below down into the plain. The changes in altitude were highlighted by sharp borders resulting from the immediate juxtaposition of architecture and landscape as well as the abrupt drop of the ground. Architecturally-embellished outlook points were created (*e.g.* exedra and *andron* A on the temple terrace or the monumental staircase between third and fourth terrace, see Williamson 2014a; Hellström 2015).

We can thus conclude that the sanctuary design of Labraunda works both ways: by transforming the terrain and appropriating it by means of architecture, it sheds even more light on the landscape's characteristics and challenges instead of expelling it. Landscape is drawn into the sanctuary's inner space, particularly at the borders between the terraces. This constant intertwining with architecture is thus deeply imbedded in its physical constitution.

The Heraion in Pergamon

The second example of entangled sanctuaries is the *temenos* of Hera in Pergamon (Fig. 9). This sanctuary, situated intramurally just above the gymnasium, was erected in one single building period during the time of Attalos II (reigned 159-138 v. Chr.), as an inscription on the architrave of the temple proves (Jacobsthal 1908, p. 402; Dörpfeld 1912, pp. 263-264; Ippel 1912, p. 283; Schazmann 1923, p. 110). As in most other parts of the city, the terrain is extraordinary steep and required thus fundamental interventions in the landscape.

Building phases

The sanctuary extends over two parallel, elongated but narrow terraces. It is accessible from the west, in the direction of the gymnasium and the Demeter sanctuary; a small rock-cut staircase at the western corner possibly provided a side entrance to the upper terrace. Except for the terrace retaining walls, only one architectural unit is situated in the middle of the lower terrace: the altar. Just behind it, to the north,

Figure 10. Sanctuary of Hera, prospect (Schazmann 1923, Pl. 8).

exists a short yet broad monumental staircase giving access to another narrow and elongated terrace. Here, another three buildings were situated: a Doric *prostylos*, on the same axis as the altar and the staircase, flanked by an exedra to the left as well as small hall to the right. It is not certain if these last two buildings were preceded by a columnar front as is the case with the temple (Schazmann 1923, p. 108); in any case, all three edifices on the upper terrace were partly sunken into the backward terrace retaining wall.

Landscape's contribution, movement and perception

In terms of movement as well as perception, the Hera sanctuary shares many features with the Labraunda sanctuary. People approaching from the west were directed along half of the lower terrace in order to arrive at the altar. Whilst moving horizontally, buildings on the upper terrace were partially blocked from view, whereas a vertiginous outlook over the gymnasium down on the landscape is given, sharply cut in half by the visually conceived line between terrace and thin air. This was accomplished by far-reaching construction engagements, the terraces and the remodelling of the ground, both of which draw attention to the steep terrain. However, the most important differences between the Heraion and the other case studies is the way in which the perception of the buildings' tri-dimensionality is diminished in favour of a laminar appearance, on one hand, as well as the orthogonal approach combining horizontal and axial movement, on the other. Access to the upper terrace is strictly frontal, quite unusually through the *pronaos*, extending to the terrace's limits (compare the paper of Philipp Kobusch in this volume). This prevents any perception of the depth extension and increases the expectation. Horizontal pacing on the upper terrace does not change the picture since all three buildings, the temple, the exedra, and the hall were partly sunken into the slope so that only the front (and inside) is fully accessible. In this case, archi-

design type	secluded sanctuaries		entangled sanctuaries	
sanctuary	Asclepieion of Athens	Demeter sanctuary of Pergamon	Zeus sanctuary of Labraunda	Hera sanctuary of Pergamon
date	Late Classical	Hellenistic	Late Classical	Hellenistic
topography	single level (hill slope)		multiple levels (hill slope)	
routes	angular	axial	alternating	orthogonal
orientation of buildings	parallel to the slope		parallel to the slope	frontal to the slope
prospective quality	marginal	inside & outside	mostly outside	all up
contact zones of architecture and landscape	outer borders	outer borders and outlooks	inner/outer borders and outlooks	

Table 1. Characteristics of secluded and entangled sanctuaries.

tecture was designed autonomous of cultic and topographical parameters normally dictating the orientation of temples to the east as well as arranging it parallel to the slope. Instead, the higher efforts of deeply cutting into the slope were accepted in favour of forming a prospect of the sanctuary together with the *gymnasion* underneath. People ascending the slope by means of the broad street passing the *gymnasion* should have been able to appreciate that prospect from distance (Fig. 10, compare also Stappmanns 2014 regarding access to and movement in that *gymnasion*).

Conclusion

The discussion between both sanctuary designs, the secluded and the entangled, showed that both encompass characteristics and tendencies that can be considered distinctive for the Late Classical and Hellenistic age (Table 1). Secluded and entangled sanctuaries are two diametrical poles in the continuum of built space. These two modes of built space should not regarded as monolithic, invariable blocks, however, into which each existing sanctuary can be pressed. They should rather be seen as models or analytical frames situated at two ends of a design continuum. They thus help to understand the characteristics of the sanctuaries in question (mostly featuring principles of both design modes). Often, features of both types are combined in such sanctuaries usually regarded as most typical of the Hellenistic age, as for example the Coan Asclepieion (Interdonato 2013 with older literature; Müller 2020) and can equally be found in 'grown' sanctuaries as well as *'Gesamtanlagen'*.

Topographically, secluded sanctuaries have a much broader scope of possible sitings; they can be found on slopes, as in cases of the Asclepieion and the Demeter sanctuary, as well as in the plain (such as the sanctuary of Asclepios in Messene, Greece, see Müth 2007, pp. 141-202) and on hilltops (such as the sanctuary of Meter in Mamurt Kale, Turkey, see Conze and Schazmann 1911). The varying topographical situations may influence their outlines, generally long and narrow on slopes as well as wide and quadrangular in plains and on spacious hilltops. Entangled sanctuaries, in contrast, exist only on slopes, since spreading over several terraces is a mandatory principle of their layout. Many of them seem to have started as single-level complexes in their earliest phases, appropriating space further up or below whilst time passes by, as was the case with the sanctuary of Labraunda. This tendency is certainly not a new one when seen against the background of entangled sanctuaries of Archaic and Classical date, as for example the sanctuary of Apollon in Delphi (Greece, see Maaß 1993). However, the Hellenistic age saw an increasing appropriation of landscape, formerly regarded as too narrow or steep, or both, to be built on.

At the same time, the case studies show a tendency towards frontality and a loss of depth visible in both design types. Instead of displaying the buildings' tri-dimensionality as well as their depth extension, which was a feature of Archaic *temenoi*, Hellenistic sanctuaries take on a façade-like character, compressing the spatial volume at certain critical points (Bergquist 1967, pp. 133-134). Routes in secluded sanctuaries shifted from an angular (Asclepieion of Athens) to an axial pacing (Demeter sanctuary in Pergamon), whilst alternating pathways (Zeus sanctuary of Labraunda) gained a vertical axis and become orthogonal (Hera sanctuary in Pergamon), merging outer and inner prospects. Due to the possibilities of vertically staging architecture modules by means of podia, temples for instance, such effects could also be established on the plain (compare, for example, the Sanctuary of Aphrodite in Kos City, see Rocco 2009). The most substantial impact was reached, however, where the prospective quality was already present in the ground and architecturally unsheathed during the Hellenistic age (*e.g.* by orienting buildings frontal to the slope), even if this required massive interventions in the natural terrain.

Yet, the situation is insufficiently described by simply equating each design type with such notions as 'closed' and 'open'. Their openness and closeness strongly depends on the ancient actor's position at the one hand as well as the topographical situation at the other. Standing directly in front of the main entrance both sanctuary types would feature the same degree of closeness. But seen from distance, there is a difference since entangled sanctuaries give a foretaste of what to expect when entering the sacred space (although not in detail). The mutual dependency of architecture and human action emerges very clearly in such situations. Secluded sanctuaries can only approximate such an effect by using podia or multi-storeyed buildings, which however demands extraordinary expenditures of labour and materials as well as technical skills. Entangled sanctuaries, in turn, can create enclosed areas by means of horizontally graduating architectural elements inside (such as the sanctuary of Athena in Lindos, Greece, see Lippolis 1988-1989). The combination options are virtually endless.

Yet, this is not to say that Hellenistic sanctuaries were by any means completely independent of landscape or challenging landscapes were simply regarded as an obstacle to overcome. On the contrary, as Lauter (1986, p. 300) observes, landscape was always firmly embedded into their design, even more so when the Hellenistic period progressed. But its interaction with architecture, fostered by vantage points, was concentrated in certain zones where their contrast interacts most strongly with human action. Usually, these are the borders of the *temenos*, outer borders in case of secluded sanctuaries as well as outer and inner borders in case of entangled sanctuaries, both of which were internalised by ancient actors whilst moving through built space. We may thus state that the interplay between architecture and landscape was more flexible during the Hellenistic age than in any period before. Even more so, when we realize that the models of secluded and entangled sanctuaries described here are only two of several options in forming Hellenistic built space. We may compare here the sanctuary of the Great Gods on Samothrace with its network of sites distributed on certain points of the natural terrain, drawn together by the interstitial space of passageways (see Wescoat *et al.* in this volume). Another type of sanctuary which has definite seclusive qualities but nevertheless draws landscape into the inner space by means of *bothroi* and a mud coating of the walls is the Thesmophorion in Pella (see the chapter by Agelidis in this volume). The Hellenistic age is thus a period characterized by a more conscious perception and sophisticated transposition of options latently present in landscape as well as architecture, in particular when it comes to their mutual relationship.

Acknowledgements

The present paper is an outcome of my research done between October 2016 and September 2017 as employee of the CRC 'Scales of Transformation' at the University of Kiel, Germany (funded by the Deutsche Forschungsgemeinschaft / DFG, German Research Foundation – Projektnummer 2901391021 – SFB 1266). I am therefore indebted to all CRC members for the enriching discussion as well as the financial support when doing my field studies.

References

Aleshire, S.B. 1991. *Asklepios at Athens: epigraphic and prosographic essays on the Athenian healing cults*. Amsterdam: J.C. Gieben.

Ariew, R. (ed.) 2000. *G. W. Leibniz and Samuel Clarke: correspondence*. Indianapolis: Hackett Publishing Company.

Baran, A. 2011. The Sacred Way and the spring houses of Labraunda Sanctuary, in: Karsslon, L. and Carlsson, S. (eds.). *Labraunda and Karia*, Proceedings of the International Symposium Commemorating Sixty Years of Swedish Archaeological Work in Labraunda: The Royal Swedish Academy of Letters, History and Antiquities Stockholm, 20-21 November 2008. Västerås: Edita Västra Aros, 51-98.

Bergquist, B. 1967. *The Archaic Greek temenos: a study of structure and function*. Lund: Gleerup.

Besci, L. 1967-1968. Il monumento di Telemachos, fondatore dell'Asklepieion ateniese. *Annuario della Scuola archeologica di Atene e delle missioni italiane in Oriente* 45, 381-436.

Bing, P. 1998. Between literature and monuments, in: Harder, M.A., Regtuit, R.F. Wakker, G.C. (eds.). *Genre in Hellenistic poetry*. Groningen: Forsten, 21-43.

Bohtz, C.H. 1981. *Das Demeter-Heiligtum*, Altertümer von Pergamon 8. Berlin: Walter de Gruyter.

Conze, A. and Schazmann, P. 1911. *Mamurt-Kaleh: Ein Tempel der Göttermutter unweit Pergamon*. Berlin: Reimer.

Dörpfeld, W. 1912. Die Arbeiten zu Pergamon 1910-1911: Die Bauwerke. *Mitteilungen des Kaiserlich Deutschen Archäologischen Instituts: Athenische Abteilung* 37, 235-276.

Ehrhardt, W. 2014. Ergebnisse des DFG-Forschungsprojektes zum Asklepieion von Kos in den Jahren 2010-2013: Ein Resümee. *Kölner und Bonner Archaeologica* 4, 75-107.

Friese, W. 2019. On the Peripatos: accessibility and topography of the Acropolis slope sanctuaries, in: Friese, W., Handberg, S., Kristensen, T.M. (eds.). *Ascending and descending the Acropolis: movement in Athenian religion*. Aarhus: Aarhus University Press, 43-62.

Girard, P. 1881. *L'Asclépieion d'Athènes: d'après de récents découvertes*. Paris: Thorin.

Gruben, G. 2001. *Griechische Tempel und Heiligtümer*. 5th ed. München: Hirmer Verlag GmbH.

Hellström, P. 2007. *Labraunda: a guide to the Karian sanctuary of Zeus Labraundos*. İstanbul: Ege Yayınları.

Hellström, P. 2011. Feasting at Labraunda and the chronology of the Andrones, in: Karsslon, L. and Carlsson, S. (eds.). *Labraunda and Karia*, Proceedings of the International Symposium Commemorating Sixty Years of Swedish Archaeological Work in Labraunda: The Royal Swedish Academy of Letters, History and Antiquities Stockholm, 20-21 November 2008. Västerås: Edita Västra Aros, 149-157.

Hellström, P. 2015. A cultic theatre at Karian Labraunda: the monumental stairs and the propylon courtyard, in: Faust, S., Seifert, M., Ziemer, L. (eds.). *Antike. Architektur. Geschichte: Festschrift für Inge Nielsen zum 65. Geburtstag*. Aachen: Shaker Verlag, 107-120.

Hellström, P. 2019. Early Labraunda: excavations on the Temple Terrace 1949–1953, in: Henry, O. and Konuk, K. (eds.). *Karia Arkhaia: la Carie des origines à la période pré-hékatomnide*, 14-16 Novembre 2013 Istanbul. Institut Française d'Études Anatoliennes Georges Dumézil: Istanbul, 61-88.

Helm-Rommel, I. 2009. *Das Theater am Burgberg in Pergamon*. Thesis (PhD). Universität Karlsruhe.

Henry, O., Anderson, E., Bost, C., Çakmakli, Ö., Cederling, F., Commito, A., Cormier-Huguet, M., Coutelas, A., Dolea, A., Ergenç, D., Freccero, A., Frejman, A., Lebouteiller, P., Lesguer, F., Löwenborg, D., Lungu, V., Marchand-Beaulieu, F., Sitz, A., de Staebler, P., Vergnaud, B. 2016. Labraunda 2015. *Anatolia Antiqua* 24, 339-457.

von Hesberg, H. 1981. Bemerkungen zu Architekturepigrammen des 3. Jahrhunderts v. Chr. *Jahrbuch des Deutschen Archäologischen Instituts* 96, 55-119.

Interdonato, E. 2013. *L'Asklepieion di Kos: archeologia del culto*. Roma: L'Erma Di Bretschneider.

Ippel, A. 1912. Die Arbeiten zu Pergamon 1910-1911: Die Inschriften. Die Einzelfunde. *Mitteilungen des Kaiserlich Deutschen Archäologischen Instituts: Athenische Abteilung* 37, 277-330.

Jacobsthal, P. 1908. Die Arbeiten zu Pergamon 1906-1907: Die Inschriften. Die Einzelfunde. *Mitteilungen des Kaiserlich Deutschen Archäologischen Instituts: Athenische Abteilung* 33, 375-441.

Kant, E. 1787. *Critique of pure reason*. Riga: Johann Friedrich Hartknoch.

Köhler, U. 1877. Der Südabhang der Akropolis zu Athen nach den Ausgrabungen der archäologischen Gesellschaft. *Mitteilungen des Deutschen Archäologischen Institutes in Athen* 2, 229-260.

Koumanoudis, S. 1877. Peri ton prepagmenon tes Archaiologikes Etairias kata to etos 1876. *Πρακτικά της εν Αθήναις Αρχαιολογικής Εταιρείας 1876-1877*, 3-49.

Lauter, H. 1986. *Die Architektur des Hellenismus*. Darmstadt: Wissenschaftliche Buchgesellschaft.

Lefantzis, M. and Tae Jensen, J. 2009. The Athenian Asklepieion on the south slope of the Akropolis: early development, ca. 420-360 B.C. in: Tae Jensen, J., Hinge, G., Schultz, P., Wickkiser, B. (eds.). *Aspects of ancient Greek cult: context, ritual and iconography*. Aarhus: Aarhus University Press, 91-124.

Lippolis, E. 1988-1989. Il santuario di Athana a Lindo. *Annuario della Scuola archeologica di Atene e delle missioni italiane in Oriente* 66, 97-157.

Löw, M. 2008. *Einführung in die Stadt- und Raumsoziologie*. 2nd ed. Opladen: Farmington Hills.

Maaß, M. 1993. *Das antike Delphi: Orakel, Schätze und Monumente*. Darmstadt: Wissenschaftliche Buchgesellschaft.

Mantis, A. 2009. The Asklepieion of Athens, in: De Miro, E., Sfmani Gasparro, G., Calì, V. (eds.). *Il culto di Asclepio nell'area mediterranea*, Atti del convegno internazionale, 20-22 Novembre 2005 Agrigento. Roma: Gangemi, 67-77.

Mitropoulou, E. 1975. *A new interpretation of the Telemachos Monument*. Athens: Pyli.

Müller, A. 2020. Hellenistic built space and human action: the Asclepieion of Cos, in: Haug A. and Merten S. (eds.). Urban practices: repopulating the ancient city, Studies in Classical Archaeology 8. Turnhout: Brepols Publishers, 149-165.

Müth, S. 2007. *Eigene Wege: Topographie und Stadtplan von Messene in spätklassisch-hellenistischer Zeit*. Rahden/Westf.: Leidorf.

Nielsen, I. 2002. *Cultic theatres and ritual drama: a study in regional development and religious interchange between East and West in antiquity*. Aarhus: Aarhus University Press.

Obbink, D. 2005. New old Posidippus and old new Posidippus: from occasion to edition in the epigrams, in: Gutzwiller, K. (ed.). *The new Posidippus: a Hellenistic poetry book*. Oxford: Oxford University Press, 97-115.

Papaefthimiou, V. 2009. Recent excavations at the Asklepieion of Athens, in: De Miro, E., Sfmani Gasparro, G., Calì, V. (eds.). *Il culto di Asclepio nell'area mediterranea*, Atti del convegno internazionale, 20-22 Novembre 2005 Agrigento. Roma: Gangemi, 79-89.

Papaefthymiou, V. 2009. Der Altar des Asklepieions von Athen, in: Tae Jensen, J., Hinge, G., Schultz, P., Wickkiser, B. (eds.). *Aspects of ancient Greek cult: context, ritual and iconography*. Aarhus: Aarhus University Press, 67-89.

Papaefthymiou, W. and Christodoulopoulou, R. 2014. Der Tempel des Asklepios und der Hygieia im Asklepieion von Athen: Neue Forschungen, in: Amedick, R., Froning, H., Held, W. (eds.). *Marburger Winckelmann-Programm 2014*. Marburg: Eigenverlag des Archäologischen Seminars der Philipps-Universität Marburg, 35-49.

Piok-Zanon, C. 2007. Dank an Demeter: Neue Gedanken zu Architektur und Bedeutung des Demeter-Kultes in Pergamon im späten 3. Jh. v. Chr. *Istanbuler Mitteilungen* 57, 323-364.

Riethmüller, J.W. 1999. Bothros and tetrastyle: the heroon of Asclepius at Athens, in: Hägg, R. (ed.). *Ancient Greek hero cult*, Proceedings of the Fifth International Seminar on Ancient Greek Cult, 21-23 April 1995 Göteborg University. Stockholm: Åström, 123-143.

Riethmüller, J.W. 2005. *Asklepios: Heiligtümer und Kulte I*. Heidelberg: Verlag Archäologie und Geschichte.

Rocco, G. 2009. Note sul santuario di Afrodite Pandamos e Pontia a Kos. *Annuario della Scuola Archeologica di Atene* 87, 599-612.

Schatzki, T. 2015. Spaces of practices and of large social phenomena. *EspacesTemps.net* https://www.espacestemps.net/en/articles/spaces-of-practices-and-of-large-social-phenomena [Accessed 28 June 2019].

Schazmann, P. 1923. *Das Gymnasion: Der Tempelbezirk der Hera Basileia*, Altertümer von Pergamon 6. Berlin: Walter de Gruyter.

Schazmann, P. 1932. *Asklepieion: Baubeschreibung und Baugeschichte*, Kos 1. Berlin: Walter de Gruyter.

Stappmanns, V. 2014. Das Gymnasion von Pergamon: Erschließungswege als Schlüssel funktionaler Gliederung, in: Kurapkat, D., Schneider, P.I., Wulf-Rheidt, U. (eds.). *Die Architektur des Weges: Gestaltete Bewegung im gebauten Raum*. Regensburg: Schnell & Steiner, 121-132.

Travlos, I.N. 1939-1941. He palaiochristianike basilike tou Asklepieiou ton Athenon. *Archaiologike Ephemeris 1939-1941*, 35-68.

Travlos, I.N. 1971. *Bildlexikon zur Topographie des antiken Athen*. Tübingen: Wasmuth.

Williamson, C. 2014a. A room with a view: Karian landscape on display through the Andrones at Labraunda, in: Karlsson, L., Carlsson, S., Blid Kullberg, J. (eds.). *Labrys: studies presented to Pontus Hellström*. Uppsala: Uppsala Univ., 123-138.

Williamson, C. 2014b. Power of place: ruler, landscape, and ritual space at the sanctuaries of Labraunda and Mamurt Kale in Asia Minor, in: Moser, C. and Feldman, C. (eds.). *Locating the sacred: theoretical approaches to the emplacement of religion*. Oxford: Oxbow Books, 87-110.

Notes on contributor

Asja Müller - Institute of Classical Archaeology, Freie Universität Berlin (present). Studies of Classical Archaeology, Prehistoric Archaeology, Experimental Archaeology and Egyptology at Leipzig and Exeter (UK); PhD Kiel 2017; Postdoc Research Fellow CRC 1266, project E3 at the Institute of Classical Studies / Classical Archaeology, CAU Kiel, 2016-2017; Travel Scholarship of the German Archaeological Institute 2017-2018; Assistant Professor at the Institute of Classical Archaeology, Freie Universität Berlin 2018-.

Roman Awe for Greek Sanctuaries: Polybius and Livy Illustrate Roman Encounters with Greek Patrimony

Jessica van 't Westeinde

Abstract

When Polybius describes Aemilius Paullus's encounter with the statue of Zeus at Olympia, he emphasises the impact of visual perception (Plb. 30,10). The Roman general acts and is acted upon. It is a case of mutual interaction between a human and built space. My analysis of the passage will study a double form of perception: that of the author (Polybius/Livy) and that of the actor: the Roman general who travels Greece. I investigate how he perceives the monumental architecture and decoration of sanctuaries and how he responds to it. I argue that agency and interaction work both ways: from the perceiver and the perceived, as is evident from Aemilius Paullus's encounter with the statue of the god, which exceeded his expectations.

Keywords: sanctuaries, human actors, perception, Polybius, Livy

Introduction

Aemilius Paullus entered the sacred enclosure at Olympia and was struck with admiration at the statue of the god (Plb. 30,10). Polybius demonstrates the visual experience of a Roman general when he enters a Greek sacred architectural complex. Interestingly, Polybius does not comment at all on the rich Classical architecture of the sanctuary, nor does he say anything about possible Hellenistic additions or transformation of it.[1] The only aspect, which he seems to consider worthwhile mentioning is the central cult object. It is not the aesthetics of the sanctuary that inspire awe in Polybius's Roman general, but the statue of Zeus. In one phrase, Polybius problematises one of the key

*Eberhard-Karls Universität Tübingen
Wilhelmstraße 36
72074 Tübingen
Germany
jessica.van-t-westeinde@uni-tuebingen.de*

1 As such, my use of the term 'Hellenistic' is temporal, *i.e.*, it refers to Polybius's time, not necessarily to the origins in which certain sanctuaries had been constructed. For the sanctuary at Olympia, see for example Kyrieleis *et al.* 2006; Taita 2007.

interests of this research volume, namely human action in Hellenistic sanctuaries. Where the modern reader would expect musings on the aesthetic beauty and impressive architectural design of Olympia, the ancient historiographer all but mentions the highlight of the sanctuary: Pheidias's statue of Zeus (McWilliam 2011). The fragment thus tells us only something about human perception of a cult object and its impact on the onlooker. The dialectics of reciprocal influence will be at the centre of attention in the current contribution.[2] The narrative fits within the literary genre that communicates and memorises a wider practice, namely that of touring conquered territories. Already Amy Russell has read Aemilius Paullus's tour of Greece as a political act to demonstrate his power (Russell 2012), and Elena Isayev has interpreted Polybius's narrative as a 'rite of passage for Rome into Imperial adulthood' (2017, pp. 233-234). I intend to fine-tune these observations with a focus on perception and interaction between actor and space, or, in case of the above, between actor and (cult) object. This focus will demonstrate how, in Polybius's and Livy's narratives, perception is transformed into mental categories. The question then is how the Greek Polybius differs from the Roman Livy: is their mental conception of sanctuaries discrete, and if so, how does this tie in with ideas of Greek and Roman cultural and political heritage? Both authors communicate for posterity Aemilius Paullus's tour of Greece, but they do so from divergent perspectives.

There are two underlying reasons why I have singled out these two authors. Polybius's account of Aemilius Paullus's travels through Greece have been recorded in Book 30 of his *Histories*. Unfortunately, only fragments of this book have been preserved. Book 30 is furthermore curious because it seems to be a later addition. Russell has argued that Book 29 in the first edition comes across as a conclusion to Polybius' *magnum opus*. It has likely been altered in his second revision, when a *Book* 30 is implied. Thus, Polybius only added Book 30 at a later stage (Russell 2012, p. 154). Livy also offers an account of Aemilius Paullus's tour of Greece. Since he appears to have largely based his work on Polybius's text, I will include the corresponding passages from Livy. Much philological scholarship has focused on the analysis of Livy's dependence on Polybius. There is still debate on the exact degree of dependency, with some scholars pointing at significant differences between the texts (Levene 2010, p. 130; Russell 2012, p. 156; Baron 2018). However, these differences do not affect my particular comparison of the two narratives, and as such Livy's account may be used to complete the fragmentary bit of text we have from Polybius. The choice of Aemilius Paullus's tour offers an opportunity to study the correlation between religious space, travel (which covers geographical landscape), human action, and perception (see also Muir 2011).

This leads to the second reason why I have chosen these two authors: an analysis of their (common) narratives will allow one to test if there is a difference in communicative strategies of Greek and Roman perception. I will test if these authors indicate any sense of perception, and in what way they project this on their actor. How do these authors, writing in different times, perceive (or have their actor perceive) the same space? Is there any significant difference, and would this signify a transformation? For example, in Polybius we have a Greek author who appears to be writing for an audience of compatriots about a Roman general who has just conquered their lands. Polybius finds himself in the rather unique position of being familiar with both worlds – having

2 My contribution is part of a wider research project into Hellenistic literary sources that sought to demonstrate if these written sources mentioned aesthetic perspectives and transformation of Hellenistic sanctuaries and human action, as part of the SFB-project 1266, Teilprojekt E3 conducted by Annette Haug, Lutz Käppel, and Asja Müller. It takes up from the work of Käppel and Pothou on human action (development) and sacred landscapes (Käppel and Pothou 2015). I have investigated historiographical texts in search of processes of transformation along three major axes, namely 'geographical', 'military-political' (with emphasis on human-environmental interaction and social transformations), and 'religious' (*i.e.* sanctuaries, with focus on interaction in human – built-space – divine ritual). However, it turned out that it is not until Pausanias that one genuinely encounters pastoral and aesthetic perception of natural and built space from a first-person perspective.

spent time in Rome – and thus he can speak with an authoritative voice. The Roman general cares to travel through Greece to see the highlights of Greek sanctuaries and cities, in other words, heritage sites of cultural importance. As such, he is presented as philhellenic (Reiter 1987). At the same time, one could postulate that, in spite of Aemilius Paullus having defeated Perseus and his army at Pydna, he is (still) overthrown once he is confronted with the statue of Zeus. In the analysis below, I will contrast Polybius's wording of the course of events with that of Livy. Conflicting accounts may hint at perception and action being employed to promote ideas of *Graecitas* versus *Romanitas*, and the sanctuaries visited by the Roman general become spaces of identity and memory.

This focus on Greek versus Roman in Polybius is not new. Scholars of Polybius have often shown a keen interest in the historiographer's perception of the Romans. The title of Numa Denis Fustel de Coulanges' 1858 PhD thesis *Polybe ou la Grèce conquise par les romains* is telling (Fustel de Coulanges 1858). Numerous studies have a cultural-political or military focus: Frank Walbank (1979), Eric Marsden (1974); more recently Tim Rood (2012), John Ma (2008), Jonathan Williams (2012), and Amy Russell (2012). Recently, Frank Daubner reflected on the way Polybius uses geographic descriptions in his *Histories* (Daubner 2014). However, even if previous scholarship did reflect on space, it was mostly political space. My contribution will complement these currents in scholarship by looking specifically at Polybius's perception of Roman action in Greek sacred space: not for the sake of extracting political ideas, but to test if we can say something about how Polybius sees his Hellenistic architectural and sacred heritage, and, as noted above, how this affects his portrayal of Roman victors acting in *his* space. Yet perhaps we should also reverse the query: how could Polybius's portrayal of Roman victors acting in his Hellenistic space tell us something about how Polybius himself perceives his Hellenistic (architectural) heritage. How does his Aemilius Paullus experience or perceive the monumental architecture, particularly that of sanctuaries; how does he respond to it? It will be argued that agency and interaction work both ways: from the perceiver and from the perceived. We will see how Polybius demonstrates this most strongly when he claims that Aemilius Paullus's encounter with the statue of Zeus 'exceeded his expectations'.

This approach implies that sites are no mere passive spaces in which action takes place, but space becomes active exactly in this interaction between perceiver and perceived. Space (and place) is multi-layered and dynamic (Gilhuly and Worman 2014). Taking up from this observation, I will try to show how for Polybius-Livy there are instances where there is mutual interaction: sites also influence the onlooker; a visitor does not necessarily just act as observer or performs an act, they are open to be influenced and affected, too. Yet, as we will see, in Polybius and Livy there are some differences in the extent to which the actor is influenced by a site. What the authors do have in common is that they are trying to create (lasting) memory and identity by attaching meaning to space, both built and unbuilt.

Whereas the original aim had been to find literary output that offers an emic perspective on perception and action in sanctuaries, our authors only offer an etic perspective. Both Polybius and Livy offer examples of *what* is perceived rather than *how* it is perceived. Yet, archaeological evidence has demonstrated a great eye for aesthetic detail and the interplay between natural landscape and built space, particularly for sanctuaries (as can be seen from other contributions in this volume, for example Asja Müller and Bonna Wescoat). This is supported by observations from later authors. For example, Cicero writes how 'the Greeks take particular delight in [religious] ornaments, in works and examples of art, statues, and paintings, things which seem to us Romans to be trifling and of no account (*levia et contemnenda*).[3] Therefore, no wrong is harder for Greeks to bear than this kind of spoliation of

3 Yet, see Jás Elsner and Michael Squire on the relation between perception and memory in Roman visual art (2015, pp. 180-204).

their shrines and towns' (Verr. 2, 4, 132-3). Jonathan Williams, who points to Cicero's observation, adds that 'the artistic nature and quality of the sacred statues despoiled by Verres matter to the Greeks.' (2012, p. 292) Yet, Hellenistic authors, historiographers in particular, do not prioritise such observations in their writings.

Aemilius Paullus travels through Greece

In Polybius's fragmentary Book 30 of the 'Histories' we find the author's account of the Roman general and (twice) consul Lucius Aemilius Paullus Macedonius, who embarks on his tour of victory after having defeated Perseus, King of the Macedonians, in the battle of Pydna (Plb. 29) in the year 168 BCE. Aemilius Paullus, as we learn from Plutarch, had been chosen consul unanimously for a second time. He was to be the commander of the Macedonian war, and in his role as a general he was to lead the army against Perseus (Plut. Aem. Paullus. 10). Polybius presents Aemilius as a newcomer to Greece and a 'would-be traveller-geographer' (Isayev 2017, p. 233). It remains to be seen if Aemilius Paullus's encounters with Hellenistic sanctuaries could be described as a touristic sightseeing tour, perhaps even a form of 'religious' tourism (Bloch 2017, pp. 5-10, 'biblical tourism'), or if it is a triumphant tour over conquered territories.

The parallel passage in Livy is found in Livy, 'The History of Rome' 45, 27-28. It will become clear that Livy's perception obviously diverts from Polybius's. In my comparison of both segments, I will highlight the differences of perception when the authors write about the same space: there are significant dissimilarities of perception between a Greek authorial perspective and a Roman authorial perspective when it comes to narratives of Roman awe for Greek sanctuaries. Both authors communicate their respective cultural political agendas: a cultural politics rooted in architecture, human action, and perception. The fragments from Book 30, 10 offer one of the finest examples of perception of human action and sanctuaries set within a geographical or natural landscape in Polybius's 'Histories'.

Delphi to Athens

> **Polybius 30, 10, 1-2:**
> '[ἐξ ὧν μάλιστα κατίδοι τις ἂν ἅμα τὴν ὀξύτητα καὶ τὴν ἀβεβαιότητα τῆς τύχης, ὅταν ἃ μάλιστ' ἄν τις αὑτοῦ χάριν οἴηται διαπονεῖν, ταῦτα παρὰ πόδας εὑρίσκηται τοῖς ἐχθροῖς κατασκευάζων:]
> [2] κίονας γὰρ κατεσκεύαζε Περσεύς, καὶ ταύτας καταλαβὼν ἀτελεῖς Λεύκιος Αἰμίλιος ἐτελείωσε καὶ τὰς ἰδίας εἰκόνας ἐπέστησεν. [3]'
>
> *'[The most striking illustration of the mutability and capriciousness of Fortune is when a man, within a brief period, turns out to have been preparing for the use of his enemies the very things which he imagined that he was elaborating in his own honour. Thus] Perseus was having some columns made, which Lucius Aemilius, finding unfinished, caused to be completed and placed statues of himself on them...'*

In these first lines, Polybius suggests that before the battle with the Romans, Perseus had ordered the construction of columns, which he had wished would serve to carry statues of himself. With Perseus beaten by the Romans, however, it is now Lucius Aemilius, the Roman conqueror, who sees his chance to complete the unfinished work by having statues of *himself* placed on Perseus's columns. One could argue that this is an instance where Aemilius Paullus interacts with (built) space. As such, Polybius illustrates a case of Roman action, interference with Greek cultural (architectural) heritage. We do not know from this fragmentary bit of text the extent of the implications since the fragment does not inform us about the spatial context. This is where we need Livy, who allows us to grasp the significance of Roman action in Greek space. In the citations from both authors' works in this contribution, it is immediately evident that there is a significant discrepancy in the amount of text. The first part of Livy's account is completely missing in Polybius.

> **Livy 45, 27, 5-11:**
> '[...] *autumni fere tempus erat; cuius temporis initio ad circumeundam Graeciam visendaque, qua nobilitata fama maoira auribus accepta sunt quam oculis noscuntur, uti statuit.* [6] *praeposito castris C. Sulpicio Gallo profectus cum haud magno comitatu, tegentibus latera Scipione filio et Athenao, Eumenis regis fratre, per Thessaliam Delphos petit, inclutum oraculum.* [7] *ubi sacrificio Apollini facto inchoatas in vestibulo columnas, quibus impposituri statuas regis Persei fuerant, suis statuis victor destinavit. Lebadiae quoque templum Iovis Trophonii adit;* [8] *ibi cum vidisset os specus, per quod oraculo utentes sciscitatum deos descendunt, sacrificio Iovi Hercynnaeque facto, quorum ibi templum est, Chalcidem ad spectaculum Euripi Euboeaeque, tantae insulae, ponte continenti iunctae descendit.* [9] *a Chalcide Aulidem traicit, trium milium spatio distantem, portum inclutum statione quondam mille navium Agamemnoniae classis, Dianaeque templum, ubi navibus cursum ad Troiam filia victima aris admota rex ille regum petiit.* [10] *inde Oropum Atticae ventum est, ubi pro deo vates antiquus colitur templumque vetustum est fontibus rivisque circa amoenum;* [11] *athenas inde, plenas quidem et ipsas vetustae famae, multa tamen visenda habentis, arcem, portus, muros Piraeum urbi iungentis, navalia, monumenta magnorum imperatorum, simulacra deorum hominumque, omni genere et materiae et atrium insignia.*'
>
> *'It was about the season of autumn; Paulus decided to employ the beginning of this season travelling about Greece and seeing the sights which are made so famous by repute that they are greater by hearsay than by visual acquaintance. Putting Gaius Sulpicius Gallus in charge of the camp, he set out with no large escort, his son Scipio and Athenaeus, the brother of King Eumenes, serving as his personal aides. He went through Thessaly to Delphi, the famous oracular shrine. There he offered sacrifice to Apollo and when he saw the columns, which had been begun at the entrance, on which they were going to place statues of King Perseus, he reserved them for his own statues as conqueror. At Lebadia also he visited the shrine of Jupiter Trophonius; there he viewed the mouth of the cave through which those who use the oracle go down to make their inquiries of the gods, and offered sacrifice to Jupiter and Hercynna, whose temple is there. Paulus then went down to Chalcis to see the spectacle of the Euripus and of that great island Euboea, which is joined by a bridge to the mainland. From Chalcis he crossed to Aulis, three miles away, with its harbour famous as the anchorage once upon a time for the thousand ships of Agamemnon's fleet, and its temple of Diana, where the renowned king of kings sought passage to Troy for his ships by bringing his daughter as a victim to the altar. Thence Paulus went to Oropus in Attica, where an ancient prophet is worshiped as a god, and there is an old temple made charming by springs and streams around it. Thence he went to Athens, which is also replete with ancient glory, nevertheless it has many notable sights, the Acropolis, the harbours, the walls joining Piraeus to the city, the shipyards, the monuments of great generals, and the statues of gods and men —statues notable for every sort of material and artistry.'*

Livy tells us how Aemilius Paullus had set out on his tour (*circumeundam*) of Greece to admire its architectural heritage in the autumn of the year 168 BCE. The Roman author sneers that the Greeks boast too much about their heritage; it is only half as impressive when seen in real life (*qua nobilitata fama maoira auribus accepta sunt quam oculisnoscuntur*). Livy's *circumeundam ... visendaque* could be interpreted as the equivalent of Polybius's *theōriā* (*thēan*, see Plb. 30, 10, 5 below). Livy proceeds to describe the tour: Aemilius Paullus and his travel companions Scipio and Athenaeus travel through Thessaly towards Delphi, move through Boeotia to Attica and Athens, then the party goes south towards the Peloponnese, starting with the Argolis and continuing on to Sparta to finish their tour at Olympia (see also Walbank 1979, p. 432). On their tour, they visit famous cities and sanctuaries. The first is 'the famous oracular shrine' (*inclutum oraculum*) at Delphi, that is, the Temple of Apollo. Aemilius Paullus chooses to perform a ritual act in this shrine: he offers a sacrifice to Apollo (*ubi sacrificio Apollini facto inchoatas*). He thus feels himself entitled as a Roman to perform such an act in a Greek sacred space. Whilst he is there, he notices columns: they had been begun at the sanctuary entrance, obviously destined to carry statues of King Perseus. An interesting aside is that excavations have shown only one column for Perseus, but both Polybius and Livy speak of a plurality of columns (respectively *κίονας* and *columnas*). Here, both authors agree. The textual reference is a bit vague, but when we compare it to the archaeological evidence we see that what is meant is that the column was erected right at the entrance to the temple (south): a very prominent place. The significance of the statues is confirmed where the Roman general appropriates space in this Hellenistic sanctuary (Kousser 2010, pp. 528-531). The temple lies halfway up the mountain and the column with statue, at a height of about nine meters (Tuck 2015, pp. 107-108), must have been quite an eye-catcher, its perception dramatized by the effect of the incline (Taylor 2016, p. 560; Boschung 2004; Kähler 1965). This is also demonstrated by the column of Prusias, which is still *in situ*. Sadly, our authors do not give that much detail. Polybius offers a more 'objective' description of Aemilius Paullus's actions, whilst Livy is keen to stipulate that the Roman general's statues should serve to signify his status as conqueror. The statue is now lost, but the inscription, on a marble slab at the base of the column, survives, supporting Livy's account:

> *'L(ucius) Aimilius L(uci) f(ilius) imperator de rege Perse / Macedonibusque cepet' || 'Aemilius, son of Lucius, Imperator, set this up from the spoils which he took from King Perseus and the Macedonians'* (*CIL* 1^2*.622).*

When they continue and reach Lebadia, Aemilius Paullus is said to have visited the shrine of Jupiter Trophonius. This sanctuary is otherwise known as the cave of Zeus Trophonius.[4] Again, the Roman general performs a ritual act, here in the temple of Zeus. Livy, of course, uses the Roman name of the gods (*sacrificio Iovi Hercynnaeque facto*). Livy also describes how Aemilius Paullus observes the *'mouth of the cave through which those who use the oracle go down to make their inquiries of the gods'* (*ibicum vidisset os specus, per quod oraculo utentes sciscitatum deos descendunt*). As such, he takes along the reader in the movement down through natural landscape formation. It is an act necessary for ritual purposes. Livy does not offer a detailed description of an oracle-seeker's experiences or any further description of the sanctuary.

Aemilius Paullus and his companions subsequently travel south to Chalcis. Here they witness the spectacle of the Euripus (*vidisset ... Chalcidem ad spectaculum Euripi Euboeaeque*): this natural phenomenon with its strong tidal currents occurs in the strait between Boiotia (the port city Chalcis is located at the narrowest point) and Euboea (the island) – and it obviously attracted tourists (sightseers). Livy explains that a bridge connects the island to the Greek mainland (*tantae insulae, ponte continenti iunctae descendit*), an observation also made by Strabo, 'Geography' 8, 5, 6.

Aemilius Paullus's next port of call is Aulis with its famous harbour and the temple of Diana (*Dianaque templum*, which is the temple of Artemis: another case of Roman cultural appropriation). Livy refers to Greek mythology, in which king Agamemnon sacrificed his daughter Iphigenia to Artemis so that they could sail

4 This site is discussed in Christina Williamson's contribution to this volume.

to Troy.[5] The journey continues into Attica, where at Oropus they see how '*an old temple has been made charming by springs and streams around it*' (*inde Oropum Atticae ventum est, ubi pro deo vates antiquus colitur templumque vetustum est fontibus rivisque circa amoenum*). Here we encounter one of the best examples of interaction between architecture and natural landscape. The reader is likely to ask: what was there first? Livy's text claims an 'old temple' was made more appealing by water features that surround it. The more reasonable explanation would be that it was a deliberate choice to build the temple exactly where there were these natural water sources flowing, which, in Greek understanding, were divine (Horster 2010, pp. 456 no. 53). Livy's description comes across as if there had been a conscious decision in the construction of the sanctuary to make it aesthetically appealing, but he does not reflect upon it in so many words. The temple Livy is referring to is the Amphiareion: it dates from the 4th century BCE and boasts a sacred spring and a stream (Roesch 1984). The sacred spring is mentioned by the 2nd century AD author Pausanias (Paus., *Description of Greece,* vol. I 1, 34, 4). He claims people tossed coins into the spring after being healed of disease. The site was famous for its baths; people visited in search for healing. Livy's wording perhaps serves to de-dramatise a site revered by the Greeks. This reading could be supported by what follows next, namely Livy's claim that Athens – the next stop on the tour – is 'also replete with ancient glory, nevertheless it has many notable sights' (*plenas quidem etipsas vetustae famae, multa tamen visenda habentis*). In other words, the Greek cultural heritage sites are overrated: they may have been admirable and glorious in ancient days, but according to Livy this is no longer the case in Roman times. Yet, Livy admits some sites are still worth seeing. He sums up: the Acropolis, the harbours, the walls connecting the harbour of Piraeus to the city of Athens, shipyards, monuments of great generals, and statues of gods and men. He speaks highly of the craftsmanship and materials used, but offers no further detail of their situation within the surrounding landscape or their aesthetic appeal.

Athens to Corinth

> **Polybius 30, 10, 3-4:**
> 'ὁ δὲ θαυμάσας τὴν τῆς πόλεως θέσιν καὶ τὴν τῆς ἀκροπόλεως εὐκαιρίαν
> πρός τε τοὺς ἐντὸς
> Ἰσθμοῦ καὶ πρὸς τοὺς ἐκτὸς ἀπολαμβανομένους τόπους. [4]
> Ἐπισημηνάμενος δὲ τοῦ
> Σικυῶνος τὴν ὀχυρότητα καὶ τὸ βάρος τῆς τῶν
> Ἀργείων πόλεως ἦλθεν εἰς Ἐπίδαυρον.'
>
> '*He admired the situation of the city* [Corinth], *and the excellent position of the acropolis for commanding the districts on both sides of the Isthmus.*'
> '*After marking the strength of Sicyon and the importance of the city of Argos, he came to Epidauros.*'

Returning to Polybius, this segment explains how Aemilius Paullus had continued from Athens to Corinth. According to our Greek author, the Roman general admires the situation of the city, with its excellently positioned acropolis: as a military officer, he must have had an eye for strategic positions. He thus must have noticed that the acropolis lends itself for the command of districts on both sides of the Isthmus; that

5 There are various myths, *e.g.* Homer's *Iliad*; Euripides's tragedy *Ipheghenia in Aulis*; Aeschylus's *Agamemnon*. In Euripides's play it is Menelaos who convinces Agamemnon to sacrifice his daughter to Artemis; the seer Calchas has revealed that this is what is to be done to satisfy Artemis, who was affronted because Agamemnon accidentally killed a deer in a grove sacred to the goddess.

is, both sides of the narrow strip of land between the Peloponnese and the Greek mainland. He brushes over Sicyon and Argos, to go to Epidaurus. Livy, again, offers a more detailed narrative:

> **Liv. 45, 28, 1-2:**
> '*sacrificio Minervae, praesidi arcis, in urbe facto profectus Corinthum altero die pervenit.* [2] *urbs erat tunc praeclara ante excidium; arx quoque et Isthmus praebuere spectaculum; arx intra moenia in immanem altitudinem edita, scatens fontibus; Isthmus duo maria ab occasu et ortu solis finitima artis faucibus dirimens.*'
>
> '*After offering sacrifice to Minerva, the Guardian of the Citadel, in Athens, Paulus set out for Corinth and reached it on the second day.* [2] *The city was then world-famous before its destruction; its citadel and the Isthmus were also sights to see; the citadel rising to a huge height, enclosed by the city wall and flowing with springs, while the Isthmus separated by its narrow passage two neighbouring seas lying toward the sunrise and sunset.*'

Still in Athens, Livy's Aemilius Paullus performs another ritual act: he offers a sacrifice to Minerva, who is the guardian of the citadel. It is self-evident that the Roman general decides to pay tribute to the goddess of wisdom and war. What is also interesting is that Livy creates a bridge from the one citadel to the next: Aemilius Paullus continues from Athens to Corinth. Livy speaks in the past tense, but in doing so he does not refer to Aemilius Paullus's time, but to his own time: Corinth has been destroyed in 146 BCE by the Roman army under Lucius Mummius. Although a Roman colony had been re-established and Julius Caesar had reinstalled it as administrative capital of Achaea in 44 BCE, apparently its sightseeing attractions had not been restored. Once, Livy observes, it had been world famous; 'its citadel and the Isthmus were also sights to see' (*arx quoque et Isthmus praebuere spectaculum*). Corinth's citadel was positioned high: 'rising to a huge height' (*in immanem altitudinem edita*), and Livy describes how it was enclosed by the city wall and was flowing with springs (*arx intra moenia ... scatens fontibus*): here we have a combination of natural features interwoven in architectural – thus, human-built, space. The Isthmus, the narrow strip of land also mentioned by Polybius, is presented by Livy as 'separating two neighbouring seas lying toward the sunrise and sunset', *i.e.* to the east and to the west. The latter sentence channels Livy's perception of natural landscape.

Corinth to Olympia

For the third section, we return to Polybius, where we jump from Corinth, a brief mention of Sicyon, Argos, and Epidauros, over the gaps in text to Olympia. Aemilius Paullus, Polybius claims, had been long anxious to see it.

> **Polybius 30, 10, 5:**
> '[5] πάλαι μετέωρος ὢν πρὸς τὴν τῆς Ὀλυμπίας **θέαν** ὥρμησε.'
>
> '*... Having been long anxious to see Olympia, he set out thither.*'

Although it is but a short phrase, it is highly significant. Namely, Polybius uses *θέα*, which means seeing or looking at. It is related to *theōriā* and *theōreō*, sightseeing (Hdt. 1.30). It evokes a deliberate act to travel somewhere in order to see and perceive something. I use 'perceive' because, as we will see below, it is not a passive onlooking. Already Karl Kerényi has attempted to situate *theōriā* and *theōreō* in their religious and cultural context. In his understanding, it implies simultaneously human vision of the gods *and* the gods' vision of their human worshippers (Rutherford 2013, p. 11, who refers to Kerényi). René Bloch, on the other hand, simply defines *theōriā* as sightseeing (2017, p. 5). However, according to Ian Rutherford, the verb *theōreō*, although the common meaning is 'to observe', often implies more than just sightseeing: it could refer to an embassy sent with political motivations. These sacred delegates could well be visiting a sanctuary, but they will have been sent there by the city they represent (Rutherford 2013, p. 4). It is only in rare circumstances, such as in the account of Herodotus, that *theōriā* implies 'travel on a voyage of exploration' (Rutherford 2013, p. 6). In Polybius, the use of *theān* is indeed the element of deliberation as well as the representative function similar to that of sacred delegates: the Roman general and victor Aemilius Paullus represents, as it were, not only the city of Rome, but Rome as the new 'super power'. Furthermore, he does visit a sanctuary, and not just any sanctuary, but Olympia. It will become clear in the next segment whether there is also an inkling of Kerényi's definition present in Polybius's understanding of Aemilius Paullus's visit to Olympia.

Livy 45, 28, 3-4:
'*...sicyonem inde et Argos, nobiles urbes, adit; inde haud parem opibus Epidaurum, sed inclutam Aesculapi nobili templo, quod quinque milibus passuum ab urbe distans nunc vestigiis revolsorum donorum, tum donis dives erat, quae remediorum salutarium aegri mercedem sacraverant deo.* [4] *inde Lacedaemonem adit, non operum magnificentia, sed disciplina institutisque memorabilem; unde per Megalopolim Olympiam escendit.*'

'*Thence Paulus went to Sicyon and Argos, both famous cities; from there he visited Epidaurus, by no means as wealthy a town, but noted for the famous temple of Aesculapius which, at a distance of five miles from the city, is now rich in the traces of gifts of which it has been robbed, but then was rich in the gifts themselves which the sick had consecrated to the god as payment for healthgiving remedies.* [4] *Next he visited Lacedaemon, notable not for the splendour of its buildings, but for its discipline and institutions; from there he went up to Olympia via Megalopolis.*'

Livy, again offering a more elaborate account, has Aemilius Paullus travel from Athens to the famous cities of Sicyon and Argos; the Roman general then continues on to visit Epidauros with its famous Aesclepieion. The sanctuary is situated five miles from the city of Epidauros: an observation that does not receive any further attention. Livy does not discuss the sanctuary's pastoral setting or its architectural design: he merely states that once it was abundant with gifts offered by those who sought healing in the sanctuary. Nowadays there are but traces of these gifts since the site has been robbed (*nunc vestigiis revolsorum donorum*). Leaving Epidauros, Aemilius Paullus continues to Lacedaemon (Sparta). The city is praised by the Roman author for its discipline and institutions – and explicitly *not* for the splendour of its architecture (*non operum magnificentia*). Livy hints here at Spartan austerity, which is reflected in built space. Leaving Sparta, the entourage travels via Megalopolis (Polybius's home turf) to Olympia – and here we are level again with Polybius. However, the striking difference here is that Livy does not take note of any alleged desire of Aemilius Paullus that he had been desperate to see Olympia. Livy simply states that the Roman general went up Olympia via Megalopolis (*unde per Megalopolim Olympiam escendit*). This brings us to the final sections.

The sanctuary of Olympia

Polybius 30, 10, 6-10:
'Λεύκιος Αἰμίλιος παρῆν εἰς τὸ τέμενος τὸ ἐν Ὀλυμπίᾳ, καὶ τὸ ἄγαλμα θεασάμενος ἐξεπλάγη καὶ τοσοῦτον εἶπεν ὅτι μόνος αὐτῷ δοκεῖ Φειδίας τὸν παρ' Ὁμήρῳ Δία μεμιμῆσθαι, διότι μεγάλην ἔχων προσδοκίαν τῆς Ὀλυμπίας μείζω τῆς προσδοκίας εὑρηκὼς εἴη τὴν ἀλήθειαν.'

'*Aemilius entered the sacred enclosure at Olympia, and when he saw the statue he was struck with awe and said he thought only Pheidias had reproduced the Zeus of Homer; for although he had great expectations of Olympia, he found the reality was greater than his expectations.*' (translation adapted from Russell 2012, p. 161)

The parallel passages in Polybius and Livy in these final sections are roughly of the same length. Polybius describes how the Roman general entered the sacred enclosure (*τέμενος*) at Olympia, and moving from the profane into the sacred space, he perceives the statue of Zeus: the Roman is struck with awe by the sight of it. Polybius uses *θεάομαι*, which has a stronger sense than merely 'to see'; it is rather 'to gaze at' or 'to behold'. There is a correlation between *θεάομαι* and *ἐκπλήσσω*: the seeing, or the perception, is enacted by Aemilius Paullus, yet simultaneously Aemilius Paullus is acted upon: he is struck. This is an 'action', so to speak, from the statue of the god. Here one might recall Kerényi's observation that vision works both ways (see above). It contrasts, and likely deliberately so, with the idea of looking at something means to claim power over it (Russell 2012, p. 157 no. 15): in this case, Polybius's Aemilius Paullus is looking, but as a result, he is conquered, disempowered. The effect of the visual experience of Aemilius Paullus is that he concludes that his encounter on Olympia exceeded his initial expectations (*προσδοκίας*). Polybius claims that Aemilius Paullus was of the opinion that the sculptor, Pheidias, '*was the only one who had represented the Zeus of Homer*' – that is, the only one having been able to accurately, or better, vividly, recreate the god. Walbank explains that the chryselephantine statue of Zeus, seated on a throne, was the most famous work of Pheidias (1979, p. 433; see also McWilliam 2011). The fact that numerous ancient authors have mentioned the statue implies that it must have attracted many a sightseer. Although one has to be wary of the fragmentary nature of this passage, it remains striking that Polybius only comments upon the effect Pheidias's statue had on his Roman general. He allows him to pass through the sanctuary and into the *temenos* without the general taking notice of the impressive architecture of the complex. The only general comment Polybius seems to be making, and which seems to be referring to the entire site – Polybius speaks of *προσδοκίαν τῆς Ὀλυμπίας* –, is that Aemilius Paullus thought that '*the reality was greater than his expectations*'. He had expected to encounter something impressive, but he perceives that reality surpasses this. As such, Polybius demonstrates that the Roman conqueror, who had obviously already heard of the reputation of Olympia, and came prepared, was still overwhelmed by the sight of it. Greek cultural heritage thus conquers Roman preconception: it has value even in Roman times; perhaps one could postulate that here, Polybius demonstrates that Graecitas surpasses Romanitas.

Livy 45, 28, 5:
'*...ubi et alia quidem spectanda ei visa;* [5]*iovem velut presentum intuens motus animo est. itaque haud secus, quam si in Capitolio immolaturus esset, sacrificium amplius solito apparari iussit.*'

'*At Olympia he saw many sights which he considered worth seeing; but he was stirred to the quick as he gazed on what seemed Jupiter's very self.* [6] *Therefore he ordered a sacrifice prepared larger than usual, just as if he had been going to sacrifice on the Capitol.*'

Livy also admits that there were a great many things at Olympia which the Roman general thought of as worth seeing. However, and here Livy agrees with Polybius, it was the statue of the god that impressed him most. The difference with Polybius is nonetheless significant. First, Livy does not specify that Aemilius Paullus is struck with awe the moment he enters the sacred space. Second, here as elsewhere in his description of Greek sanctuaries, Livy uses the Latin equivalent to name the Greek gods. Of course, this is commonplace for Latin authors, yet in the context of the current paper, it deserves special mention. Namely, it contains an element of perception, and it deals with the communication of cultural knowledge and the communication of memory for posterity. Livy's choice seems deliberate, reflecting a political agenda of cultural appropriation. Moreover, it is only because Aemilius Paullus had the impression he had just encountered Jupiter himself, which caused him to feel moved to his soul (*iovem velut praesentem intuens motus animo est*), and that then he decided to order a sacrifice. The sacrifice ordered is specific: due to the magnitude of the general's experience, the sacrifice had to be larger than usual (*amplius solito apparari iussit*): that is, larger than any of the sacrifices offered in the Greek sanctuaries he had encountered earlier on his tour. Yet, it is not because he revered this particular Greek sacred space so much that he decided to offer such a sumptuous sacrifice, rather it is because he makes a cognitive connection with Rome. This is evident from Livy's expression: the Roman general acted as if (*quam si*) he had been going to sacrifice on the Capitol; that is to Jupiter Capitolinus, in Rome.

Conclusion

Polybius's description of Aemilius Paullus's tour of Greece begins in Delphi and culminates in the sacred enclosure of Olympia. It commenced with the Roman general's observation that Perseus's columns had been left unfinished and his decision to adorn them with statues of himself. The Roman conqueror thus appropriates Greek space and makes it his own, demonstrating the change of times. Interestingly, when Aemilius Paullus ends his tour of Greece on top of Olympia, there is another statue. This time, however, the Roman general is struck with awe. Polybius cleverly inverses the roles: the Roman general does not act, but is acted upon. He perceives Pheidias's statue of Zeus and is overwhelmed by it. He is so impressed that he admits that the reality of Olympia exceeded his expectations. Where his tour started with a show of military and political superiority which he manifested by his actions of appropriating Greek sacred space, in the end it is Greek cultural heritage that conquers this Roman attitude of superiority. Olympia retains its Greek identity. The only other places which Aemilius Paullus visits in Polybius's narrative are Corinth, Sicyon, Argos, and Epidauros. He only comments on the situation of Corinth, where he demonstrates his military expertise: he perceives the position of the acropolis and the Isthmus as excellent – an observation made from a perspective of military strategy.

Livy's narrative describing Aemilius Paullus's travels across Greece has been preserved better. The Roman author offers an at times detailed description of the tour through cities and sanctuaries, from monumental ones to destroyed and looted ones to caves. However, instead of reflecting on the natural or built setting of these sanctuaries, Livy largely ignores such aesthetic observations. Livy starts by stating that Greek cultural heritage is overrated: the Greek claims about the sanctuaries being so important to them as spaces of identity are denigrated by Livy. Subsequently, other than in Polybius, Livy's Aemilius Paullus offers sacrifices at most of the sanctuaries he visits: in this act, he both acknowledges the religious identity of the site as well as appropriates it. He considers himself, as a Roman, entitled to sacrifice in foreign sanctuaries. Furthermore, as I have alluded to above, Livy's architectural observations are minimal (*e.g.* the bridge connecting the great island Euboea with the mainland), and the only pastoral aesthetic observation occurs in Livy 45,27,10 where he mentions springs and streams that make the old temple (Amphiareion) charming. Livy does briefly describe built space, monuments, and statues in Athens, but only in passing. His description of Corinth has more of an aesthetic character: he describes the high citadel enclosed by city walls and flowing with springs; the Isthmus separates two seas towards east and west. His description largely follows Polybius: it offers more aesthetic detail, yet it seems to be missing the military character of the observation found in Polybius. This is interesting, because in this passage Livy's Aemilius Paullus seems to appear less in his role of military conqueror and more in his role of a visitor who perceives 'sights worth seeing', whereas in Polybius emphasis is placed on Aemilius Paullus's military expertise. This temporary switch of roles is however short-lived: it changes radically once Livy's Roman general arrives in Olympia. Compared to the other passages in his narrative, Livy's description of Aemilius Paullus's visit to Olympia is, in contrast to the description offered by Polybius, a bit of an anti-climax. The Roman general chose to see the sights which *he* thought worth seeing, and yes, he was amazed when he gazed upon the statue of Zeus, which Livy described as *'what seemed Jupiter's very self'*. Yet, rather than being immobilized with awe, Livy's Aemilius Paullus ordered a sacrifice, *'just as if he had been going to sacrifice on the Capitol'*: as such, Livy shifts the impact to ultimate Roman appropriation. The religious identity of the Greek sanctuary is compatible with that of the Roman capitol. It is not because of the greatness of the Greek sanctuary itself, but because of its similarity to the Roman capitol that the Roman general's sacrifice is ordered larger than usual.

Overall, both Polybius and Livy often testify of cultural (re-)appropriation of Greek sanctuaries by the Roman actor, the general Aemilius Paullus. We may follow Amy Russell's suggestion that Polybius presents 'his non-Roman reader' with an illustration of a Roman looking at the Greek world so that they can form a judgement of the moral nature of the Romans. Russell argues that as such, this doubling of perspectives allows for mutual construction of Greek and Roman identity (2012, p. 151). Although the moral element is to some extent connected to aesthetic appreciation – the Roman general looks at the Greek sanctuaries, enters with respect, but he does not ransack the sacred space – Polybius does not elaborate on Aemilius Paullus's perception of the aesthetic harmony of Greek sanctuaries in their natural or built setting. The Roman conqueror is struck with aesthetic awe only once: when he is in the sacred enclosure at Olympia, gazing upon Pheidias's statue of Zeus. As I already hinted at above, Polybius's Aemilius Paullus even subjects himself to one of the Greek sanctuaries: he is humbled by the view of the statue of Zeus, and he admits that the sanctuary at Olympia surpassed his expectations. Greek architecture and statuary thus has the power to impress, to act upon the Roman visitor (conqueror), in a way turning Roman victory lopsided. Therefore, I would not be inclined to follow Russell that Polybius's Aemilius Paullus becomes a mere spectator: he remains very much an actor trying to appropriate Greek sacred space, yet also open to be acted upon. Although Russell stipulates that Aemilius Paullus does not wholly lose his role as an actor, she chiefly sees his role centred on his practice of viewing sites (2012, p. 157). This brings us to sightseeing, and thus Polybius's use of *thēorēo* (in the form of *θέα*). Considering the political connotations of this concept of sightseeing, as well as its reciprocal character (that is to say, the reciprocity of influence between perceiver and perceived), it is striking that although Polybius describes Aemilius Paullus's tour of Greece and his visits to 'touristic' hotspots such as Greece's most famous sanctuaries, the author uses a *thēorēo*-connotation only once. The fragmentary Polybius appears to be primarily concerned about perception of cultural politics and moral standards, not about perception of built space in architectural or aesthetical terms or how they sit in their pastoral context or how ritual actions within these sanctuaries are perceived. This only occurs sporadically without the author offering much detail. Livy's narrative complements Polybius, but it may also be interpreted as shifting the perspective. The Roman author emphasises Roman action within Greek space: the aspect of appropriation is much stronger than in Polybius. Even when the Roman general appears to be influenced by what he perceives, Livy inverses the effect and creates a correlation with Rome, thus emphasising Rome's supremacy. In the end, this may demonstrate a transformation of action (socio-cultural awareness), transformation of architecture or decoration, and transformation of the *omphalos*: the centre of the world no longer is Greece, but it is relocated to Rome. This perception of *omphalos* is significant on several levels: social, cultural, and environmental; it includes agency, the relation built space-natural space, sanctuaries, and the idea of divine presence and providence. Sanctuaries in particular are considered spaces of identity, and they are being (re)appropriated. Although both authors recognise Greek cultural patrimony, Polybius seeks to emphasise its continued legacy now that Rome has risen to power, whereas Livy demonstrates that Rome can dominate and appropriate Greek cultural heritage. The two narratives represent different media strategies to communicate cultural knowledge and memory for posterity: in both accounts, sightseeing and perception is key, but the difference lies in who affects whom. In Polybius, the ultimate standoff between Roman actor and Greek sanctuary culminates in Greek victory (in the 'person' of Zeus) on Olympia. In Livy, human action tends to dominate the space in which it takes place. In other words, although Rome is now the ruling power in the world, at least for Polybius, Greek sanctuaries retain their power to influence sightseers, even Roman conquerors.

Acknowledgements

I would like to express my gratitude to Annette Haug for the inspiring conversations, introduction into new methodologies, and the intellectual challenges that have opened up new ways of approaching ancient literary sources. It has been a wonderful opportunity to work in such a genuinely interdisciplinary environment. Furthermore, I would like to thank Annette Haug and Asja Müller for offering the opportunity to contribute to this volume, and I thank the other contributors for their feedback on a first draft of this paper, which was presented at the Hellenistic Architecture and Human Action International Conference in Kiel, November 2018 (funded by the Deutsche Forschungsgemeinschaft / DFG, German Research Foundation – Projektnummer 2901391021 – SFB 1266). I also thank the reviewers for their constructive feedback and suggestions, and the editors for their corrections.

References

Baron, C. 2018. The historian's craft: narrative strategies and historical method in Polybius and Livy, in: Miltsios, N. and Tamiolaki, M. (eds.). *Polybius and his legacy*, Trends in Classics: Supplementary Volumes 60. Berlin: De Gruyter, 203-221.

Bloch, R. 2017. *Andromeda in Jaffa: Mythische Orte als Reiseziele in der jüdischen Antike* (Franz-Delitsch Vorlesung 2015). Münster.

Boschung, D. 2004. Überlegungen zum Denkmal des Aemilius Paullus in Delphi, in: Evers, C. and Tsingarida, A. (eds.). *Rome et ses provinces: genèse et diffusion d'une image du pouvoir* (Lucernae Novantiquae). Brussels: Le Livre Timperman, 59-72.

Daubner, F. 2014. Zur Rolle der geographischen Schilderungen bei Polybios, in: Grieb, V. and Koehn, C. (eds.). *Polybios und seine Historien*. Stuttgart: Franz Steiner Verlag, 113-126.

Elsner, J. and Squire, M. 2015. Sight and memory: the visual art of Roman mnemonics, in: Squire, M.J. (ed.). *Sight and the ancient senses*. London: Routledge, 180-204.

Fustel de Coulanges, N.D. 1858. *Polybe ou la Grèce conquise par les romains*. Thesis (PhD). Unisersité Paris-Sorbonne.

Gilhuly, K. and Worman, N. (eds.) 2014. Introduction, in: Gilhuly, K. and Worman, N. (eds.). *Space, place, and landscape in ancient Greek literature and culture*. Cambridge: Cambridge University Press, 1-20.

Horster, M. 2010. Religious landscape and sacred ground: relationships between space and cult in the Greek world. *Revue de l'histoire des religions* 4, 435-458.

Isayev, E. 2017. *Migration, mobility and place in ancient Italy*. Cambridge: Cambridge University Press.

Kähler, H. 1965. *Der Fries vom Reiterdenkmal des Aemilius Paullus in Delphi*, Monumenta artis Romanae 5. Berlin: Gebr. Mann.

Käppel, L. and Pothou, V. (eds.) 2015. Prologos – Prefatory Note, in: Käppel, L. and Pothou, V. (eds.). *Human development in sacred landscapes*. Göttingen: Vandenhoeck & Ruprecht, 11-18.

Kousser, R. 2010. Hellenistic and Roman Art, 221 BC - AD 337, in: Roisman, J. and Worthington, I. (eds.). *A companion to ancient Macedonia*. Oxford: Blackwell, 522-542.

Kyrieleis, H., Eder, B., Benecke, N. (eds.) 2006. *Anfänge und Frühzeit des Heiligtums von Olympia: Die Ausgrabungen am Pelopion 1987-1996* (Deutsches Archäologisches Institut). Berlin: De Gruyter.

Levene, D. 2010. *Livy on the Hannibalic War*. Oxford: Oxford University Press.

Ma, J. 2008. Chaironeia 338: topographies of commemoration. *The Journal of Hellenic Studies* 128, 72-91.

Marsden, E.W. 1974. Polybius as a military historian. *Entretiens sur l'Antiquité classique* 20, 267-301.

McWilliam, J. (ed.) 2011. *Statue of Zeus at Olympia: new approaches*. Newcastle: Cambridge Scholars Publishing.

Muir, S. 2011. Religion on the road in ancient Greece and Rome, in: Harland, P.A. (ed.). *Travel and religion in antiquity*. Waterloo: Wildrid Laurier University Press, 29-47.

Reiter, W.A. 1987. *Aemilius Paullus: conqueror of Greece*, London: Routledge.

Roesch, P. 1984. L'Amphiaraion d'Oropos, in: Roux, G. (ed.). *Temples et sanctuaires: séminaire de recherché 1981-1983*, Travaux de la Maison de l'Orient 7. Lyon: Maison de l'Orient et de la Méditerranée Jean Pouilloux, 173-184.

Rood, T. 2012. Polybius, in: de Jong, I.J.F. (ed.). *Space in ancient Greek literature: studies in ancient Greek narrative*. Leiden, Boston: Brill, 179-197.

Russell, A. 2012. Aemillius Paullus sees Greece: travel, vision, and power in Polybius, in: Smith, C.J. and Yarrow, L. (eds.). *Imperialism, cultural politics, and Polybius*. Oxford: Oxford University Press, 152-167.

Rutherford, I. 2013. *State pilgrims and sacred observers in ancient Greece: a study of Theōriā and Theōroi*. Cambridge: Cambridge University Press.

Taita, J. 2007. *Olimpia e il suo vicinato in epoca arcaica*. Milan: LED.

Taylor, M.J. 2016. The battle scene on Aemilius Paullus' Pydna Monument: a reevaluation. *Hesperia* 85 (3), 559-576.

Tuck, S.L. 2015. *A history of Roman art*. Malden, MA: Wiley Blackwell.

Walbank, F.W. 1979. *A historical commentary on Polybius*, vol. III (books XIX-XL). Oxford: Clarendon Press.

Williams, J. 2012. From Polybius to the Parthenon: religion, art, and plunder, in: Smith, C.J. and Yarrow, L. (eds.). *Imperialism, Cultural Politics, and Polybius*. Oxford: Oxford University Press, 278-297.

Translations of Ancient Authors

Godley, A.D. 1920. *Herodotus: the Persian wars, Volume I: Books 1-2*, Loeb Classical Library 117. Cambridge, MA: Harvard University Press.

Jones, W.H.S. 1918. *Pausanias: description of Greece, Volume I: Books 1-2 (Attica and Corinth)*, Loeb Classical Library 93. Cambridge, MA: Harvard University Press.

Olson, S.D. and Paton, W.R. 2012. *Polybius: the histories, Volume VI: Books 28-39. Fragments*, Loeb Classical Library 161, revised by F.W. Walbank and C. Habicht. Cambridge, MA: Harvard University Press.

Perrin, B. 1918. Plutarch, Aemilius Paulus, in: Hendersen, J. (ed.). *Lives, Volume VI: Dion and Brutus. Timoleon and Aemilius Paulus*, Loeb Classical Library 98. Cambridge, MA: Harvard University Press, 357-457.

Schlesinger, A.C. 1951. *Livy: the History of Rome, Volume XIII, Books 43-45*, Loeb Classical Library 396. Cambridge, MA: Harvard University Press.

Notes on contributor

Jessica van 't Westeinde - Department of Ancient History, Faculty of Philosophy, Eberhard-Karls University Tübingen, and Department of Ancient History, Faculty of History and Philosophy, University of Bern (present). Studies in Theology and Religious Studies with major in History in Leuven; PhD Durham 2016; Visiting Fellow at Aarhus University 2016; Teach at Tübingen Excellence Fellow 2016-2017; Postdoctoral Research Fellow CRC 1266, project E3 at the Institute of Classical Studies / Classical Archaeology, CAU Kiel, October 2017 – March 2018.

Man-Made Space versus Natural Space in Greek Sacred Caves

Katja Sporn

Abstract

The chapter deals with man-made interventions in or around Greek sacred caves. Although very limited artificial alterations are characteristic for sacred caves in the Greek motherland, a synoptic view of the evidence shows that many of the caves display but one or two. After a brief summary of the evidence and the problem of defining a sacred cave, various artificial elements present in the caves will be discussed. They concern both alterations to the natural setting and the building and setting up of features such as architecture (buildings, walls, terraces, altars), images of gods (sculpture and rock-cut elements), inscriptions and plantations. Although the cave was itself considered sacred, man-made modifications were used for delineating and defining space, both inside and outside the caves, for ritual and non-ritual purposes.

Keywords: Sacred caves, architecture, space, ritual, Greece

A peculiar feature of caves or rock-shelters in Greece is their use for cultic purposes.[1] The earliest confirmed sacred caves in Greece can be traced back on Crete to at least MM I, *i.e.* around 2000 BCE (the Idaean Cave, Amnisos, Skoteino, Psychro *etc.*). For the Idaean Cave a date in the 3rd millennium BCE or even earlier (Stampolidis and Kotsonas 2013, p. 188, with further references) had been proposed before, but according to the recent publication of the excavations, the Neolithic finds seem to be related to short-term residents (Sakellarakis and Sapouna-Sakellaraki 2013, pp. 167-168). The focus of this contribution will not be on prehistory, but rather on Greek sacred caves in historical times, especially in the Classical and Hellenistic periods, when an apogee of cultic use can be discerned (see Sporn 2013, pp. 204-205 on the chronological range of sacred caves).

German Archaeological Institute, Athens
Fidiou 1
10678 Athens
Greece
katja.sporn@dainst.de

1 Many thanks to Doniert Evely for improving the English text and Franziska Lehmann and Irini Marathaki for their help.

The paper is divided into five short parts: After a general overview of the evidence of Greek sacred caves in the historical periods, I will briefly refer to the problem of identifying a sacred cave. A discussion of man-made features in sacred caves follows, especially of features which could be related to defining ritual space, such as images of gods and mortals, altars, artificial structures, and inscriptions. This chapter will not deal with the detailed analysis of finds of other possible votive material in the caves, such as pottery, unless their find spots are important for helping define space. In the fifth part I will draw some conclusions.

Greek sacred caves in historical times – the evidence

The present analysis is based on a catalogue composed over the last 25 years – and since it is continuously being augmented, the work is still in progress – of over 180 caves in the ancient Greek and Roman world, about 130 of which are situated within the limits of modern Greece. The collected material is primarily of an archaeological nature, although there are some 20 sacred caves only known through literary evidence. The caves are spread all over Greece (Sporn 2013, p. 214 Fig. 12.1), though there is a certain bias towards Crete, which is particularly rich in caves. Around 4000 caves, *varathra*, and rock-shelters were known about already back in the 1960s. Comprehensive studies of Cretan caves have been undertaken especially by Paul Faure, Loeta Tyree, Bodgan Rutkowski and Kristof Nowicki (Faure 1964; Tyree 1974; Rutkowski and Nowicki 1996; Tyree 2013), although there was always a certain emphasis on the Minoan and Mycenaean periods. Only more recently, the periods after the Bronze Age came more into focus (Sporn 2002, passim and pp. 346-348; Prent 2005, pp. 200-209 and passim; Stampolidis and Kotsonas 2013). In his last book on that topic, Faure (1996) collected 82 Cretan caves which he considered sacred, of which 49 provided material of Classical and Hellenistic times. This number seems to my mind far too large, principally because Faure did not define his criteria precisely enough. Already Tyree (1974, pp. 148-161) has suggested in her thesis on 'Cretan Sacred Caves' that only 10 of them can be considered sacred in these periods, while in my study of Cretan sanctuaries and cults in Classical and Hellenistic times I have gathered 10 definite and five probable and five possible sacred caves of the same dating (Sporn 2002, pp. 346-348).

Thanks to the study by Jere Wickens (1986) on 'The Archaeology of Cave Use in Attika', there exists a detailed analysis of Attic caves used in Antiquity, which according to his study numbered 345. The cultic use of caves started in Attica fitfully in Geometric times, with the cave connected with the altar of Zeus Parnesios on Mount Parnes (Palaiokrassa-Kopitsa and Vivliodetis 2015), and even in Archaic times such practice was still not really common: Wickens counts only four definite cult caves. The prime time for cave use for cultic purposes in Attica was the Classical years: out of 37 definitely or probably utilized caves, 13 to 19 were sacred. This is most obviously connected with the importance of the cult of Pan, first brought to Attica from Arcadia in the early 5th century BCE, thanks to his mythical help in the Persian wars. Altogether, 10 Attic caves were sacred to Pan and the Nymphs.

Comprehensive studies covering regions in Greece other than Crete or Attica are rare (see Sporn 2007, 2010, 2013). Only occasionally have cult caves been thoroughly investigated and published: the more famous ones being the rock-shelter of Polis on Ithaka with its cult activities going back as early as the late 9th century BCE (see Deoudi 2008; Mylonopoulos 2016), the Idaean Cave on Crete (Sakellaraki and Sapouna-Sakellaraki 2013), the Corycian cave above Delphi (Amandry 1984), and more recently the Schisto Cave at Keratisini in Attica (Mavridis *et al.* 2013; Zambiti 2013), the Leibithrion Cave on mount Helicon with its enormous yield of finds (Vassilopoulou 2013; 2016), and the cave of Lechova close to Sikyon in Corinthia (Kormazopoulou *et al.* 2006) to which the thorough publication of the cave of the Nymphs at Pharsala in Thessaly, excavated in the early 20th century, should now be added (Wagman 2016).

Identification of a sacred cave

It is a very difficult task to decide whether a cave should be considered as being sacred or not in antiquity. Because caves are natural spaces and commonly not altered by architectural features – at least in the Greek mainland, as opposed *e.g.* to various parts of Anatolia, they do not possess specific layouts: in this they stand in contrast to buildings whose architectural form is connected to a certain function, *e.g.* the *peripteros* to a temple. It is therefore necessary to observe a combination of various elements (see also Sporn 2007, pp. 43-46). According to Faure (1996, p. 16) a cave has to fulfil six criteria in order to be considered as sacred:

1. Presence of water
2. *Votives*
3. Traces of ashes
4. Specific natural features (stalagmites, stalactites, rock formations)
5. Literary traditions concerning the cult
6. Proximity to a settlement

Criteria 1, 4 and 6 are not absolute conditions, and even criteria 3 and 5 are not strictly necessary. Only the finds – *votives* – can be considered as definite indicators of cultic use if there is no definite epigraphic evidence on the site. In line with finds made in possible cult caves, items with clear cultic connotations (or indeed finds that are not in keeping with cult or pagan use: for those, see now Wickens 2013 as regards Attica) are:

- items made of precious material (marble or metal);
- votive clay items such as terracotta figurines, *pinakes*, miniature vessels and fine ware, *i.e.* materials which had no place in caves being otherwise used;
- ceramics used for drinking and eating in the cave might indicate *ritual* dining and drinking, and an enormous quantity of lamps (not individual pieces used in some everyday lighting needs of a random visitor, but lamps found *en masse*).

Even so, precious materials are but rarely found in these caves: bronze *votives* disappear more or less completely after the Archaic period in Greek sanctuaries. Marble is found in exceptional cases, such as in Attica, as votive reliefs to Pan and the Nymphs and statues, or in the Corycian Cave, but rarely in other areas such as Crete or now the Leibethrion Cave (Table 2; see also Sporn 2007, p. 52).

Ritual space in Greek sacred caves?

Having thus defined some criteria for identifying a sacred cave, it is important to ask whether the ritual space, the area(s) used for cultic purposes, can be defined within this. Walter Connor (1988, p. 181 no. 81) has argued that in the cave of Vari there were clearly defined spaces for both ritual and non-ritual purposes: the interior of that cave is divided by a natural rock feature into two parts – and all the votive material has been found in the southern part. Connor (1988) compares this with the caves of Daphni in Attica, divided by a wall (Travlos 1937, p. 400 Pl. 1), and of Psychro on Crete (Rutkowski and Nowicki 1996). Connor (1988) wonders whether this has to do with the 'doubling' of caves, which is sometimes mentioned in literary sources. For example, Virgil (Aen. 6) mentions a cave with two entrances, one to enter by and the other to exit. Nevertheless, it is perhaps straining the evidence to detect a difference between an entrance space and an exit space in a sacred cave.

	Place	Constructed features (architecture, plantations)	References
1.01	Athens, Ilissos area	Artificially smoothened vertical walls, cuttings for beams, originally supporting roof, beddings for wall on one side	Wickens 1986, 2, pp. 313-319, no. 58
1.02	Attica, Hymettos, Liontari	Cave divided by rubble walls and stalactites into rooms	Karali et al. 2006
1.03	Attica, Penteli, quarry	Marble door frame and part of lintel still visible, slabs for trapeza, parts of clay water pipeline, maybe path with marble plaques leading to the cave	Zoridis 1977; Wickens 1986, 2, pp. 202-211, no. 39
1.04	Attica, Parnes	Rubble wall inside, pebbled floor	Mastrokostas 1983, p. 340
1.05	Attica, Vari	Kepos and oikos for the Nymphs	Schörner and Goette 2004
1.06	Attica, Anavyssos, Kastela i Spilia	Rock shelter closed by a wall at entrance	Lohmann 1993, 1, p. 230
1.07	Attica, Brauron, grave of Iphigeneia	Cave behind temple, inside the cave built structure (depository room, dining space or residential area?)	Ekroth 2003
1.08	Attica, Daphni, cave of Pan	Outside opposite the entrance, two walls, the lower one a terrace wall, the upper a temenos wall, confining an artificially levelled terrace; stepped entrance (steps); wall in the first room inside the cave; initially plastered floor	Travlos 1937; Wickens 1986, 2, pp. 287-298, no. 53
1.09	Attica, Eleusis, Plutonion	Walls in front of the rock shelter, defining a terrace (4th c BC), temple (4th c BC), replacing an older building (Archaic)	Wickens 1986, 2, pp. 279-287, no. 52
1.10	Attica, Lavrion, Kitsos	Altar (3 x 2 m) in the middle of the cave, built or rock-cut?	Wickens 1986, 2, pp. 4-15, no. 11
1.11	Attica, Keratsini, Schisto	Various retaining walls of large blocks and some rock-cut steps facilitate steep way into the cave	Mavridis and Kormazopoulou 2007/2008, p. 12
1.12	Phokis, Korykaion	Built rectangular altar in front of the cave	Amandry 1984, pp. 413-414
1.13	Thessaly, Krounia	Many remains of architecture (blocks, column drums, capitals)	Agouridis et al. 2006
1.14	Thessaly, Pharsala	Kepos and laurel tree	Wagmann 2016
1.15	Macedonia, Mieza	Bench, tiles, sima etc.	Rhomiopoulou 1999, pp. 12-15
1.16	Thrace, Oisyme	Worked stone blocks found in the interior might be from a built wall	Bakalakis 1938, p. 97, no. 6
1.17	Cyclades, Ikaria, Drakospilo	Interior of the cave is divided by walls into three rooms (one might be recent)	Katsaros 2006, pp. 157-158
1.18	Thera, Herakles and Hermes	The entrance is closed with a huge wall in isodomic masonry	Hoepfner 1997, pp. 33-34 (C. Witschel)
1.19	Syros, Alithini	Terrace or temple in front of cave	Iannoulidou 1974, p. 28
1.20	Ikaria, Hieron	Paved path, steps leading to two smaller caves	Katsaros 2006, pp. 158-159
1.21	Kasos, Ellinokamara	Walls in front and inside the cave, three terraces in front of the cave	Sakellarakis 2006
1.22	Kos, Aspripetra	Ash altar in the interior	Levi 1925/1926
1.23	Skopelos, Panormos	Artificially widened entrance, terrace wall (5th c BC)	Sampson 2000, p. 132
1.24	Ithaka, Polis	Interior: step and a retaining wall of tuff, construction of stones (altar?)	Deoudi 2008, pp. 322-323

Table 1. Architecture and plantations in or around Greek sacred caves (table: Katja Sporn).

In order to define a ritual space, it is important to look for man-made interventions in the cave. Built architecture such as the *oikos* (probably in front of the cave) at Vari (Table 1.05), the constructions at the cave in the quarry at Penteli (Table 1.03), at the Plutonion at Eleusis (Table 1.09), the artificial sacred caves such as the Megaron of Demeter at Megara (Table 2.10), the artificial rooms with benches in the Asclepieion of Corinth (Table 2.25), or the artificially made chamber in the cave sanctuary at Christos on Thera (Table 2.33) are quite rare in Greece.

Also not commonly encountered are artificially smoothed surfaces of the vertical inner sides of caves, among the exceptions here being the rock-shelter of Pan at the Ilissos river in Athens and a cave at cape Tainaron in Laconia (Table 1.01. 2.22). The fountain house at Mieza (Table 1.15) is often quoted as another example. In fact, although in the excavations at Mieza a large *stoa* and benches connected with the three grottoes were found, there could not be traced any clear indications for cult-activity at the site, which leaves the identification as a sacred cave open.

Are there clearly marked areas to accommodate the supposed presence of the god, corresponding to cult statues in built sanctuaries and, for sacrifices, corresponding to the altar? The answer is no, at least not always, and especially not in caves without organized, institutionalized ritual (*i.e.* with collective feasts, processions *etc.*). Because the cave as a natural feature was itself considered sacred, often there might not have been the need for a further clearly defined ritual space. There can be discerned an important difference between cave cults with an established and organized ritual, where collective feasts and offerings of a larger community were executed, and caves that were only sporadically visited by individuals for personal reasons, but nevertheless still considered sacred. This second group comprises, for example, caves visited by people frequenting the mountains, especially shepherds, and caves close to the seashore frequented by seafarers. Both these shepherds´ and seafarers´ caves are usually in remote places and not close to settlements.

Images of gods and mortals

In general, there was no need in a cave for a central image of a god, a cult image (Table 2 and Sporn 2007, p. 53). The instance of a three-dimensional rock-cut statue, such as in the case of the sitting figure, probably Cybele, in the cave of Vari, is so far unique to Greece. Actual finds of marble statues and votive reliefs depicting gods and heroes have mainly been made in Attica, or only at major sanctuaries outside Attica (the Corycian Cave, the Leibithrian Cave *etc.*) and rarely in smaller, regional caves (*e.g.* Crete, Liliano). The actual finds of free-standing statuary are small scale or at least less than life size, the largest one so far recorded being a marble statue of a satyr from the Corycian Cave; it has a height of 1.09 m without its head, but even with a plinth, it is still under life-sized. Most of the actual sculpture finds connected with the caves are fragments of reliefs of the Nymphs (and Pan). Inscriptions do mention the setting up an *agalma* and an *eikon* of Pan in the Lychnospilia on Mount Parnes (Table 2.05 and 3.03), and in the long 4th century BCE inscription in the cave of the Nymphs at Pharsala 'the sacred things inside, the plantings, the tablets, statues, and the many gifts' are explicitly stated as belonging to the gods worshipped, along with the entire construction (Table 3.11) – although it is not stated whom these statues depict. Intriguing is the mention of *pinakes*, paintings on tablets, since the only preserved painted *pinakes* from a Greek cave so far known are mainly the six wooden examples from Pitsa in the Corinthia, which only survived due to the specific circumstances of their deposition (Brecoulaki *et al.* 2017; for a double-sided, possibly originally painted marble slab from the Lychnospilia at Parnes, see Wickens 1986, Part 2, p. 261). Those at Pitsa depict rather the *adorants* and the ritual, rather than the gods. The gods seem to have been represented mainly in statues and reliefs in the caves – the carved relief of the dedicant Archedamos in Vari in a prominent position next to the rock-cut altar is again an exception.

The only references to cult statues come from Pausanias (Table 2), who at least in some cases seems to refer to much older pieces since he calls some of them *xoana*. But these *xoana* might sometimes refer to rock formations in the shape of a human being, which were but partly artificially enhanced. A few examples should be sufficient to make the point: the rock resembling a bear in the Arkoudospilia on Crete; the various shapes in Skoteino on Crete (Tyree *et al.* 2005/2006); the rocks

	Place	Rock cut features	Carvings, rock-cut reliefs
2.01	Athens, north slope, Apollo Hypakraios	Niches for inscriptions (Roman)	
2.02	Athens, south slope		
2.03	Attica, Daphni, cave of Pan	Niches at the entrance, in front of the wall rectangular, artificially flattened rock with channel on top (altar?); starting from 5th c BC, walls and plaster Byzantine ?	
2.04	Attica, Marathon, Oinoe II	Around the East entrance in front of cave carved niches for votives, near the entrance, 5th c BC - Roman	
2.05	Attica, Parnes, Lychnospilia	In front of the entrance, to the south, three rock-cut niches, in earlier times iron clamps were preserved, cuttings on the steep rock to the north are today used as a ladder, their date is unsure	
2.06	Attica, Penteli, Ikarion	At the front edge right above the entrance cutting for stele; in the interior, rock-cut niche in higher level	
2.07	Attica, Vari	12 rock cut steps leading down into the cave, various cuttings and niches, sculpture rock cut altar inside	varia: relief of Archedamos, seated figure
2.08	Attica, Kastella i Spilia	Cuttings for setting up statues	
2.09	Attica, Kitsos		
2.10	Megara, Demeter	Artificial cave, terrace in front	
2.11	Boeotia, Leibethrion	Niches in front of the cave	
2.12	Phokis, Corycian cave	Cuttings and niches in front of the cave, one with semicircular upper frame above the entrance	
2.13	Phokis, Tihorea, Schober-cave	Steps leading inside, plinths, worked surfaces	standing male figure, seated figure (natural?)
2.14	Phokis, Tihorea, cave of Pan	Triangular cuttings at the walls (for lamps?)	rock-cut and carved figures: Pan and others
2.15	Thessaly, Pharsala	Niche, `trapeza´, Steps leading up inside,	
2.16	Thessaly, Krounia	Niche, `trapeza´/bench	
2.17	Thrace, Oisyme	Niches	
2.18	Thasos, Pan	Artificial niche, with rock cut figures of Pan and others (4th c BC)	rock cut relief of Pan and others
2.19	Achaia, Boura, cave of Herakles	Steps leading inside, on both sides of the entrance cuttings (artificial facade?),	
2.20	Achaia, Katarraktes	Rock cut bench at entrance, various rather deep niches	
2.21	Arcadia, Kyllene	Cuttings for setting up of torches inside	
2.22	Laconia, Tainaron	Artificially smoothened vertical slope	
2.23	Laconia, Kyphas, cave of Asclepius	Artificial cuttings and water basins in cave	
2.24	Corinthia, Isthmia NE Cult Cave	banqueting halls, 5th - 4th/3rd c BC	
2.25	Corinthia, Corinth, Asclepieion	Artificial rooms with klinai	
2.26	Laconia, Tainaron	Artificially smoothened wall at one side of the cave's interior; cuttings for inserting stelai inside	
2.28	Cyclades, Delos, Herakles	Artificial terrace in front of cave	
2.29	Cyclades, Nisyros, Nyphio	In front of cave cutting for stele, in the interior man made column and votive niches	
2.30	Cyclades, Paros, Kounados	Niches (either inside or outside, today the ceiling is collapsed), Archaic-Roman	
2.31	Cyclades, Paros, Marathi		rock-cut relief of the Nymphs with inscription

Table 2. Rock cuttings, niches, sculpture in or around Greek sacred caves (table: Katja Sporn).

Sculpture	Reference
	Nulton 2003
Paus. 1. 21. 3: figures of Niobe and children (material unclear)	
	Travlos 1937; Wickens 1986, pp. 287-98
Paus. 1. 32. 7: in interior rooms and baths and so-called flock of goats of Pan, the rock formations reminding one of goats´ beards	Wickens 1986, 2, pp. 223-233, no. 43
Eight marble votive reliefs, mostly of Pan and the Nymphs; agalma and eikon of Pan were to be set up. Fragment of a relief with the cloven hoof of an animal (IG II2 4839, Rhomaios 1918, 154-5 fig. 10), IG II2 4834 seems to	Rhomaios 1918; Wickens 1986, 2, pp. 245-269, no. 47
have been used on both sides (painted?)	
Two votive reliefs with inscriptions	Edwards 1985, pp. 478-495, no. 22
Votive reliefs	Schörner and Goette 2004 (5th – 2nd c BC)
	Lohmann 1993, 1, p. 230
Votive relief of the Nymphs is said to have been found here	Peek 1942, p. 54, no. 86; Wickens 1986, 2, p. 12
	La Torre 1992/1993
Marble statues	Vassilopoulou 2013
Small head in daedalic style, larger head (600-500 BC), small Archaic female statuette, marble torso of satyr (2nd c BC), h. 1.09 m without head, marble statuette of Pan (4th/3rd c BC), marble torso of Pan, relief of Nymphs (325-300 BC)	Amandry 1984, p. 307-337 (J. Marcadé). 339-344
	Katsarou et al. in preparation
	Katsarou et al. in preparation
Pinakes kai agalmata dora de polla (inscription, 4th c BC)	Wagman 2016, pp. 29. 68. 73
	Agouridis et al. 2006, pp. 251. 261, fig. 6
6 Fragments of bases of statuettes and one possible trapeza or perirrhanterion, found inside the cave some with inscriptions	Bakalakis 1938, pp. 90-97
	Owen 2000
Paus. 7. 25. 10: statue of Herakles inside	Katsonopoulou and Soter 1993
	Zapheiropoulos 1952, pp. 396-398
	Kusch 1999, p. 260
	Mylonopoulos 2003, p. 232
Paus. 3. 24. 2: statue of Asclepius inside	Iannoulidou 1972, p. 146
	Gebhard 2002
	Rœbuck 1951
	Mylonopoulos 2003, p. 232
	Hellmann 2002, p. 267, fig. 12
	Economakis 2001, p. 58
Marble votive reliefs (Roman)	Pingiatoglou 1981, pp. 36. 120-123
	Edwards 1985, pp. 795-809, no. 89 (end of 4th/ early 3rd c BC)

	Place	Rock cut features	Carvings, rock-cut reliefs
2.32	Cyclades, Siphnos, Kamares, quarry	Rock-cut altar with inscription in the cave	
2.33	Cyclades, Thera, Christos	Cave consists of an artificially made chamber	
2.34	Cyclades, Thera, Pilarou	Four niches, and a bedding for a stele , outside the cave	
2.35	Cyclades, Nisyros, Nyphio	In front of the cave a bedding for a stele, inside niches and rock-cut column	
2.36	Ikaria, Drakospilo		
2.37	Ikaria, Hiero	A larger and two smaller caves, to the smaller caves lead rock-cut steps	
2.38	Sporades, Rhodos, Lindos	Four large rooms behind natural terrace, not clear whether artificial or not	
2.39	Sporades, Cos, Aspripetra	Niches inside were used for setting up votives	
2.40	Crete, Idaean Cave	Large rectangular rock-cut altar in front of the cave with a channel at its base along the long side	
2.41	Crete, Liliano		
2.42	Crete, Lera	Three niches outside the cave	

Table 2 continued.

resembling a face and a quadruped in the Schisto Cave in Attica (for the cave, see Mavridis *et al.* 2013; Spathi 2013; Zambiti 2013; on the features, see Katsarou *et al.* in preparation); a feature like a human head-and-shoulders in a cave on Syros (Iannoulidou 1972, pp. 28-29); or the various figures in a cave above Tithorea (Katsarou *et al.* in preparation). These natural formations sometimes seem to have been the focus of ritual deposits, as far as excavation has provided us with information, *e.g.* in the Melidoni cave on Crete (Tzedakis and Gavrilaki 1995), but also on Seriphos (Doumas 1963, p. 284). We have to consider though that caves were mostly used for many centuries as sheep shelters and only in very few instances were the strata intact when found and excavated.

More frequent than free standing sculpture were reliefs, either on stone (mainly marble) slabs brought to the caves or in rarer cases rock-cut reliefs (Table 2). A fine example, now destroyed, of a rock-cut relief was the one of the Nymphs on Paros, dedicated by Adamas to the Nymphs in the late 4th to early 3rd centuries BCE (Table 2.31 and Fig. 1). The marble reliefs brought to the caves are all to date those to the Nymphs and Pan (for the type, see Edwards 1985): they are mostly restricted to Attica, with one other example known from the Corycian Cave. Nevertheless, the existence of beddings for slabs (see below) in other caves means that initially there were others too.

Altars

In some caves the remains of altars can be detected, rarely in a neat-enough rectangular shape as in front of the Corycian Cave (Table 1.12) or a rock altar. They can be both natural (Skoteino: Tyree *et al.* 2005/2006, p. 55 Fig. 7, Siphnos, Kamares, here with an inscription of around 500 BCE; Table 3.22) and artificially enhanced; sometimes one cannot be sure of which (Arcadia, Demeter Melaina, Paus. 8, 42 refers to an altar in front of the cave). The artificially enhanced altars are rarely as large as the rectangular altar on an elevated position that fronts the Idaean Cave (Table 2.40), whilst the one decorated with a volute crowning inside the cave of Vari (Table 2.07) seems to be rather small for the sacrifice of any larger offering. Some of these altars contain small channels, which were either intended for collecting the blood or for cleaning (*e.g.* Idaean Cave Table 2.37, maybe Daphni Table 2.03).

Burnt offerings simply indicated by ash layers might indicate the existence of altars as well, both inside a cave (*e.g.* Daphni, Wickens 1986, pp. 287-294) and outside (Parnes, Mastrokostas 1983). Although in prehistoric times the main area for ritual

Sculpture	Reference
	IG XII 5, 483
	Giallelis 1997
	Kose 1997
	Economakis 2001, p. 58
	Katsaros 2006, pp. 157-158
	Katsaros 2006, pp. 158-159
	Dyggve 1960, pp. 445- 447
	Levi 1925/1926, p. 239
	Sakellarakis and Sapouna-Sakellaraki 2013, 1, pp. 120-122
Fragment of a marble statue	Sporn 2002, p. 102
	Sporn 2002, pp. 273-275

Table 2 continued.

activity was in the inner areas of the cave (see for example the altar inside the cave of Skoteino), eventually there seems to have been a shift to the outer areas. Menander's *Dyskolos* 407-409 contains a description of an offering made by an Athenian woman in a sanctuary to Pan, which was probably a cave: its location, according to Vanderpool (1967; cautiously accepted by Wickens 1986, p. 175) may be identified with the cave of Liontari on Mount Hymettos close to Paiania, though this is doubted by the directors

Figure 1. The rock-cut relief of the Nymphs at Marathi on Paros (now destroyed) (photo: D-DAI-ATH-Paros-070).

No.	Place	Inscription	Reference
3.01	Athens, north slope, Apollo Hypakraios	68 Fragments of inscriptions on marble slabs (Imperial Times)	Nulton 2003, pp. 41-88
3.02	Attica, Marathon, Oinoe II	Dedication by ephebes, including lex sacra concerning vestment restrictions, was set up in front of cave	SEG 37, 267 (61/60); Lupu 2001
3.03	Attica, Parnes, Lychnospilia	ca. 12 Inscriptions found inside and outside: rupestral inscriptions, 2 possible perirrhanteria, 5 marble plaques - 2 Plaques with metrical prayers for Pan, one from a dadouchos from Eleusis (IG II2 4831), the other from three Thracian hetairoi (IG II2 4838) - 3 Votive dedications (IG II2 4834. 4836. 4839) - IG II2 4933 (perirrhanterion, fragmentary) - IG II2 4835 (perirrhanterion, reading disputed) Inscriptions on votive reliefs of Pan and Nymphs: - EAM 1448, Τηλεφάνης ἀνέθηκε Πανὶ καὶ Νύμφαις - EAM 1859, 15 male personal names - Fragment: Ἀριστίων	Wilhelm 1929 Wilhelm 1924, pp. 57-60, no. 5 (3rd c AD) Wilhelm 1924, pp. 55-57, no. 4 Peek 1942, pp. 61-63, nos. 105. 107. 109 Peek 1942, p. 61, no. 104 (4th c) Peek 1942, p. 62, no. 106 (4th c) Kaltsas 2001, p. 219, no. 456 (end of 4th c) Kaltsas 2001, p. 221, no. 460 (ca. 300) Skias 1918, pp. 108-110, no. 2
3.04	Attica, Vari	13 Inscriptions in the interior, amongst them: - Block with dedication to the Nymphs by shepherd Skyron - Building inscription of the cave (on the rock) and the garden (on a stele), by the Theran Archedemos the Nympholeptos - Name of Archedemos, both next to his depiction and at other place - Ἀπόλλωνος, Ἕρσο, above the altar - Lex sacra in the interior, close to entrance, referring to cleaning of intestines - Χάριτος below a niche with a plinth for a statue - Πανός, below large niche and below a smaller one Inscriptions on votive reliefs of Pan and Nymphs: - EAM 2008, Εὐκλείδης Εὐκλῆς Λακράτης Νύμφαις - EAM 2012, Ε[ὐκλ]ῆς Λακλέου Ἁλαιεύς	Hallof 2004 (full publication) Hallof 2004, pp. 55-56, no. 10 (before 450) Hallof 2004, pp. 42-44. 51-54, nos. 1.9 (425-400) Hallof 2004, pp. 46-47. 50, nos. 4. 7 (before 400) Hallof 2004, pp. 47-49, no. 5 (430-400) Hallof 2004, pp. 44-46, no. 3 (450-425) Hallof 2004, pp. 44, no. 2 (430-400) Hallof 2004, pp. 49-51, nos. 6. 8 (before 400) IG II2 4651; Kaltsas 2002, p. 218, no. 451 (340/330) IG II2 4653; Kaltsas 2002, p. 218, no. 452 (330/320)
3.05	Attica, Eleusis, Plutonion	- Votive relief with banquet scene, Demeter crowning Kore, Pluto and Persephone, EAM 1519, Λυσιμαχίδης ἀνέθηκε, Θεᾶι, Θεῶι	Kaltsas 2001, p. 230, no. 484 (350-325); Clinton 2005, pp. 89-90, no. 83 (335-320?)
3.06	Attica, Penteli	Inscriptions on votive reliefs of Pan and Nymphs: - EAM 4465, Τηλεφάνης, Νικήρατος, Δημόφιλος ταῖς Νύνφαις ἀνέθησαν - EAM 4466, Ἀγαθήμερος Νύμφαις ἀνέθηκε	Edwards 1985, pp. 467-474, no. 22 (330/320) Edwards 1985, pp. 478-488, no. 22; Kaltsas 2001, p. 221, no. 459 (ca. 330)
3.07	Attica, Kitsos	Fragment of votive relief with Nymphs and inscription Θειρεσίδης Νύνφαις εὐχήν said to be found here	Peek 1942, p. 54, no. 86; Wickens 1986, 2, p. 12 (5th c?)
3.08	Boeotia, Leibethrion	Rock-cut inscription at the entrance, Κορωνεία Νύμφη	Vasilopoulou 2013
3.09	Boeotia, Leibadeia	Rock-cut votive inscriptions at the entrance, Δαμοτὶς Πανὶ ἀνέθηκε, Τιμάρετος Πανί	IG VII 3094
3.10	Phokis, Corycian Cave	9 Inscriptions, mostly on bases or blocks, three rock-cut: - Rock-cut inscription to the right of the entrance and below an oval cutting (0.14 m x 0.115 m) for the plinth of a statuette by Eustratos from Ambrysos and his companions: Εὔστρατος Ἀλκιδάμου Ἀμβρύσιος, συμπερίπολοι, Πανί, Νύμφαις - Rock-cut inscription to Pan and the Nymphs, above a rock- cut base - Various offerings either to the Nymphs or to the Nymphs and Pan, or to Pan, the Nymphs and Apollo Nymphagetes, by males, one from Skotoussa	Empereur 1984 (publication) Empereur 1984, pp. 345-346, no. 9 (250-200) Empereur 1984, pp. 344-345, no. 8 (uncertain date) Empereur, passim, dating from 4th until 2nd c
3.11	Thessaly, Pharsala	Two rock-cut inscriptions in front of entrance: a dedication by Pantalkes to the goddesses of a tree or the ergon, and the laurel (5th c BC) and a long inscription denoting the place as sacred to the Nymphs, Pan, Hermes, Apollo, Herakles, Chiron, Asklepios and Hygieia ('theirs are the entire construction and the sacred things inside, the plantings, the tablets, statues, and the many gifts', translation Wagman)	Wagman 2016, pp. 57-93 (5th/4th c)
3.12	Thessaly, Goritsa	Rock-cut inscription Διὸς Μιλιχίου in a distance of 2,5 m diagonally above the entrance	Bakhuizen 1992, pp. 306-307 (3rd c)

* Unless otherwise stated all dates are BC.

Table 3. Rock-cut and stone inscriptions in Greek sacred caves (table: Katja Sporn).

No.	Place	Inscription	Reference
3.13	Thessaly, Ossa	8 Fragments of stelai with dedications to the Nymphs, at least 2 of them by women	Wace and Thompson 1908/1909
3.14	Thasos, Aliki	Rock-cut inscription … ν Ἀπόλλωνι σ]πήλαιον	Salviat and Bernard 1967; SEG 31, 775 (late 4th/ beginning 3rd c)
3.15	Thrace, Oisyme	- Base of a statuette with inscription of various male hetairoi to the Nymphs - Part of an inscribed slab found in the excavation of the niche: ἀπ'Αὐλ[ῶνος] συνπόται εὐξάμ[ε]νοι πελαν[οῦ] μνημέον ἀνέθηκεν - Fragment of a round base or perirrhanterion, ΝΤΩΣΙ	Bakalakis 1938, pp. 90-94, no. 1, fig. 12 (late 4th c) Jameson 1956 (second half 4th c) Bakalakis 1938, p. 96, no. 3
3.16	Arcadia, Lykosoura	Rock-cut inscription Πανός inside a cave	IG V2, 530; Jost 1985, pp. 459-460
3.17	Arcadia, Kyllene	A fair number of names inscribed on the rock in the cave, some of them should be ancient, one on a stalagmite (not yet studied)	Kusch 1999, pp. 259-260 (4th c)
3.18	Cyclades, Andros	Latin rock-cut inscription: sancto deo	CIL XI 1821
3.19	Cyclades, Naxos, Engares	Rock-cut inscription in the interior, Νυμφέων Μυχιέων	IG XII 5, 53 (4th c)
3.20	Cyclades, Paros, Marathi	Rock cut inscription Ἀδάμας Ὀδρύσης Νύμφαις below the rock-cut relief of the Nymphs	IG XII 5, 245 (late 4th/start 3rd c)
3.21	Cyclades, Pholegandros, Chrysospilia	Around 400 graffitti painted with clay inside the cave, 7th c to Byzantine times, but mainly from the 4th c, including kalos-inscriptions and dedications by persons from the Aegean	Vassilopoulou 2018
3.22	Cyclades, Siphnos, Kamares	Rock-cut inscription Νυφέων ἱερόν on the so-called altar inside the cave	IG XII 5, p. 483 (6th/5th c)
3.23	Cyclades, Astypalaia, Drakontospilia	Rock-cut inscription (no reading given)	Ross 1843, p. 65-66 (non vidit)
3.24	Cyclades, Thera, Christos	Rock-cut inscription (lex sacra) close to the cave, Ἀρταμιτίου τετάρται πεδ ἰκάδα θυσέοντι ἰαρόν, Ἀγορηΐοις δὲ δεῖπνον καὶ ἱερὰ πρὸ τοῦ σαμηΐου	IG XII 3, 452; Giallelis 1997, pp. 50-51. 59, fig. 7 (beginning 4th c)
3.25	Cyclades, Thera, Pilarou	Δαμάτριος και Κόρας (Hiller) or Ζεὺς Δαμάτριος (Kose) at the exterior below niche with bedding for stele, Ζεὺς Εὔπολις in the interior on the wall	IG XII 3, 418; Kose 1997, p. 74-77 (4th c) Kose 1997, p. 81
3.26	Kos, Aspripetra	3 Fragments of a marble stele with a name list found inside the cave at various places	Levi 1925/1926, pp. 252-253 (3rd c)
3.27	Rhodes, Lindos	Rock-cut inscription ἱερεὺς Ἀθάνας Λινδίας Λούκιος Αἴλιος Ἀγλώχαρτος in cave A, incised 1.6 m above the ground	Dyggve 1960, p. 447 (2nd c AD)
3.28	Crete, Melidoni	- Ἵπποναξ Διοκλεῖος Ἑρμᾶι εὐχάν (outside the cave) - Epigram from a woman called Artemis referring to the Tallaian mountains and Hermes (in the vestibule) - Pilgrims from Eleutherna (…Διοκλῆς …. πόλεως ὅλης τῆς Ἐλευθέρνης προσκυνήσαντες) (in the vestibule)	IC II. xxviii 1 (2nd/1st c) IC II. xxviii 2 (2nd c AD) IC II. xxviii 3; Tzifopoulos 2011 (2nd- 3rd c AD or later)

Table 3 continued.

of the more recent investigations there (Karali *et al.* 2006). Together with a maid and a cook, this Athenian woman visited the cave of Pan. While she rested in front of it, the preparation of the food and its cooking was made in the interior of the cave. A private offering, well enough mirrored in the famous depiction on a painted wooden plaque from the cave of Pitsa (540/530 BCE) (Brecoulaki *et al.* 2017). In this last instance, as in Vari, where the altar is also inside, the burnt offerings were dedicated by smaller, private groups. By contrast, on Mount Ida on Crete and at the Corycian Cave, the ritual was institutionalized: there were collective offerings and processions by larger groups, and the altars are situated in front of the cave. Maybe the same was the case on Mount Parnes, where the altar of Zeus Parnesios was situated some meters away from the cave and where Euthymios Mastrokostas (1983, p. 239) cautiously referred to the existence of a 'procession road'. Due to its situation in a present-day military zone, it is hard to approach this sanctuary and to check that opinion.

Even the depictions on the reliefs of Pan and the Nymphs show the altar (in these cases, mostly natural ones) at the mouth of a cave and not deep inside (Edwards 1985), although this impression might be due to the simplified two-dimensional depiction of the cave. Although it is not possible to establish a clear chronological development connecting altars inside the cave to altars outside, it can be said at least that there is no altar in front of a cave dating to the Bronze Age, the earliest one known being the altar in front of the Karabola Cave on Mount Parnes in Attica, dating to Archaic times. The date of the impressive rock altar in front of the Idaean Cave is not clear – it could even be as late as the probable Roman bases for bronze statues found on the terrace at the front (Sakellarakis and Sapouna-Sakellaraki 2013, pp. 122-123 Fig. 82), and would thus be part of a general refurbishment of that date. In general, a lot of archaeological material has been found either in front of the caves, *e.g.* at the cave of Pan above Daphni (Travlos 1937, p. 400), at the cave of the Nymphs at Pharsalos (Levi 1923/1924, p. 32; on the cave see now Wagman 2016) or in general in the outer areas of caves such as at Koudonotripa at Ambrakia (Petsas 1952, pp. 53-54). This gives one the impression that the area in front of the caves was important in the ritual, either in its preparation or the conduct itself. But this impression will need to be tested through a look at other mobile and immobile features of the caves.

Niches, cuttings

Again, mainly in the entrance areas of the caves, artificial cuttings for slabs or niches or even for plinths of statues can be found (Table 2.01. 2.03. 2.04. 2.05. 2.06. 2.08. 2.11. 2.12. 2.15. 2.16. 2.17. 2.18. 2.19. 2.29. 2.30 [unclear]. 2.33. 2.34. 2.42 and see earlier Sporn 2007, pp. 54-55; Sporn 2013, p. 206). In rare cases, they are located right above the entrance of the cave (Table 2.06. 2.12). These cuttings were used for various purposes (Table 1). If they are rectangular and elongated, they could have been used for setting up slabs with inscriptions or for votive reliefs which were thus standing upright (for actual finds see below and Table 2 and 3). The niches are mostly rectangular and limited in size and therefore intended for medium- to small-scale statuary. In only once instance, a rock-relief, depicting Pan, had been carved inside a niche and is still preserved (Thasos, Table 2.18). One of the niches at the Corycian Cave, the one above the entrance, has a semi-circular upper frame (Table 2.12). This shape is generally intended for statuary and the earliest clearly datable examples are Late Classical to Early Hellenistic (compare the niche for Herakles at Panopeus, dated the earliest to mid-4th century BCE, Camp *et al.* 1997, p. 262). Sometimes the niches were combined with a rectangular bedding for the setting up of a slab inside (*e.g.* Thera, Pilarou 2.34). Although mainly found close to the exterior of the caves´ entrances, in some cases the niches are set in the interior of the caves (Table 2.07. 2.08. 2.26. 2.35. 2.39). But even in these cases, they served the same purposes.

In some cases, there are rectangular or oval rock-cuttings horizontally placed and intended for setting up bases, possibly for statues (*e.g.* Table 2.07. 2.12. 2.13). In the case of the cave of Schober at Tithorea, where these cuttings are situated inside, both the larger rectangular cutting and the oval one seem to have intended for statues that were oriented towards the entrance and the first part of the cave. Here, the plane rock in front of and below the statues was possibly intended for setting up additional objects. In the Corycian Cave, all the cuttings were outside the cave.

Sometimes very small rounded or triangular cuttings can be discerned at eye level. By their locations at the height of 1.5-2 m they can sometimes justifiably be interpreted as cuttings for setting up torches (Table 2.21) or lamps (Table 2.14).

Trapezai, benches, water basins

Other worked areas in the caves include spaces with prepared surfaces, which can be either interpreted for the setting up of *votives*, such as *trapezai*, or for the accommodation of pilgrims to sit upon in the form of benches (Table 2.15, 2.16. 1.03. Achaia, Katarraktes; Table 2.20). Nevertheless, there is no clear evidence for their function, except in the case of the bench at the fountain house of Mieza (Table 1.15). Singular rock-cut seats in the manner of thrones are not yet testified in sacred caves (contrary to Wagman 2016, p. 29).

The presence of water is one of the most common features of sacred caves. Nevertheless, there are rarely constructions for the regulation or collection of the water, such as channels, rock-cut water basins or *perirranteria* (Table 1.03. 2.23. 3.03. 3.15), although natural cavities are of course common.

In front of the caves: plantations, terraces, paths, steps

At the exterior of the cave-mouths there were sometimes man-made areas (Table 1) such as a *kepos* planted by Pantalkes in front of the cave at Pharsala (Wagman 2016) or a *kepos* and an *oikos* at Vari (Schörner and Goette 2004). Artificial gardens and green spaces were common in public areas in ancient Greece (Neumann 2018).

Open spaces in front of caves were used or, in their absence, terraces installed deliberately: these were intended for the setting up of *votives* and the gathering of the community. An example is seen at the Ellinokamara cave on Kasos (Table 1.21 and Fig. 2). This cave is particularly interesting because it combines terraces in front of the entrance – three sloped terraces altogether – with divisions in the interior and also features a massive wall built in *isodomic* masonry at its opening – one of the few such examples in Greece. This wall and especially the two doors which could be locked make it difficult to believe that the cave was used only for cultic purposes – it recalls a treasury just as much, but maybe the publication of the finds can provide further information on this point. Walls closing the entrance of caves and giving only limited access through a door were quite uncommon (see Table 1.03. 1.18. 1.21).

Delineations of terraces outside the caves seem to be especially common in places, especially where the natural space is not sufficient, *i.e.* at the cave at Daphni (Table 1.08) and the cave of Herakles on the western slope of Mount Kynthos at Delos (Table 2.28), but also in front of artificial caves such as the cave of Demeter at Megara (Table 2.10).

The access to the caves was sometimes further facilitated by paths, both paved and merely delineated, but this seems to have been the case only in caves favoured with a larger number of visitors. A man-made path, partly stepped, is known at Delphi leading to the Corycian Cave, but another also exists from the ancient Polis Drakano to the Hieron cave on Ikaria (Table 2.12. 2.37). At the quarry of Penteli, a path paved with marble plaques probably gave access to the cave (Table 1.03). Whenever it was necessary, partly worked steps were made in order to facilitate the way into the caves. Examples are to be seen at Schisto, Lychnospilia, Vari, Tithorea, Pharsala, Boura, and two caves at Ikaria (Table 1.11. 2.05. 2.07. 2.13. 2.15. 2.19. 2.37. 2.38).

Inscriptions in and around caves

Both rock-cut and inscriptions incised on slabs and then inserted into the rock (Table 3) are known from the caves, mainly in their outer part, close to the entrance. Mostly, these inscriptions name the cave as sacred to a god (Table 3.08. 3.12. 3.16. 3.18. 3.19), or are votive inscriptions of one or more dedicants to the god or gods there worshipped (Table 3.09. 3.10. 3.11. 3.20), or they are related to dedications originally set up there (Table 3.25). Rarely are these rock-cut inscriptions as long

Figure 2. The Ellinokamara cave on Kasos with the large wall at the entrance (photo: D-DAI-ATH-Sporaden-0013).

and detailed as in the case of the Pharsala cave, where one of the inscriptions is quite extensive and refers in detail to the gods worshipped and the setting of the cave (Table 3.11). In some cases, the inscriptions are *leges sacrae*, *i.e.* they concern ritual regulations on the worship related to the cave (Table 3.02. 3.05. 3.24). The *lex sacra* from Marathon, Oinoe II (Table 3.02) is well studied – written on a slab, it was set up in front of the cave by the *ephebes* and refers to clothing restrictions. The one from the cave of Lympholeptos is a rock-cut inscription situated in the entrance area inside the cave, dating to 450-425 BCE (Table 3.04). It set out instructions to ensure the cleaning of the intestines outside and the washing away of the muck. Close to the Christos cave at Thera lies another rock cut inscription with a cult regulation whose content is not fully clear (Table 3.23). It seems to concern some offering in the month of Artemitios and a feast of Agoraia for the gods. In general, the cultic regulations seem to have been set up in the entrance area of the caves.

The inscription found in the Plutonion of Eleusis (Table 3.05) was again written on a separate slab. It does not refer to the cave itself, but to the refurbishment of some architectural features associated with the rest of the sanctuary (door frames, capitals, altar, *etc.*), so it is in a strict sense not referring to the cave itself.

Generally, the number of inscriptions in a cave are very restricted and only rarely do the amount to more than one or two at a time (exceptions: Table 3.01. 3.03. 3.04. 3.10. 3.15. 3.21). A very peculiar case is Chrysospilia on the island of Pholegandros (Table 3.21). This cave is situated right at the sea level, and although there seems to have been a short path leading from the island to the mouth of the cave, it was possibly more easily reached with a boat. There, more than 400 graffiti painted in a clayey colour have been found, dating from the 7th century BCE until

Byzantine times, but mainly dating to the 4th century BCE. The graffiti include mostly male names, sometimes connected with an *ethnikon*, which shows that the visitors came from the the Cyclades and around like Delos and Nisyros, but also from a bit more remote places in the Aegean, such as Euboia, Lesbos, Chios, Samos, Rhodes, Cos, Crete, Cyrenaika, and Cyprus. Since some of the names are accompanied by the specification *kalos*, they might have been connected with some homoerotic ritual (see Vassilopoulou 2018). The inscriptions are painted inside the cave, all over its walls. They still remain to be fully published. Only then can it be determined whether the cave was connected with a ritual in the worship of a god or whether it was related to a rather profane ritual.

In general, the inscriptions are visible, although sometimes written in small letters, but were not easily discernible from any distance. Quite often, they are located in the vicinity of the entrance, either flanking the entrance or the path leading to it (*e.g.* Table 3.10. 3.11). Sometimes they were even located rather high up, above the entrance, as in the example of the Leibithrian cave on Mount Helicon (Table 3.08), where the inscription Κορωνεία Νύμφη is carved at a 2 m height and right above the entrance (Vassilopoulou 2013). The *stelai* with their inscriptions seem to have been set up mostly close to the entrance, but this can mainly be deduced from the cuttings made in the rock intended for taking the slabs. Sometimes, however, the inscriptions are situated inside, as in the cave of Vari in Attica, where 12 inscriptions have been found (Table 4.04), or again at Kamares on Siphnos, with its inscription Νυφέων ἱερόν on a rock, the so-called altar, dating as early as the 6th/5th centuries BCE (Table 3.22), or even the 400 graffiti mainly of personal names, including *kalos*-inscriptions, in Chrysospilia on Pholegandros, mainly dating to the 4th century BCE (Table 3.21).

Conclusion

This paper set out to give an overview of the results of man-made activities in sacred caves in Greece. The first activity of man related to caves was to visit it and to consider it sacred. Why one cave was considered sacred and another was not isn't clear to us. Reasons can be multiple, starting from a particular position in the landscape and a visibility from a distance. This must have been the case at the Corycian cave above Delphi, which according to Pausanias (Paus. X 32, 2) was most worth seeing of all the caves he knew due to its size and the natural light inside. If a cave had a large mouth and was visible from a distance, it would easily attract people, as the Corycian cave, the Idaean cave, or Skoteino Pediados, to name just a few. In this way, the sublime could be one reason for regular visits followed by cultic activity (on the notion of sublime, see Williamson in this volume; in general for the use of natural elements in cult sites see Sporn 2015; Sporn 2019). Natural ornaments such as multiple or peculiar stalagmites, stalactites, and rock formations could have attracted visitors also. In some instances it becomes clear through the findspots of votive material that they seem to have been to focus of activity, as in the Arkoudospilia or Melidoni, both on Crete. Caves supplying natural water sources, mainly through active stalactites, especially seem to have attracted visitors. In remote places the existence of water was essential for every passer-by and could have been the starting point of regular visits and led to worship.

The caves were natural spots and as such mostly kept their natural lay-out. Although human alterations were limited in scale, most of the caves had experienced some form of intervention in one way or the other. These interferences aimed both at defining ritual space where necessary as well as facilitating the experiences of *adorants* and visitors. A specific distinction of ritual spaces was not always necessary, as the natural place itself was considered sacred, especially in the case of caves that attracted only limited numbers of visitors at a time. This seems to have been the case for many caves, although we have to take into account that they are mostly not or only partly excavated so we only know of a fraction of the material used and left. In historical times, the ritual sometimes involved larger gatherings, which were not limited to the inner areas of the cave but included the broader outer area and the space in front of the caves. Although the artificial terraces detected in front of various caves in Attica, such as Daphni, cannot yet be precisely dated due to lack of published material, they seem to be related rather to caves which yield material from Classical and Hellenistic times. This use of the areas in front of the caves might have been a result of larger communities participating in organized cults (with processions, feasts, ritual dancing, *etc.*), which aspect has been noticed for the Hellenistic period in general. Nevertheless, organized cults related to caves seem to have been limited in number. But even the intentions of these organized cults were mainly private ones, destined for the individual and not for the community or the state as a whole (see on the cults in the caves Sporn 2013, pp. 206-207 Fig. 12.1).

The caves with more considerable man-made structures – be they either outside the cave, with rock cut or built altars, rock cut or set-up inscriptions, terraces, *oikoi*, *stoai*, garden-like structures, walls or doors or both closing the cave, or inside the cave when divided into rooms by walls, with set-up marble statuary or reliefs, carved relief figures – in Greece are in general the exception to the rule. These features seem to have increased in broad terms from Classical times, being mainly developed in the Hellenistic years. The inscriptions related to caves – both rock cut and set up –date mainly from these periods, with Archaic and Classical ones being still very limited in number (Table 3). Sculptural finds – in general limited to Attica and some exceptions in major cave sites in other regions such as the Corycian cave above Delphi and Leibethrion in Boiotia – also date mainly from the 4th century BCE onwards. Access to the caves was mainly not restricted by blocking the entrance with a wall including a door. Again, the known exceptions (Table 1) – the large wall with the double door at Kasos (where the cultic use is disputed) or the marble door at the cave in the quarry of Penteli – can tentatively be dated due to various indications to Classical but mainly to Hellenistic times. Then, too, there existed a counter-balancing trend towards an artificially-built 'nature' combined with architecture that one found even in private houses, as the rock-cut dwellings on the Pnyx in Athens, on Crete, and the grottoes in Rhodes show (Neumann 2016). But this is another story.

References

Agouridis, C., Zygouri, G., Rontiri, V. 2006. Το σπήλαιο στη θέση «Κρούνια», in: Politismou, Y. and Thessalias, P. (ed.). Αρχαιολογικό έργο Θεσσαλίας και Στερεάς Ελλάδας, Πρακτικά επιστημονικής συνάντησης, 27 Φεβρουάριος-2 Μάρτιος 2003 I Βόλος. Volos: Ypourgeio Politismou, Panepistimio Thessalias, 249-262.

Amandry, P. (ed.) 1984. *L'antre Corycien II*, Bulletin de Correspondance Hellénique Suppl. 9. Paris: De Boccard.

Bakalakis, J. 1938. Ἀνασκαφὴ ἐν Καβάλᾳ καὶ τοῖς περίξ. Πρακτικά της εν Αθήναις Αρχαιολογικής Εταιρείας, 75-102.

Bakhuizen, S.C. (ed.) 1992. *A Greek city of the 4th century B.C.* Roma: L'Erma di Bretschneider.

Brecoulaki, H., Kavvadias, G., Kantarelou, V., Stephens, J., Stephens, A. 2017. Colour and painting technique on the Archaic panels from Pitsa, Corinthia, in: Mols, S.T.A.M. and Moormann, E.M. (eds.). *Context and meaning*, Proceedings of the Twelfth International Conference of the Association Internationale pour la peinture murale antique, 16-20 September 2013 Athens, Bulletin antieke beschaving Suppl. 31. Leuven: Peeters, 15-23.

Camp, J., Ierardi, M., McInerney, J. 1997. An Athenian dedication to Herakles at Panopeus. *Hesperia* 66, 261-269.

Clinton, K. 2005. *Eleusis: the inscriptions on stone*, The Archaeological Society of Athens Library 236. Athens: The Archaeological Society.

Connor, W.R. 1988. Seized by the nymphs: nympholepsy and symbolic expression in Classical Greece. *Classical Antiquity* 7, 155-189.

Deoudi, M. 2008. Ιθάκη: *Die Polis-Höhle, Odysseus und die Nymphen*. Thessaloniki: University Studio Press.

Doumas, C. 1963. Σέριφος, *Archaiologikon Deltion II. Chronika* 18, 284.

Dyggve, E. 1960. *Lindos: fouilles de l'Acropole 1902-1914 et 1952 III: Le sanctuaire d'Athana Lindia et l'architecture lindienne*. Berlin: de Gruyter and Gad.

Economakis, R. 2001. *Nisyros: history and architecture of an Aegean island*. Athens: Melissa.

Edwards, C.M. 1985. *Greek votive reliefs to Pan and the Nymphs*. Thesis (PhD). New York University.

Ekroth, G. 2003. Inventing Iphigeneia? On Euripides and the cultic construction of Brauron. *Kernos* 16, 59-101.

Empereur, J.-Y. 1984. Inscriptions, in: Amandry, P. (ed.). *L' Antre corycien II*, Bulletin de Correspondance Hellénique Suppl. 9. Paris: De Boccard, 339-346.

Faure, P. 1964. *Fonctions des cavernes crétoises*, Travaux et mémoires des anciens membres étrangers de l'école et de divers savants 14. Paris: École française d'Athènes.

Faure, P. 1996. *Ιερά Σπήλαια της Κρήτης*. Heraklion: Vikelaia Bibliotheke.

Gebhard, E.R. 2002. Caves and cults at the Isthmian sanctuary of Poseidon, in: Hägg, R. (ed.). *Peloponnesian sanctuaries and cults*, Proceedings of the Ninth International Symposium at the Swedish Institute at Athens, 11-13 June 1994, Skrivter utgivna av Svenska institutet i Athen 48. Stockholm: Svenska Institute i Athen, 63-74.

Giallelis, N. 1997. Die Kultstätte im Bezirk Christos, in: Hoepfner, W. (ed.). *Stadtgeschichte und Kultstätten am nördlichen Stadtrand*, Das dorische Thera 5, Schriften des Seminars für Klassische Archäologie der Freien Universität Berlin. Berlin: Mann, 47-72.

Hallof, K. 2004. Inschriften, in: Schörner, G. and Goette, H.R. (eds.). *Die Pan-Grotte von Vari*, Schriften zur historischen Landeskunde Griechenlands 1. Mainz am Rhein: von Zabern, 42-99.

Hellmann, M.-C. 2002. *Les principes de la construction*, L'architecture grecque 1. Paris: Librairie Générale Française.

Hoepfner, W. 1997. *Stadtgeschichte und Kultstätten am nördlichen Stadtrand*, Das dorische Thera 5 Berlin: Mann.

Iannoulidou, K.M. 1972. Ιστορικά σπήλαια της αρχαιότητας. *Platon* 24, 130-161.

Iannoulidou, K.M. 1974. Ιστορικά σπήλαια της αρχαιότητας III. *Platon* 26, 22-38.

Jameson, M.H. 1956. The vowing of a *Pelanos*. *American Journal of Philology* 77, 55-60.

Jost, M. 1985. *Sanctuaires et cultes d'Arcadie*, Études péloponnésiennes 9. Paris: Librairie Philosophique J. Vrin.

Kaltsas, N. 2002. *Εθνικό Αρχαιολογικό Μουσείο: Τα γλυπτά*. Athens: Kapon.

Karali, L., Mavridis, T., Kormazopoulou, L. 2006. Σπήλαιο Λεονταρίου Υμηττού Αττικής: Ένα πετρώδες και ορεινό περιβάλλον. *Archaiologika Analekta ex Athinon*, 31-44.

Katsaros, T.T. 2006. Σπήλαια της Ικαρίας με αρχαιολογικό ενδιαφέρον: Ικαριακά Σύμμεικτα. Athens: Etaireia Ikarikon meleton, 155-182.

Katsarou, S., Kormazopoulou, L., Laufer, E., Neumann, S., Sporn, K., Zygouri, I., in preparation. Surveying the caves above Tithorea in 2016, in: Sporn, K., Laufer, E., Farnoux, A. (eds.). *Ancient Phokis: new approaches to its history, archaeology, and topography*, Proceedings of the conference held at the German Archaeological

Institute at Athens, 30 March-1. April 2017 Athenaia. Athens: Deutsches Archäologisches Institut/École française d'Athènes.

Katsonopoulou, D. and Soter, S. 1993. Το μαντικό σπήλαιο του Βουραϊκού Ηρακλή. *Archaiologia* 47, 60-64.

Kormazopoulou, L., Zigouri I., Papathanasiou, B. 2006. Η ανασκαφή του σπηλαίου Νυμφών στην Λέχοβα Κορινθίας, in: Society of Peloponnesian Studies (ed.). Πρακτικά του Ź Διεθνούς Συνεδρίου Πελοποννησιακών Σπουδών, 11-17 Σεπτεμβρίου 2005 = *Acts of the seventh international congress of Peloponnesian Studies: Pyrgos, Gastouni,* Amaliada 11-17 September 2005 Peloponnēsiaka, Parartēma 27. Athenes: Εταιρεία Πελοποννησιακών Σπουδών, 97-112.

Kose, A. 1997. Die Höhle Pilarou beim Felsheiligtum Christos, in: Hoepfner, W. (ed.). *Stadtgeschichte und Kultstätten am nördlichen Stadtrand,* Das dorische Thera 5, Schriften des Seminars für Klassische Archäologie der Freien Universität Berlin. Berlin: Mann, 73-149.

Kusch, H. 1999. Die 'Hermes-Höhle': Eine Kultstätte am Ziria, in: Tausend, K. (ed.). *Pheneos und Lousoi: Untersuchungen zur Geschichte und Topographie Nordostarkadiens.* Frankfurt: Lang, 253-262.

Levi, D. 1923/1924. L'antro delle ninfe e di Pan a Farsalo in Tessaglia. *Annuario della R. Scuola Archeologica di Atene e delle Missioni Italiane in Oriente* 6/7, 27-42.

Levi, D. 1925/1926. La Grotta di Aspripetra di Coo. *Annuario della R. Scuola Archeologica di Atene e delle Missioni Italiane in Oriente* 8/9, 235-311.

Lohmann, H. 1993. *Atene: Forschungen zur Siedlungs- und Wirtschaftsstruktur des klassischen Attika.* Köln: Böhlau.

Lupu, E. 2001. The sacred law from the cave of Marathon (SEG XXXVI 267). *Zeitschrift für Papyrologie und Epigraphik* 137, 119-124.

Mastrokostas, E. 1983. Αλάβαστρα του 700 π.Χ. εκ της ανασκαφής του βωμού του Διός επί της κορυφής της Πάρνηθος. *Annuario della Scuola Italiana di Atene* 61, N.S. 65, 339-344.

Mavridis, F. and Kormazopoulou, L. 2007/2008. Ανώνυμο σπήλαιο Σχιστού Κερατσινίου: Η ανασκαφή των ετών 2006-2007. *Archaiologika Analekta ex Athinon* 40/41, 13-24.

Mavridis, F., Kormazopoulou, L., Papadea, A., Apostolikas, O., Yamagushi, D., Tankosic, Z., Kotzamani, G., Trantalidou, K., Karkanas, P., Maniatis, Y., Papagianni, K., Lampropoulos, D. 2013. Anonymous cave of Schisto at Keratsini, Attika: a preliminary report on a diachronic cave occupation from the Pleistocene/Holocene transition to the Byzantine Times, in: Mavridis, F. and Jensen, J.T. (eds.). *Stable places and changing perceptions: cave archaeology in Greece,* BAR international series 2558. Oxford: Archaeopress, 248-284.

Mylonopoulos, J. 2003. Πελοποννῆσος οἰκητῆριον Ποσειδώνος – *Heiligtümer und Kulte des Poseidon auf der Peloponnes,* Kernos Suppl. 13. Liège: Centre international d'Étude de la religion grecque antique.

Mylonopoulos, J. 2016. Terracotta figurines from Ithaca: local production and imported ware, in: Muller, A., Lafli, E., Huysecom-Haxhi, S. (eds.). *Figurines de terre-cuite en Méditerranée grecque et romaine,* Bulletin de Correspondance Hellénique Suppl. 54. Paris: Boccard, 239-251.

Neumann, S. 2016. *Grotten in der hellenistischen Wohnarchitektur,* Marburger Beiträge zur Archäologie 4. Marburg: Seminar der Philipps-Universität.

Neumann, S. 2018. Öffentliches Grün in griechischen Städten, in: Schimpf, F., Berrens, D., Hillenbrand, K., Brandes, T., Schidlo, C. (eds.). *Naturvorstellungen im Altertum: Schilderungen und Darstellungen von Natur im Alten Orient und in der griechischen Antike.* Oxford: Archaeopress, 308-311.

Nulton, P.E. 2003. *The Sanctuary of Apollo Hypoakraios and Imperial Athens.* Providence, Rhode Island: Brown University.

Owen, S. 2000. New light on Thracian Thasos: a reinterpretation of the cave of Pan. *Journal of Hellenic Studies* 120, 139-143.

Palaiokrassa-Kopitsa, L. and Vivliodetis, E. 2015. The sanctuaries of Artemis Mounichia and Zeus Parnessios: their relation to the religious and social life in the Athenian city-state until the end of the 7th century B.C, in: Vlachou, V. (ed.). *Pots, workshops and Early Iron Age society: function and role of ceramics in Early Greece*, Proceedings of the International Symposium held at the Université libre de Bruxelles, 14-16 November 2013, Études d'archéologie 8. Bruxelles: CReA-Patrimoine, 155-180.

Peek, W. 1942. Attische Inschriften. *Mitteilungen des Deutschen Archäologischen Instituts: Abteilung Athen* 67, 1-217.

Petsas, P. 1952. Εἰδήσεις ἐκ τῆς 10ης ἀρχαιολογικῆς περιφερείας (Ἠπείρου). *Archaiologike Ephemeris Chronika*, 1-15.

Pingiatoglou, S. 1981. *Eileithyia*. Tübingen: Königshausen und Neumann.

Prent, M. 2005. *Cretan sanctuaries and cults: continuity and change from Late Minoan IIIC to the Archaic Period*, Religions in the Graeco-Roman World 154. Leiden: Brill.

Rhomaios, K. 1918. Εὑρήματα ἀνασκαφῆς τοῦ ἐπὶ τοῦ Πάρνηθος ἄντρου. *Archaiologike Ephimeris*, 99-158.

Rhomiopoulou, K. 1999. *Levkadia: Das antike Mieza*. Athens: Ypourgeio Politismou.

Rœbuck, C. 1951. *Corinth XIV: The Asclepieion and Lerna*. Princeton: The American School of Classical Studies at Athens.

Ross, L. 1843. *Reisen auf den griechischen Inseln des ägäischen Meeres 1*. Stuttgart: Cotta.

Rutkowski, B. and Nowicki, K. 1996. *The Psychro cave and other sacred grottoes in Crete*, Studies and Monographs in Mediterranean Archaeology and Civilisation Series 2 (1). Warsaw: Art and Archaeology.

Sakellarakis, G. and Sapouna-Sakellaraki, E. 2013. Το Ιδαίο άντρο: Ιερό και μαντείο, Βιβλιοθήκη της εν Αθηναις Αρχαιολογικής Εταιρείας 279. Athens: Archaiologike Etaireia.

Sakellarakis, I. 2006. Ελληνοκαμάρα Κάσου, in: Archaiologiko Institouto Aigiakon Spoudon, (ed.). *XARIS XAIRE: Μελέτες στη μνήμη της Χάρης Κάντζια 2*. Rhodes: Ypourgeio Politismou. Archaiologiko Institouto Aigiakon Spoudon, 333-345.

Salviat, F. and Bernard, P. 1967. Inscriptions de Thasos. *Bulletin de Correspondance Hellénique* 91, 578-621.

Sampson, A. 2000. Σκόπελος: Ιστορική και γεωγραφική αφήγηση. Skopelos: Σκληρό εξώφυλλο.

Schörner, G. and Goette, H.R. 2004. *Die Pan-Grotte von Vari*, Schriften zur historischen Landeskunde Griechenlands 1. Mainz: Zabern.

Skias, A. 1918. Τὸ παρὰ τὴν Φυλὴν ἄντρον τοῦ Πανὸς κατὰ τας ἀνασκαφὰς τῶν ἐτῶν 1900 καὶ 1901, *Archaiologike Ephemeris 1918*, 1-28.

Spathi, M.G. 2013. The cave of the Nymphs at Keratsini, Attica: a new location for the popular female cult of the classical period and some intriguing finds, in: Sioubara, E. and Psaroudakis, K. (eds.). *Θεμέλιον: 24 μελέτες για τον Δάσκαλο Πέτρο Θέμελη*. Athens: Frangeskakis, 395-415.

Sporn, K. 2002. *Heiligtümer und Kulte Kretas in klassischer und hellenistischer Zeit*, Studien zu antiken Heiligtümern 3. Heidelberg: Archäologie und Geschichte.

Sporn, K. 2007. Höhlenheiligtümer in Griechenland, in: Frevel, C. and von Hesberg, H. (eds.). *Kult und Kommunikation: Medien in Heiligtümern der Antike*, Schriften des Lehr- und Forschungszentrums für die antiken Kulturen des Mittelmeerraumes 4. Wiesbaden: Reichert, 39-62.

Sporn, K. 2010. Espace naturel et paysages religieux: le cas des grottes dans le monde grec, in: Scheid, J. and de Polignac, F. (eds.). *Qu'est-ce qu'un «paysage religieux»?*:

représentations cultuelles de l'espace dans les sociétés anciennes, Revue de l'histoire des religions 4. Paris: Presses Universitaires de France, 553-572.

Sporn, K. 2013. Mapping Greek sacred caves: sources, features, cults, in: Mavridis, F. and Jensen, J.T. (eds.). *Stable places and changing perceptions: cave archaeology in Greece*, BAR international series 2558. Oxford: Archaeopress, 202-216.

Sporn, K. 2015. Natur – Kult – Raum: Eine Einführung in Methode und Inhalt, *in*: Sporn, K., Ladstätter, S., Kerschner, M. (eds.). *Natur – Kult – Raum*, Akten des Internationalen Kolloquiums, 20.-22. Jänner 2012 Paris Lodron-Universität Salzburg, Sonderschriften des Österreichischen Archäologischen Instituts 51. Wien: Österreichisches Archäologisches Institut, 339-356.

Sporn, K. 2019. Natural features in Greek cult places: the case of Athens, in: Scheer, T. (ed.). *Natur – Mythos – Religion im antiken Griechenland/Nature – Myth – Religion in Ancient Greece*, Potsdamer Altertumswissenschaftliche Beiträge 67. Stuttgart: Franz Steiner, 29-48.

Stampolidis, N. and Kotsonas, A. 2013. Cretan cave sanctuaries of the Early Iron Age to the Roman Period, in: Mavridis, F. and Jensen, J.T. (eds.). *Stable places and changing perceptions: cave archaeology in Greece*, BAR international series 2558. Oxford: Archaeopress, 188-200.

La Torre, G.F. 1992/1993. La grotta di Mourmouni: una nota sulla topografia di Megara Nisea. *Annuario della Scuola Archeologica di Atene* 70, 355-363.

Travlos, I. 1937. Σπηλαίον τοῦ Πανὸς παρὰ το Δαφνὶ. *Archaiologike Ephemeris*, 391-408.

Tyree, L. 1974. *Cretan sacred caves: archaeological evidence*. Thesis (PhD). University of Missouri, Columbia.

Tyree, L. 2013. Defining Bronze Age ritual caves in Crete, in: Mavridis, F. and Jensen, J.T. (eds.). *Stable places and changing perceptions: cave archaeology in Greece*, BAR international series 2558. Oxford: Archaeopress, 176-187.

Tyree, L., McCoy, F.W., Kanta, A., Sphakianakis, D., Stamos, A., Aretaki, K., Kamilaki, E. 2005/06. Interferences for use of Skoteino Cave during the Bronze Age and later based on a spelological and environmental study at Skoteino Cave, Crete. *Aegean Archaeology* 8, 51-63.

Tzedakis, G. and Gavrilaki, I. 1995. Η ανασκαφή στο Σπήλαιο Μελιδονίου, in: Πεπραγμέγνα του 7ου Διεθνούς Κρητολογικού Συνεδρίου 1.2. Rethymnon: Papadogiannakis, 887-894.

Tzifopoulos, Y.Z. 2011. Eleuthernean pilgrims inside the Melidoni cave (Tallaeum antrum), in: Palagia, O. and Goette, H.-R. (eds.). *Sailing to Classical Greece: papers on Greek art, archaeology, and epigraphy, presented to Petros Themelis*. Oxford: Archaeopress, 79-84.

Vanderpool, E. 1967. Pan in Paiania: a note on lines 407-409 of Menander's Dyskolos. *American Journal of Archaeology* 71, 309-311.

Vassilopoulou, V. 2013. Prehistoric use and ancient ritual worship at the cave of Hagia Triada on Helikon, in: Mavridis, F. and Jensen, J.T. (eds.). *Stable places and changing perceptions: cave archaeology in Greece*, BAR international series 2558. Oxford: Archaeopress, 319-328.

Vassilopoulou, V. 2016. Aphrodite figurines from the sanctuary of `Nymph Koronia´ at Mount Helicon, in: Muller, A., Lafli, E., Huysecom-Haxhi, S. (eds.). *Figurines de terre-cuite en Méditerranée grecque et romaine*, Bulletin de Correspondance Hellénique Suppl. 54. Paris: Boccard, 473-480.

Vassilopoulou, V. 2018. The Island of Pholegandros and the graffitti of Chryssospilia cave, in: Angliker, E., and Tully, J. (eds.). *Cycladic archaeology and research: new approaches and discoveries*. Oxford: Archaeopress, 339-345.

Wace, A.J.B. and Thompson, M.S. 1908-1909. A cave of the Nymphs on Mount Ossa. *Annual of the British School at Athens* 15, 243-247.

Wagman, R.S. 2016. *The Cave of the Nymphs at Pharsalus: studies on a Thessalian country shrine,* Brill Studies in Greek and Roman Epigraphy 6. Leiden: Brill.

Wickens, J.M. 1986. *The archaeology and history of cave use in Attica, Greece from prehistoric through late Roman times.* Thesis (PhD). Indiana University.

Wickens, J. 2013. Non-ritual use of caves in the Classical and Late Roman Periods: the Case of Attica, in: Mavridis, F. and Jensen, J.T. (eds.). *Stable places and changing perceptions: cave archaeology in Greece*, BAR international series 2558. Oxford: Archaeopress, 239-246.

Wilhelm, A. 1924. Ἑλληνικῶν ἐπιγραμμάτων ἑξάς. *Archaiologike Ephemeris*, 50-62.

Wilhelm, A. 1929. Inschriften von der Grotte des Pan und der Nymphen bei Phyle. *Jahreshefte des Österreichischen Archäologischen Instituts in Wien* 25, 54-69.

Zambiti, A. 2013. Schisto Cave at Keratsini (Attika): The pottery from Classical through Roman Times, in: Mavridis, F. and Jensen, J.T. (eds.). *Stable places and changing perceptions: cave archaeology in Greece,* BAR international series 2558. Oxford: Archaeopress, 306-313.

Zapheiropoulos, N. 1952. Ανασκαφικαί έρευναι εις περιφέρειαν Φαρών Αχαΐας. *Πρακτικά της εν Αθήναις Αρχαιολογικής Εταιρείας,* 396-412.

Zoridis, P. 1977. Η σπηλιά των Νυμφών της Πεντέλης. *Archaiologike Ephimeris 1977,* Chron, 4-11.

Notes on contributor

Katja Sporn - German Archaeological Institute, Athens (present). Studies of Classical Archaeology, Philosophy and Ancient History at Heidelberg, Athens and London; PhD Heidelberg 1998; Habilitation Freiburg 2009; positions at the German Archaeological Institute at Athens, the Universities of Cologne, Freiburg and Salzburg; Director of the German Archaeology Institute at Athens 2014-; Director of the excavations at Kalapodi, 2014-; Co-Director of the Landscape Archaeological Project at the Kephissos Valley 2018-.

Part 3
Beyond sanctuaries: the agora

The Upper Agora at Ephesos in Hellenistic Times: in Search of the 'State Market'

(in honour of Wilhelm Alzinger, 1918-1998, on his centenary)

Dirk Steuernagel

Abstract

The chapter addresses the concept of 'state market' in relation to the archaeological evidence at Ephesos. A short reconsideration of the Aristotelian background of the notion shows that it designated a public space subject to rather strict social control and regulations of conduct. Against this background, the layout and possible functions of the Upper Agora at Ephesos during Hellenistic times are discussed. For that purpose, reference is made to some new insights into the Hellenistic appearance of the square as conveyed by recent fieldwork.

Keywords: Ephesos, Upper Agora, Free Agora (Aristoteles), Processions

Introduction: the two *agorai* of Ephesos

The Upper Agora is one out of two major public squares within the city of Ephesos (İzmir, Turkey), beside the Lower Agora (Fig. 1, nos. 2. 4). The latter was largely uncovered during the first decade of the 20th century by excavations under the direction of the architect Wilhelm Wilberg. Renewed field activities went on from 1977 to 2001. Results from the two most intensive research periods have been submitted in two monographs (Wilberg and Keil 1923; Scherrer and Trinkl 2006). Although some marginal buildings were already known, the Upper Agora became subject to systematic excavations only in the 1960s. It is located in the inner part of ancient Ephesos, at a distance of about 500 m from one inland-oriented city-gate, the Magnesian gate. Both *agorai* are connected by an arterial road cutting obliquely through the city's grid-plan, the so-called 'Kuretes Street' (Fig. 1, no. 3; the ancient name might have been *embolos*). To date, no monographic publication on the Upper Agora has appeared, but two of the main public buildings on the northern fringe of the area were presented in single volumes of the 'Forschungen in Ephesos' series by Martin Steskal (2010) and Lionel Bier (2011) respectively. The grand

Universität Regensburg
Universitätsstraße 31
93053 Regensburg
Germany
dirk.steuernagel@psk.uni-regensburg.de

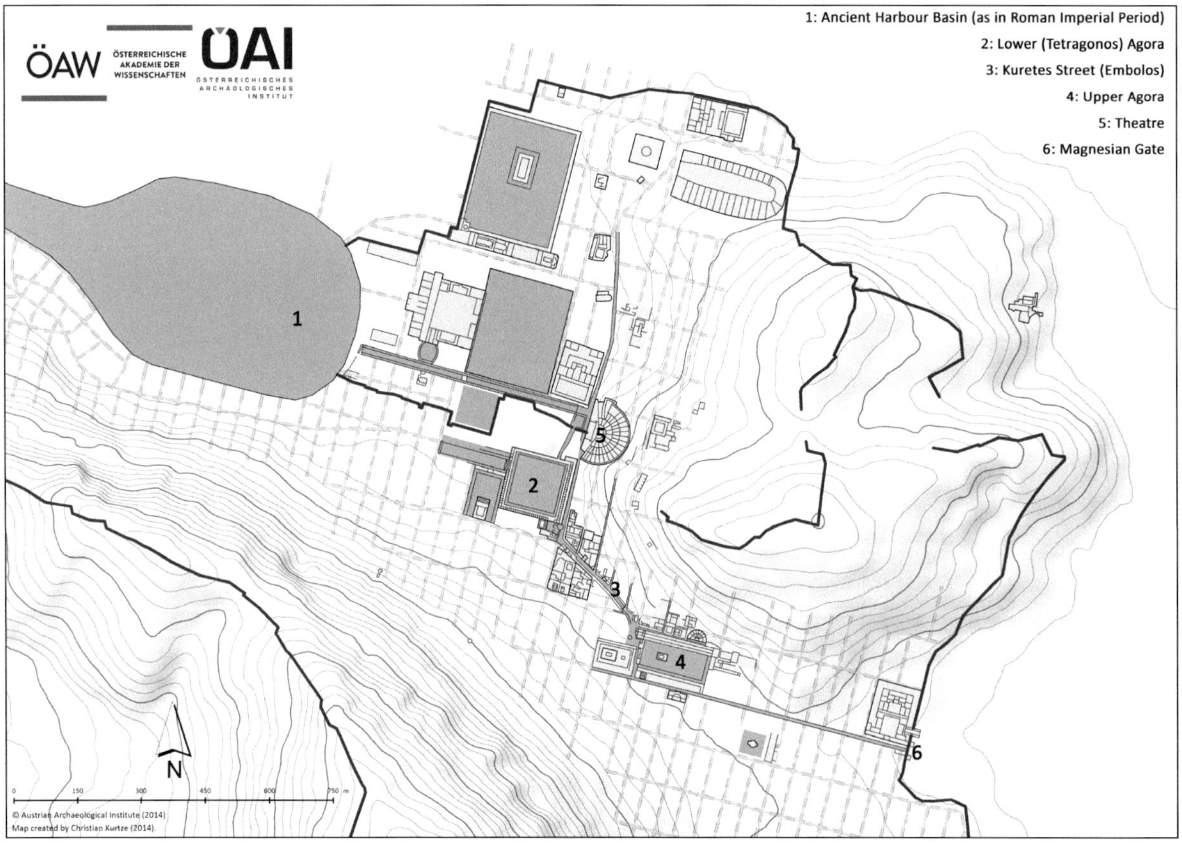

Figure 1. Ephesos. General plan of the ancient city (plan: © ÖAW-ÖAI, Christian Kurtze, 2014; labelling by Dirk Steuernagel).

Basilika Stoa, which separates those buildings from the square, was presented in smaller format by Elisabeth Fossel-Peschl (1982). As for the rest, one has to rely on a number of preliminary publications, mainly by Wilhelm Alzinger (*e.g.* Alzinger 1972-1975; cf. Lang-Auinger 2007). In 2014, a new research project on the Upper Agora started. It was funded by DFG and generously sustained by the Austrian Archaeological Institute (ÖAI), under the direction of Sabine Ladstätter. The research team, headed by Thekla Schulz-Brize (TU Berlin) and the author, has undertaken archive studies at the ÖAI head-office at Vienna as well as fieldwork at Ephesos, including stratigraphic sondages and surveys of some more important building structures (cf. Steuernagel 2020). Some insights gained during these activities will be mentioned in this article. However, given the provisional state of the project, in expectation of the final appraisal and publication of all relevant results,[1] I will confine myself to a kind of preview. Moreover, my main issue here is different, and it is twofold. Firstly, I will go briefly into the concept of the 'state' or 'civic' *agora* and its relevance for historical and archaeological studies. Secondly, some observations will be made on the probable state of the Ephesian Upper Agora during the Hellenistic period, reassessing whether its architectural layout gives any clue for the function of the square as a 'state *agora*'.

The distinction between a 'commercial *agora*' and a 'civic *agora*', as outlined in ancient philosophical writings on political theory, which we will discuss shortly, was introduced to the archaeology of ancient Ephesos already by Edward Falkener, in his pioneer-work on 'Ephesus and the Temple of Diana' (1862, pp. 61-71). This is most interesting, inasmuch as none of the city's public squares had been excavated before then. Nevertheless, Falkener (1862) was able to identify one *agora* – or at least the

1 Two PhD-theses are under way in the context of the project, one by Stefan Langer (Classical Archaeology, University of Regensburg), and the other by Daniel Musall (Historical Building Research, TU Berlin).

location of the Lower Agora – correctly; in his view, this was the 'commercial *agora*' (or '*agora venalis*', as he puts it). On the other hand, he mistook the portico-lined square further north for the *agora civilis* – actually it was a training ground in connection to the harbour gymnasium and today it is commonly known under the name of *Verulanushallen*. Later, the discussion was fuelled by findings of inscriptions which seem to attest the existence of different *agorai* at Ephesos (cf. Alzinger 1972-1975, col. 241). One of the denominations, 'τετράγωνος ἀγορά', *i.e.* 'Quadrangular Agora' (IEph 3005; 4123), refers without doubt to the Lower Agora, as the finding spot of one inscription and the coincidence between name and appearance of the square clearly show. More problematic is the mentioning of a 'Western Agora' (δυτική ἀγορά; IEph 1381). Since the respective inscription is only badly preserved and because it dates to the first years of the city newly founded by Lysimachos, we cannot be sure if 'Western Agora' is another labelling for the same site later known as *tetragonos agora* or if one has to look for another square elsewhere (Keil 1943, p. 101 no. 1; Scherrer and Trinkl 2006, p. 11; Groh 2006, p. 68; Ladstätter 2016, p. 247).[2] In any case, it is inconceivable that 'Western Agora' was the name for the Upper Agora, as the latter is situated in the eastern part of the city. Thus, to date the ancient denomination of the Upper Agora remains unknown, also because no other inscription has been found that mentions it explicitly and unambiguously (cf. Pont 2010, p. 74).

Nevertheless, Alzinger from the beginning gave the name of 'State Market' to that area in the upper part of the city which the Austrian excavations touched for the first time in 1960 (cf. Eichler 1962, p. 42; Eichler 1965, p. 96).[3] He reasoned that a wide plain area immediately south of the *prytaneion*, the seat of the communal government discovered just a few years earlier, could not have been anything else than 'the actual city centre' ('*das eigentliche Zentrum der Stadt*': Alzinger 1972-1975, col. 241). And Alzinger concluded, referring to Aristoteles (*ibid.*):

> '*Es muß zwei Marktplätze gegeben haben, wie dies schon Aristoteles für eine anständige Stadt fordert, eine* ἐλευθέρα ἀγορά, *die frei von Schmutz und Geschrei der feilschenden Händler sein sollte, der hohen Politik vorbehalten, sowie eine* ἀγορὰ τῶν ὠνίων, *auf der hauptsächlich Verkaufsbuden untergebracht waren.*'

The notion of 'Free Agora' in Greek philosophical writings

As already Alzinger's paraphrase reveals, 'state market' or 'free *agora*' are not purely descriptive terms for outlining the functional contours of a specific urban space; in fact, these notions are ethically charged to a high degree, implying certain behavioural patterns while excluding others, and are even socially discriminatory. The normative character becomes even more evident when we quote Aristoteles somewhat extensively. According to the philosopher, in the exemplary city, just beneath its sacred centre, an agora has to be established,

> '*such as that which the Thessalians call the 'freeman's agora'* (ἐλευθέρα ἀγορά*); from this all trade should be excluded, and no artisan, farmer, or any such person allowed to enter, unless he be summoned by the magistrates. It would be a pleasing*

2 Scherrer (2001, p. 68; Scherrer and Trinkl 2006, pp. 43. 46) supposes that the 'Western Agora' 'supported the political institutions' in the early period of the Lysimacheian city and tentatively locates it west of the Lower Agora; however, geophysical prospections in this area have not revealed clear traces of such a structure, cf. Ladstätter 2014, p. 28.

3 Excavation diary, entry September 4, 1960: 'Südlich in Höhe des Prytaneions zeigt sich im Gelände ein ebener im Süden durch eine Geländestufe abgeschlossener Platz. Alzinger vermutet hier die Agora (zweite).'

> *use of the place, if the gymnastic exercises of the elder men were performed there. For in a noble practice different ages should be separated, and some of the magistrates should stay with the boys, while the grown-up men remain with the magistrates; for the presence of the magistrates is the best mode of inspiring true modesty and ingenuous fear. There should also be a traders' agora (τῶν ὠνίων ἀγορά), distinct and apart from the other, in a situation which is convenient for the reception of goods both by sea and land. [...] The magistrates who deal with contracts, indictments, summonses, and the like, and those who have the care of the agora and of the city respectively, ought to be established near an agora and some public place of meeting; the neighbourhood of the traders' agora (ἀναγκαία ἀγορά) will be a suitable spot; the upper agora (ἄνω ἀγορά) we devote to the life of leisure, the other is intended for the necessities of trade.'* (Aristot. Pol. 7, 12 = 1331 a 30-1331 b 13; transl. by S. Everson, Cambridge 1988, cf. Martin 1951, pp. 306-307; Dickenson 2017, pp. 54-55)

What might seem strange at first glance is the exclusion of certain social groups from the *'free'* or *'freeman's agora'*, namely artisans and farmers and, at least implicitly, traders. Why this is so, becomes clear when one adduces other passages from the same work. Especially in the sixth book of the *Politica*, Aristoteles declares the necessary qualifications for what he classifies the *'best form of democracy'*. In his view, the state should be based on agriculture and on peasantry since the people living and working in the countryside *'have no leisure, and therefore do not often attend the assembly ...'* On the contrary, the humble classes of the urban population – artisans, traders and labourers – *'because they are continually hanging around in the city and in the agora, can easily hold an assembly'*[4] (Aristot. Pol. 6, 4 = 1318 b 7-1319 a 34; cf. Schwaabe 2012, pp. 167-170). These groups are estimated as *'inferior'* in relation to the rural population because their professions would not follow morality. But even the farmers are not considered citizens in the proper sense (Schütrumpf 2005, p. 434, *ad locum*). The crucial point of our concern is that Aristoteles generally tends to rule out uncontrolled assemblies, deliberations, and decisions organised by the common people. Instead, he recommends relying on the expertise of a political upper class: the ἐπιεικεῖς, as he calls them, *i.e.* the 'decent' men (cf. Lane 2013, esp. pp. 249. 266).

In practice, a 'rule of the ἐπιεικεῖς' could turn out to be a *'régime des notables'*, which has been described as a common Hellenistic form of civic government, especially for the later Hellenistic period, by Philippe Gauthier (1985, esp. pp. 67-68. 72-73) and others. This is not the place to enlarge upon the topic of democratic participation and oligarchic tendencies in *poleis* subdued to monarchic domination, which has been debated intensively over the last years (cf. *e.g.* Grieb 2008; Mann and Scholz 2012). Nor will I, for lack of personal competence, go into the type of constitution considered best by Aristoteles. Suffice it to say, that the constitutional model he proposes combines democratic and oligarchic elements (cf. *e.g.* Bien 1985, pp. 323-328; Schwaabe 2012). Thessaly, from where Aristoteles claims to have drawn his model of the *'free agora'*, certainly had an oligarchic political order (cf. Martin 1951, pp. 296-297). The same holds true for Persia as portrayed by another author of the 4th century BCE, Xenophon, in his *Cyropaedia*. Actually, he does not seem to describe a monarchy, but rather a republic in the Spartan style (Nadon 2001, pp. 29-42). As a central location of the public education system, Xenophon mentions an 'ἐλευθέρα ἀγορά'; it was situated close to the royal palace and enclosed other governmental buildings. On the other hand, all kind of wares and the traders,

4 The last quotation is given in my own translation; the second part of the phrase, one could also translate as *'can easily attend an assembly'* (Greek ἐκκλησιάζει).

> *'their cries and their vulgarities are banished from there to another place, in order that their tumult may not intrude into the decent behaviour of the educated.'* (Xen. Cyr. 1, 2, 3; transl. by Dirk Steuernagel)

The last words, in Greek 'πεπαιδευμένων εὐκοσμία', make sufficiently clear that Xenophon also defines his 'free *agora*' as a place controlled by a social and cultural élite that imposes certain standards of behaviour. 'Free' in this context refers not so much to politically free citizens of an autonomous *polis* but to a socially prominent group of 'peers' or 'gentlemen'. This might correspond to Aristoteles's use of the term, given his presentation of the *'free agora'* as a spot for leisure-time activities. Even the educational aspect appears at least implicitly in Aristoteles's description of a *'free agora'* from his alluding to the *'presence of the magistrates'* as *'the best mode of inspiring true modesty and ingenuous fear'*.

To sum up, the 'state', 'civil' or 'free *agora*', in accordance with ancient philosophical and historical writings, can be defined as a public space that is subject to rather strict regulations, fencing off economic activities as well as certain social groups, thus avoiding spontaneous and unrestrained popular action in the field of politics. If the 'state *agora*' was meant to serve predominantly ceremonial acts or if it should also foster political decision-making processes within elitist circles, as Hans Lauter (1986, p. 79) has supposed, remains an open question.

The Upper Agora at Ephesos in its Hellenistic state

Starting from these considerations, I would like to ask whether the Upper Agora at Ephesos, in its Hellenistic phase, meets the requirements of a thus-defined 'state *agora*', particularly whether a presence of civic institutions is attested for that period. Moreover, it will be questioned if the architectural design was apt for eliciting or encouraging certain behavioural modes. Therefore, it is necessary to outline briefly the shape and endowment of the square between the 3rd and 1st centuries BCE. Some first remarks on the other, the Lower or 'Tetragonos' Agora, will help to draw contours more sharply.

The area of the Lower Agora was located near the harbour and at a crossing point of different pre-Hellenistic streets (Fig. 1, no. 2) (Scherrer and Trinkl 2006, p. 55). It was prepared by levelling works already in the first years of the Lysimacheian foundation. About 270/60 BCE the first building was erected, which already betrays an economic function: a double row of internally connected chambers, probably storerooms or shops (Scherrer and Trinkl 2006, p. 15: '*Magazinbau*'), oriented both to the east, *i.e.* onto the supposed open space of the *agora*, and to the west, in direction of the harbour zone. Still in the course of the 3rd century, a second building of similar shape was constructed on the same north-south axis, with chambers opening to its east and north sides. The eastern façade was screened by a portico and a corresponding element was added to the earlier structure. A street leading to the harbour passed north of the two buildings. For the late Hellenistic period, a court-like enclosing of the Lower Agora on four sides through *stoai* seems probable, even if the archaeological evidence is rather meagre (Scherrer and Trinkl 2006, pp. 18-19; cf. Sielhorst 2015, p. 123). Also in the late Hellenistic period, between 60 and 50 BCE, the supervising and beneficial activity of an *agoranomos* is firstly attested in relation to the Lower Agora (IEph 3004; cf. Kirbihler 2016, p. 116). There are many more inscriptions mentioning *agoranomoi* from the Roman Imperial period (1st to 3rd century AD: IEph 930a-939a; 3011-3018), and the association of Italo-Roman traders, the *conventus civium Romanorum qui Asiae negotiantur*, seems to have operated business here at least between the proto-Augustan age and the reign

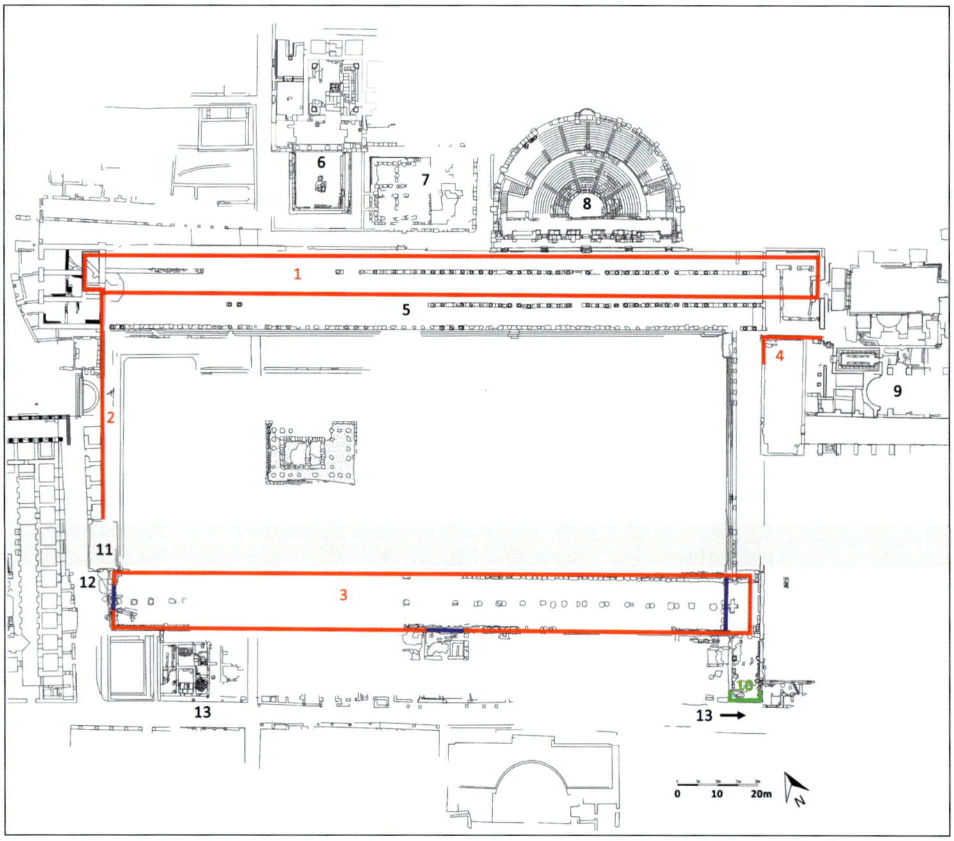

Ephesos, Upper Agora
State plan (as in 2018)

Elaboration by Stefan Langer and Dirk Steuernagel, based on digital city map (ÖAW-ÖAI)

Red: outlines of structures of 2nd century BCE-date
Green: secondarily added during 1st century BCE
Blue: secondarily created sidewall and entrances to the South Stoa
Shaded grey: possible course of street before c. 100 BC

1) Hellenistic North Stoa
2) Hellenistic western retaining wall
3) Hellenistic South Stoa
4) Hellenistic North-East-Building
5) Basilike Stoa
6) Prytaneion
7) so-called Rhodian Peristyle
8) Bouleuterion
9) Thermae
10) Propylon
11) so-called Sockelbau A
12) Domitian's Lane
13) South Street (arrow pointing in direction of Magnesian Gate)

Figure 2. Ephesos, Upper Agora. State plan with Hellenistic buildings (plan based on digital city plan [ÖAI/ÖAW], elaboration by Stefan Langer and Dirk Steuernagel, 2019).

of Claudius (IEph 409, 658, 3019; cf. Scherrer 2007, pp. 63-65). A '*stoa of the moneychangers*' is attested at the end of the 1st century AD (IEph 3065). Thus, the Lower Agora of Ephesos seems to fit very well the image of an 'ἀναγκαία ἀγορά' as characterised by Aristoteles. Actually, many things are corresponding, from the topographical situation and the architecture to the presence of traders and magistrates who were concerned with matters of daily life. Even a '*public place of meeting*', as the philosopher had demanded, was nearby: the theatre, built not before the second quarter of the 2nd century BCE, but scheduled perhaps since the times of Lysimachos (Fig. 1, no. 5; Hofbauer *et al.* 2017, pp. 513-514). This neighbourhood may also explain why there are such numerous bases of honorary monuments for emperors, Roman officials, and local dignitaries found in the Lower Agora (cf. Wilberg and Keil 1923, pp. 107-109).

The mix of economic and political aspects attested for the Lower Agora in Roman Imperial times leaves open the question if the city planners of newly-founded Ephesos had envisaged a functional splitting between different *agorai*, perhaps with Aristoteles in mind. A strong contradicting argument is that for the early Hellenistic period we have no evidence for an architecturally shaped public space on the spot of the later Upper Agora (or 'ἄνω ἀγορά', as we could name it with Aristoteles). Admittedly, the area in question was included from the beginning into the circuit of the city walls. Ceramic and other findings seem to attest even some settlement activities, intensified just before the middle of the 3rd century BCE, but no monumental architecture of that period has been identified yet (Ladstätter 2016, p. 246). Instead, the earliest large-scale building activities can be dated to the turn of the 2nd century. Then, probably between 220 and 180 BCE, the predecessor of the better-known Basilike Stoa was built: a *stoa*, which was about 180 m long, as attested by its (in parts only poorly preserved) foundations, and which constituted the northern limit of the square (Alzinger 1972-1975, col. 281; Alzinger 1988, pp. 21-23; for chronology see Lang-Auinger 2007, p. 6) (Fig. 2, no. 1). Within the same timeframe, the square as such must have been laid out. This connection is now more clearly demonstrated by the results of Daniel Musall's intensive building survey, pointing out more than one structural link between the Hellenistic North Stoa and the huge retaining wall in the west.[5] The construction of this wall (Fig. 2, no. 2) was, in turn, an indispensable precondition for levelling the entire developable area. With that said, it also becomes evident that the architectural complex of the Upper Agora from the beginning cut through the course of a road, which in Archaic and Classical times had crossed the zone transversally, in prolongation of the 'Kuretes Street' (*pace* Thür 2007a, p. 79; Sielhorst 2015, p. 116).[6]

On the southern side, a huge, two-aisled *stoa* architectonically defined the limit of the square (Fig. 2, no. 3). Longer sections of the *crepidoma* and of the back wall, which integrates a bench seat over the whole length, were uncovered in larger parts already during excavations between the 1960s and '80s (Fig. 3). Nevertheless, the South Stoa has remained more or less unpublished to date (cf. Alzinger 1972-1975, col. 282). Therefore, it is one of the main objects of study within the research project mentioned at the outset. By carefully cleaning and surveying the preserved aboveground remains as well as by sinking a couple of sondages into the foundation layers, we have explored the South Stoa over three field campaigns. In accordance to an analysis of ceramic findings, we are confident in dating the building to more or less the same time as its northern counterpart, in any case not after the first half of the 2nd century BCE.[7] Regarding the first Hellenistic building phase, a number of new discoveries have changed the image as produced by the former state of research. Detailed argumentation is reserved for publications to come, so I will mention only briefly two most essential insights: (1) The original *stoa* was longer than it appears today. A subsequent shortening took place at its eastern end, probably in relation to the creation of a new entrance to the Upper Agora during Late Hellenistic times (see below). Following some clues given by the documentation of the earlier excavations and guided by an intuition of Stefan Langer, we have detected parts of the original eastern *euthynteria* (Fig. 4) and therefore are now able to reconstruct the original length of *c.* 161 m (instead of 154 m in the second state). (2) The first building had closed sidewalls. An opening of the western wall, documented by the present state of the ruin, became necessary only when, probably during the 1st century AD, a large monument with massive concrete core (so-called pedestal building, *Sockelbau A*: Fig. 2, no. 11) was set immediately against the northern *crepidoma* of the *stoa* at its western end (Fig. 5: C; cf. Steuernagel 2020, p. 100). At the same moment, an access from the side of 'Domitian's Lane' (cf. Fig. 2, no. 12), which must have previously existed in front of the South Stoa, was closed. It was

5 In addition to a reinforcing the interconnection between the foundations of the Hellenistic north *stoa* and the western retaining wall ('*Schräge Mauer II*', mentioned by Lang-Auinger 2007, p. 6), Daniel Musall (see above, footnote 1) now can prove a structural linking of that wall and the westernmost extension of the Hellenistic north *stoa*, which bridges the difference of altitude between the stoa and the 'Kuretes street' (predecessor of the western *chalcidicum* resp. the '*Sockelbau*' of the Basilike Stoa, cf. Alzinger 1972-1975, p. 281; Fossel-Peschl 1982, p. 8).

6 '*Schräge Mauer I*', considered a wall flanking the earlier road by Fossel-Peschl, Thür and Sielhorst, all following Bammer 1972-1975, col. 384, actually is a subsequent installation of yet unexplained purpose into the western extension of the north *stoa*, as Daniel Musall will show in his PhD thesis. Moreover, there was no need to respect the road course in the planning process, as it probably was not part of an old processional way, see Ladstätter 2016, pp. 256-257.

7 The spectrum of ceramic wares and forms, analysed by Bettina Springer-Ferazin in her master-thesis (unpublished, University of Regensburg, 2018), resembles very much the one described for the foundation layers of the north *stoa* for which cf. Mitsopoulos-Leon 2007, p. 65.

Figure 5. Ephesos, Upper Agora. South Stoa, western end (photo: © ÖAW-ÖAI, Niki Gail, 2014).

only from then on that the pierced western pediment wall of the *stoa* (Fig. 5: B) functioned as a kind of *propylon* to the square.[8]

As for the eastern limit of the Upper Agora, information on the primary state, of the 2nd century BCE, is rather sparse. One building (Fig. 2, no. 4), baptised 'North-East Building' by us for lack of knowledge about its original shape and function, might date to the same period as the South Stoa since the two share some structural characteristics.[9] What we have are parts of the northern and western faces composed of large marble *orthostats*, which are superimposed on bench blocks (Fig. 6). Thus, a bench externally girdled the building. This bench went out of use when the Basilike Stoa (Fig. 2, no. 5) was erected late in the reign of Augustus, with its *crepidoma*-steps abutting against and partly overlapping the bench. Before, a passageway, about 10 m wide, must have existed between the shallower Hellenistic North Stoa and the 'North-East Building'. Interestingly, the 'North-East Building' was not destroyed in the course of the Augustan remodelling, but remained upright, at least partly, until the later Imperial period (cf. Alzinger 1974, p. 50). So far as observable today, it extended min. 15 m in the west-east and min. 9 m in the north-south direction. The original dimensions could have been much larger, but due to the integration of the Hellenistic into late-antique structures, the reconstruction remains pure guesswork.

8 In the illustration, letter A identifies the trunk of the western sidewall, B the *toichobate* of a wall-section that was removed, C the *Sockelbau A*. – An independent *propylon*-building, mentioned by former publications (*e.g.* Alzinger 1974, p. 51; Thür 2007a, p. 80; Sielhorst 2015, p. 118), never existed in the southwest of the Upper Agora; the assumption is based on misunderstandings which occurred in the first period of excavation, in the years 1960-1962.

9 A small sondage within the north-western corner of this building yielded only insignificant material from the construction layers; furthermore, the unexpected suspension of excavation-works at Ephesos in 2016 prevented further investigations. The building was partly explored and described by Alzinger in the diaries and documents of excavations between 1968 and 1971, but hardly ever mentioned in the publications, cf. Eichler 1969, p. 133; Steuernagel in press, p. 103.

Figure 3 (opposite above). Ephesos, Upper Agora: South Stoa, section of back wall (photo: Dirk Steuernagel, 2015).

Figure 4 (opposite below). Ephesos, Upper Agora. South Stoa, original eastern euthynteria (photo: Dirk Steuernagel, 2016).

Figure 6. Ephesos, Upper Agora. North-East-Building with integrated bench seat, from the west (on the left hand side, crepidoma of Basilike Stoa) (photo: © ÖAW-ÖAI, archives, 1968).

Figure 7 (opposite above). Ephesos, Upper Agora. Propylon, from the south (photo: Dirk Steuernagel, 2018).

Figure 8 (opposite below). Ephesos, Upper Agora. Portal in the central section of the South Stoa's back wall, from north (photo: © ÖAW-ÖAI, Niki Gail, 2015).

One main alteration of this first layout of the Upper Agora during the Late Hellenistic period was the opening of a new entrance to the square in its south-eastern corner. South of the eastern end of the South Stoa, a small *propylon*-building was constructed (Fig. 2, no. 10), facing the so-called South (or Magnesian) Street which, at a distance of about 15 m, runs parallel to the South Stoa (Fig. 2, no. 13) (Thür 1996; Steuernagel 2020, pp. 95-98). Today, this *propylon* is preserved only in a partial reconstruction from late antiquity (most probably 5th century AD) (Fig. 7). A sondage within the south-western corner of the building, however, brought forth strong arguments for locating the original building on the same spot since the 1st century BCE, more probably since the first half of the century.[10] Apparently, the aforementioned shortening of the South Stoa is related to the building of the *propylon*, inasmuch as the western column of the *propylon's* façade is approximately aligned with the secondary western wall of the *stoa*. In addition, a quite splendid, nearly 10 m wide portal, installed secondarily into the central section of the South

10 I would like to thank Nikolaus Schindel, Johanna Struber-Ilhan, and Bettina Springer-Ferazin for information on preliminary assessments of the numismatic and ceramic evidence.

Stoa's back wall, created another connection between the Upper Agora and the South Street (Fig. 8). By way of hypothesis, one could interpret these alterations as an attempt to link the Upper Agora with a newly traced out arterial road, the very South Street. Since the latter is oriented onto the Magnesian Gate in the East (cf. Fig. 1, no. 6), and since this gate according to Alexander Sokolicek (2009, esp. pp. 337. 341) occupied its present position not before *c.* 100 BCE, the South Street, in turn, might not date further back (Sokolicek 2010, esp. p. 363). Thus, we can hypothesise the existence of an older street that would have run alongside the South Stoa, traversing the Upper Agora.[11] Hence, the spatial constellation would have been comparable to the so-called Ionian Agorai in western Asia Minor (modern province of Aydın, Turkey): the *agora* of Priene, with the 'Westtorstraße' passing in front of the 'Hiera Stoa'; the South Agora at Miletus, with the street running parallel to the *stoa* of Antiochos; the *agora* at Magnesia, with the street in front of the southern *stoa* (cf. *e.g.* von Gerkan 1924, pp. 94-101; von Kienlin 2004, pp. 131-137. 140-142).

A state agora?

To sum up, the Upper Agora at Ephesos in its original Hellenistic aspect probably resembled more the public squares just mentioned than a *temenos*-like enclosure – a shape it assumed only in later phases, starting already in the 1st century BCE. Against this background, we now return to the functional aspects for which unfortunately no external information is available from the Hellenistic period. While the line-up of clearly recognisable buildings like *prytaneion* and *bouleuterion* on the northern fringe of the square and a *peripteral* temple on its central axis give evidence for the administrative and cultural functions since Augustan times, the picture is much more indistinct when we consider the preceding era. An inscription from *c.* 50 BCE, found within the *prytaneion* (IEph 740 b; cf. Kirbihler 2016, p. 84), recalls the renovation of a *bouleuterion* which Alzinger (1988; 1999) tried to identify with a mural structure connected to the Hellenistic North Stoa. Lionel Bier (2011, pp. 47-48) was able to disprove the main points of Alzinger's argumentation, but still admitted that the zone north of the North Stoa must have been built up in Hellenistic times. The same is also suggested by some disconnected remains of monumental style integrated into the architectonical patchwork of the so-called Rhodian Peristyle, west of the Imperial *bouleuterion*.[12] With regards to the *prytaneion*, Alzinger first assumed that a predecessor must have existed in the place of the present structure, which probably was built in the last decade BCE. He later abandoned the idea as contradicted by the archaeological evidence (Alzinger 1974, pp. 1972-1975 col. 248; cf. Steskal 2010, pp. 77-78). Nevertheless, a Hellenistic *prytaneion* might have existed somewhere in the neighbourhood of the Upper Agora. One possible indicator is an inscription, reused in late antiquity in the paving of the northeast corner of the South Stoa (where it is still to be found). It mentions a donation made by a freedman of Julius Caesar for sacrifices on occasion of the festival of the *Epheseia* that should be offered at the 'sacred hearth of the city' (ἐπὶ τῆς ἱερᾶς ἑσ[τίας τῆς πόλεως]; Engelmann 1990, pp. 92-94).[13] Since the normal place of the hearth would be the *prytaneion*, the inscription in any case does attest the existence of such a building in pre-Augustan times. That the Hellenistic *prytaneion* can be located near the finding spot of the inscription is far from certain, but should not be ruled out completely in view of our still-incomplete

11 Geophysical prospections revealed the existence of a sewer (?), which lines what could be the northern edge of the supposed street course.

12 Stefan Langer is preparing a survey of these remains within his PhD thesis (see above, footnote 1).

13 Some scholars assume that the donator is identical with C. Iulius Nicephorus, *prytanis* for lifetime under Augustus, cf. *e.g.* Kirbihler 2016, pp. 408. 421.

Figure 9. Ephesos, Upper Agora. South Stoa, section of back wall, with dowel holes (photo: Dirk Steuernagel, 2015).

knowledge of the area (cf. the somewhat divergent position expressed by Scherrer 2007, pp. 68-69). Some more inscriptions from proto-Augustan and Augustan times, found in the Upper Agora or its immediate surroundings, reinforce the impression that competing groups within the civic élite tried to put their mark on this place through donations of different types (buildings, statues, ceremonies *etc.*) (cf. Pont 2010, esp. pp. 389-390; Kirbihler 2016, pp. 420-436).

Additional, though unfortunately not datable, evidence for a political function of the Upper Agora comes from the South Stoa. Inside this building, drilled into the surface of *orthostats* and ashlars of the back wall, there are numerous holes, some still containing dowels and pins (Fig. 9). Apparently, no regular pattern exists, thus the holes most probably served for fixing wooden or bronze inscribed tablets. Closely comparable evidence comes from the Hellenistic Northwest-Stoa at Morgantina (Aidone, Sicily), where according to Malcom Bell (2007, p. 122) official documents were displayed.[14] As for Asia Minor, one can cite, for example, the walls of the '*Hiera Stoa*' at Priene and the Western Stoa of the *agora* at Magnesia, which bear public

14 The wall beneath the so-called temple of Minerva at Assisi (Umbria, Italy) offers another close parallel, also from the western Mediterranean: Gros and Theodorescu 1985, esp. pp. 891-893.

decrees of Hellenistic date, only that the latter were inscribed directly on the stone (Kern 1900, pp. 11-12; Hiller von Gaertringen 1906, pp. 82-83).

As we can see, there are some, albeit not finally decisive, arguments for ascribing political and ceremonial functions to the Upper Agora in Hellenistic times. Therefore, we should also take a divergent interpretative model into consideration, brought forward by Helmut Engelmann (1993, pp. 288-289), Peter Scherrer (2001, pp. 71-72; 2007, pp. 68-69) and Hilke Thür (2007b). These scholars hold the view that the area was one of the city's *gymnasia* before it changed its appearance and intended purpose under Augustus. Their main arguments are: (1) A cluster of inscriptions refers to *gymnasion*-related institutions and activities in the zone of the Upper Agora. (2) The length of the Hellenistic North Stoa, about 180 m, corresponds to the length of a *stadion*. (3) The bench seats within the South Stoa and on the eastern side of the square were apt to accommodate spectators of athletic competitions. These arguments, however, are anything but conclusive. Firstly, they do not take into account that an *agora* could well be a stage for '*gymnastic exercises*' and competitions, as mentioned also by Aristoteles, even if this practice seems less well testified for Hellenistic than for earlier times (Krinzinger 2011, p. 124; cf. Sielhorst 2015, p. 33; Dickenson 2017, pp. 108-113). Moreover, the inscriptions could stem from the area east of the Upper Agora, where two of them actually have been found. Already Alzinger (1970, coll. 1618-1619) guessed that a *palaistra* might have been located there, in relation to the thermal building of probable 2nd century AD date (Fig. 2, no. 9; cf. Thür 2007b, pp. 406-407). Secondly, the measure of a *stadion* does not give a definite clue for the function of a columned hall. For example, Antiochos stipulated that the *stoa* he donated to the Milesians should be a *stadion* long ([στοὰ στα]δίαια), although the building had nothing to do with a *gymnasion* (Bringmann and von Steuben 1995, pp. 341-343 no. 281, ll. 12-13; cf. von Hesberg 1990, pp. 237-238). Finally, the argumentation is based on a partially outdated state of research: no matter how we reconstruct the Hellenistic shape of the Upper Agora, according to the investigations briefly reported on above, it certainly did not have the character of enclosure which is presupposed by (and necessary for) an interpretation as *gymnasion*.[15]

To the proponents of the interpretation as *gymnasion*, though, appertains the merit of having highlighted the conspicuous presence of bench seats in the Upper Agora. As noted above, such seats are lined up not only in the interior of the South Stoa, where they are integrated into the back wall, but also under the open sky, on the east side of the square, as part of the 'North-East Building'. This remarkable feature may help to understand in a more general way the kind of use that was made of the square. In this respect, and in conclusion, I would like to return to the characterisation of a 'state *agora*' as given above: a public space subject to rather strict social control and regulations of conduct that is destined for predominantly ceremonial or ritualised action. Actually, the pure capacity of the seating fosters longer stays on the spot. It offers a space for conversation rather than for dispute. Moreover, it invites users or visitors to adopt a steady and calm attitude and to behave as spectators. Spectating was also facilitated by the long *crepidomas* of the North Stoa and South Stoa which provided a sort of stands. Thus, the architectural framing allows for perception of events and actions staged in the area of the square. The first thing one would think of at Ephesos were celebrations and processions in honour of Artemis. Though the existence of a processional route traversing the area of the new city is questioned for the period anterior to Lysimachos (above,

15 In addition, Scherrer's interpretation (2001, pp. 71-72) of '*Schräge Mauer I*' as '*oblique W end*' of a terrace-wall that serves as '*the foundation for the terraces of an early stadium*' clearly fails to recognise chronological sequence and architectural context of that wall (above, footnote 6).

footnote 6), it is beyond debate for later times. Only the testament of C. Vibius Salutaris, however, describes the route explicitly, in 104 AD. According to the last will of this rich Ephesian citizen, images of Artemis, personifications, heroes, and rulers should be carried around in a parade that started from the Artemision; it then entered the city at the Magnesian Gate, continued to the theatre and the Koressian Gate before returning to the sanctuary (Rogers 1991, pp. 86-89; original text and translation *ibid.*, pp. 152-183, esp., ll. 91-92. 556-568). It is generally assumed that this routing traces back to an older processional track, although it may traditionally have been walked in the reverse direction (Knibbe and Langmann 1993, pp. 28-32; Feuser 2015). Consequently, every procession would at least have touched the zone of the Upper Agora since the participants must have used the South Street when proceeding from or heading to the Magnesian Gate (cf. Fig. 1, no. 6). If the supposition that the South Street was created only about 100 BCE proves correct (see above), one might imagine, for the 2nd century BCE, processions that pass along the length of the South Stoa. In that case, the comparison with the *agorai* at Priene and Miletus could regard not only architectural, but also performative aspects (cf. von Gerkan 1922, p. 92; von Kienlin 2004, pp. 129. 141).[16]

Unfortunately, for the Hellenistic phase of the Ephesian Upper Agora we have no evidence comparable to what we have for Priene, *i.e.* of monuments in the open square that followed, enforced, or thwarted the guidelines for movement in space given by the main buildings. Thus, a valuable source for understanding the effects of an architectural endowment as well as the repercussions effected by social action is missing. Nevertheless, assessing the situation at Ephesos, and particularly the salient importance of bench seats, I would like to vindicate a main point within the interpretative model conceptualised by Hans-Joachim Schalles (1982) for the Athenian *agora*. Against his approach, some reasonable objections have been raised in more recent publications. Above all, changed views of Hellenistic urban society and of the role of *poleis* within the Hellenistic kingdoms (as well as under Roman rule) induced to abandon visions of a 'depoliticised' and 'musealised' urban space (Sielhorst 2015, pp. 74-75; cf. Dickenson 2017, pp. 157-170). As distinct from the idea of processions as spectacles of a purely 'theatrical' character, which people could watch from terraces in front of columned halls, Ruth Bielfeldt (2012, esp. pp. 107. 113) has rightly stressed the active involvement of (in theory) the whole citizenry. On the other hand, one cannot ignore that processions and similar activities in Hellenistic times appear much more regulated, with regard even to organisational details, than they had ever been before. By regimentation of this kind, the self-image of the *polis* was shaped in the face of non-citizens, foreigners, and foreign rulers – *i.e.*, the present or virtual spectators (Chaniotis 1995, pp. 157. 162; 1997, pp. 246-248; cf. von Hesberg 1990, p. 234). The *mis-en-scène* may well have encouraged a rather passive, receptive mode of perceiving the enactments of civic pride and their architectural setting, as claimed by Schalles (1982, esp. pp. 110-111; cf. Köhler 1996, p. 152). It is in this sense, as a possible place for ceremonial self-representation, that the Upper Agora at Ephesos in its Hellenistic phase seems to match the Aristotelian notion of 'free' or 'state *agora*' – whatever its real ancient name might have been. Given the chronological priority of the Lower Agora (and its multi-layered functionality), the need to have such a stage seems to have been felt, though not in the foundation period of Hellenistic Ephesos, but only after a certain lapse of time.

16 Schneider 1987, pp. 103-104, has called the inner-urban course of the processional route at Miletus, as proposed by von Gerkan, into question; nevertheless, the discovery of an Hellenistic altar just north of the entrance to the South Market seems to support von Gerkan's view, cf. Cain and Pfanner 2009; Sielhorst 2015, p. 128; generally on the use of long *stoai* as a kind of stands cf. Lauter 1986, p. 104.

References

Alzinger, W. 1970. *Paulys Realencyclopädie der classischen Altertumswissenschaft*, Suppl. XII, 1588-1704 s.v. Ephesos B. Archäologischer Teil. Stuttgart: J. B. Metzler Verlag.

Alzinger, W. 1972-1975. Grabungen in Ephesos von 1960-1969 bzw. 1970: Das Regierungsviertel. *Jahreshefte des Österreichischen Archäologischen Instituts* 50, coll. 229-300.

Alzinger, W. 1974. *Augusteische Architektur in Ephesos*. Wien: Österreichisches Archäologisches Institut.

Alzinger, W. 1988. Die Lokalisierung des hellenistischen Rathauses von Ephesos, in: Büsing, H. and Hiller, F. (eds.). *Bathron: Festschrift zur Architektur und verwandten Künsten für Heinrich Drerup zu seinem 80. Geburtstag*. Saarbrücken: Saarländische Druckerei und Verlag, 21-29.

Alzinger, W. 1999. Das Zentrum der lysimacheischen Stadt, in: Friesinger, H. and Krinzinger, F. (eds.). *100 Jahre österreichische Forschungen in Ephesos*. Akten des Symposions, Wien 1995, Denkschriften (Österreichische Akademie der Wissenschaften. Philosophisch-Historische Klasse) 260 = Denkschriften (Österreichische Akademie der Wissenschaften. Philosophisch-Historische Klasse), Archäologische Forschungen 1. Wien: Verlag der Österreichischen Akademie der Wissenschaften, 389-392.

Bammer, A. 1972-1975. Grabungen in Ephesos von 1960-1969 bzw. 1970: Architektur. *Jahreshefte des Österreichischen Archäologischen Instituts* 50, coll. 381-406.

Bell III, M. 2007. Apronius in the agora: Sicilian civil architecture and the lex Hieronica, in: Prag, J.R.W. (ed.). *Sicilia nutrix plebis Romanae: rhetoric, law, and taxation in Cicero's Verrines*, Bulletin of the Institute of Classical Studies Suppl. 97. London: Institute of Classical Studies, 117-134.

Bielfeldt, R. 2012. Polis made manifest: the physiognomy of the public in the Hellenistic city with a case study on the agora in Priene, in: Kuhn, C. (ed.). *Politische Kommunikation und öffentliche Meinung in der antiken Welt*. Stuttgart: Franz Steiner, 88-122.

Bien, G. 1985. *Die Grundlegung der politischen Philosophie des Aristoteles*. 3rd ed. München: Alber.

Bier, L. 2011. *The bouleuterion at Ephesos*, Forschungen in Ephesos 9, 5. Wien: Verlag der Österreichischen Akademie der Wissenschaften.

Bringmann, K. and von Steuben, H. (eds.) 1995. *Zeugnisse und Kommentare*, Schenkungen hellenistischer Herrscher an griechische Städte und Heiligtümer 1 Berlin: Akademie.

Cain, H.-U. and Pfanner, M. 2009. Die Agora Milets in der Kaiserzeit und Spätantike, in: Dally, O., Maischberger, M., Schneider, P.I., Scholl, A. (eds.). *ZeitRäume: Milet in Kaiserzeit und Spätantike*. Regensburg: Schnell & Steiner, 83-95.

Chaniotis, A. 1995. Sich selbst feiern? Städtische Feste des Hellenismus im Spannungsfeld von Religion und Politik, in: Wörrle, M. and Zanker, P. (eds.). *Stadtbild und Bürgerbild im Hellenismus*, Kolloquium München 24.-26. Juni 1993, Vestigia 47. München: C.H. Beck, 147-172.

Chaniotis, A. 1997. Theatricality beyond the theater: staging public life in the Hellenistic world, in: Le Guen, B. (ed.). *De la scéne aux gradins: théâtre et représentation dramatiques après Alexandre le Grand*, Pallas 47. Toulouse: Presses Unversitaires du Mirail, 219-259.

Dickenson, C.P. 2017. *On the agora: the evolution of a public space in Hellenistic and Roman Greece (c. 323 BC-267 AD)*. Leiden: Brill.

Eichler, F. 1962. Die österreichischen Ausgrabungen in Ephesos im Jahre 1961. *Anzeiger der Österreichischen Akademie der Wissenschaften. Phil.-Hist. Klasse* 99 (6), 37-53.

Eichler, F. 1965. Die österreichischen Ausgrabungen in Ephesos im Jahre 1964. *Anzeiger der Österreichischen Akademie der Wissenschaften. Phil.-Hist. Klasse* 102 (6), 93-110.

Eichler, F. 1969. Ephesos: Grabungsbericht 1968. *Anzeiger der Österreichischen Akademie der Wissenschaften. Phil.-Hist. Klasse* 106 (6), 131-146.

Engelmann, H. 1990. Ephesische Inschriften. *Zeitschrift für Papyrologie und Epigraphik* 84, 89-94.

Engelmann, H. 1993. Zum Kaiserkult in Ephesos. *Zeitschrift für Papyrologie und Epigraphik* 97, 279-289.

Falkener, E. 1862. *Ephesus and the temple of Diana*. London: Day & Son.

Feuser, S. 2015. *A stroll along the sea: the processional way in Ephesus and the littoral* [online]. Available from: http://www.chs-fellows.org/2015/02/20/a-stroll-along-the-sea/ [Accessed 19 June 2019].

Fossel-Peschl, E.A. 1982. *Die Basilika am Staatsmarkt in Ephesos*. Graz: Selbstverlag.

Gauthier, P. 1985. *Les cités grecques et leurs bienfaiteurs (4e-1er siècles av. J.-C.): contribution à l'histoire des institutions*, Bulletin de Correspondance Hellénique Suppl. 12. Paris: De Boccard.

von Gerkan, A. 1922. *Der Nordmarkt und der Hafen an der Löwenbucht*, Milet 1, 6. Berlin: De Gruyter.

von Gerkan, A. 1924. *Griechische Städteanlagen: Untersuchungen zur Entwicklung des Städtebaues im Altertum*. Berlin: De Gruyter.

Grieb, V. 2008. *Hellenistische Demokratie: Politische Organisation und Struktur in freien griechischen Poleis nach Alexander dem Großen*, Historia Einzelschriften 199. Stuttgart: Franz Steiner.

Groh, S. 2006. Neue Forschungen zur Stadtplanung in Ephesos. *Jahreshefte des Österreichischen Archäologischen Instituts* 75, 47-116.

Gros, P. and Theodorescu, D. 1985. Le mur nord du 'forum' d'Assise: ornementation pariétale et spécialisation des espaces. *Mélanges de l'École française de Rome. Antiquité* 85, 879-898.

von Hesberg, H. 1990. Platzanlagen und Hallenbauten in der Zeit des frühen Hellenismus, in: Deutsches Archäologisches Institut (ed.). *Akten des XIII. Internationalen Kongresses für Klassische Archäologie*, Berlin 1988. Mainz: Zabern, 231-241.

Hiller von Gaertringen, F. 1906. *Inschriften von Priene*. Berlin: Reimer.

Hofbauer, M., Öztürk, A., Styhler-Aydın, G. 2017. Zusammenfassung und chronologischer Überblick, in: Krinzinger, F. and Ruggendorfer, P. (eds.). *Das Theater von Ephesos*, Forschungen in Ephesos 2 (1). Wien: Verlag der Österreichischen Akademie der Wissenschaften, 513-522.

Keil, J. 1943. Drei neue Inschriften aus Ephesos. *Wiener Jahreshefte (Jahreshefte des Österreichischen Archäologischen Instituts)* 35, 101-108.

Kern, O. 1900. *Die Inschriften von Magnesia*. Berlin: Reimer.

von Kienlin, A. 2004. *Die Agora von Priene* [online]. Thesis (PhD). TU München. Available from: http://mediatum.ub.tum.de/doc/601008/601008.pdf [Accessed 18 June 2019].

Kirbihler, F. 2016. *Des Grecs et des Italiens à Ephèse*, Scripta Antiqua 88. Bordeaux: Ausonius.

Knibbe, D. and Langmann, G. 1993. *Via Sacra Ephesiaca 1*, Berichte und Materialien (Österreichisches Archäologisches Institut) 3. Wien: Schindler.

Köhler, J. 1996. *Pompai. Untersuchungen zur hellenistischen Festkultur.* Frankfurt a. M.: Lang.

Krinzinger, F. 2011. Spectacula und Kaiserkult, in: Ebner, M. and Esch-Wermeling, E. (eds.). *Kaiserkult, Wirtschaft und spectacula: Zum politischen und gesellschaftlichen Umfeld der Offenbarung*, Novum Testamentum et Orbis Antiquus 72. Göttingen: Vandenhoek & Ruprecht, 103-137.

Ladstätter, S. 2014. *Wissenschaftlicher Jahresbericht des Österreichischen Archäologischen Instituts 2014*. Wien: Österreichisches Archäologisches Institut 2014. Also available from: https://www.oeaw.ac.at/fileadmin/ Institute/OEAI/pdf/Kommunikation/Jahresberichte/OeAI_Jahresbericht_2014.pdf. [Accessed 6 June 2019].

Ladstätter, S. 2016. Hafen und Stadt von Ephesos in hellenistischer Zeit. *Jahreshefte des Österreichischen Archäologischen Instituts* 85, 233-272.

Lane, M. 2013. Claims to rule: the case of the multitude, in: Deslauriers, M. and Destrée, P. (eds.). *The Cambridge Companion to Aristotle's politics*. Cambridge: Cambridge University Press, 247-274.

Lang-Auinger, C. 2007. Zum Grabungsbefund, in: Mitsopoulos-Leon, V. and Lang-Auinger, C. (eds.). *Die Basilika am Staatsmarkt in Ephesos: Funde klassischer bis römischer Zeit*, Forschungen in Ephesos 9, 2, 3. Wien: Verlag der Österreichischen Akademie der Wissenschaften, 1-8.

Lauter, H. 1986. *Architektur des Hellenismus*. Darmstadt: Wissenschaftliche Buchgesellschaft.

Mann, C. and Scholz, P. (eds.) 2012. *Demokratie im Hellenismus: Von der Herrschaft des Volkes zur Herrschaft der Honoratioren?*, Die hellenistische Polis als Lebensform 2. Mainz: Verlag Antike.

Martin, R. 1951. *Recherches sur l'agora grecque: études d'histoire et d'architecture urbaines*. Paris: De Boccard.

Mitsopoulos-Leon, V. 2007. Die Lampen, in: Mitsopoulos-Leon, V. and Lang-Auinger, C. (eds.). *Die Basilika am Staatsmarkt in Ephesos: Funde klassischer bis römischer Zeit*, Forschungen in Ephesos 9, 2, 3. Wien: Verlag der Österreichischen Akademie der Wissenschaften, 64-113.

Nadon, C. 2001. *Xenophon's prince: Republic and Empire in the 'Cyropaedia'*. Berkeley: University of California Press.

Pont, A.-V. 2010. *Orner la cite: enjeux culturels et politiques du paysage urbain dans l'Asie gréco-romaine*. Bordeaux: Ausonius.

Rogers, G.M. 1991. *The sacred identity of Ephesos: foundation myths of a Roman city*. London: Routledge.

Schalles, H.-J. 1982. Die hellenistische Umgestaltung der Athener Agora im 2. Jh. v. Chr. – Ausdruck von Rationalität oder Entpolitisierung? *Hephaistos* 4, 97-116.

Scherrer, P. 2001. The historical topography of Ephesos, in: Parrish, D. (ed.). *Urbanism in Western Asia Minor: new studies on Aphrodisias, Ephesos, Hierapolis, Pergamon, Perge and Xanthos*, Journal of Roman Archaeology Suppl. 45. Portsmouth, RI: Journal of Roman Archaeology, 68-87.

Scherrer, P. 2007. Der *conventus civium Romanorum* und kaiserliche Freigelassene als Bauherren in Ephesos in augusteischer Zeit, in: Meyer, M. (ed.). *Neue Zeiten – neue Sitten: Zu Rezeption und Integration römischen und italischen Kulturguts in Kleinasien*. Wien: Phoibos Verlag, 63-75.

Scherrer, P. and Trinkl, E. 2006. *Die Tetragonos Agora in Ephesos,* Forschungen in Ephesos 13 (2). Wien: Verlag der Österreichischen Akademie der Wissenschaften.

Schneider, P. 1987. Zur Topographie der Heiligen Straße von Milet nach Didyma. *Archäologischer Anzeiger*, 101-129.

Schütrumpf, E 2005. *Aristoteles. Politik Buch VII/VIII: über die beste Verfassung*, Werke in deutscher Übersetzung 9, 4. Berlin: Akademie.

Schwaabe, C. 2012. Demokratie und Oligarchie, in: Zehnpfennig, B. (ed.). *Die 'Politik' des Aristoteles*. Baden-Baden: Nomos, 158-176.

Sielhorst, B. 2015. *Hellenistische Agorai: Gestaltung, Rezeption und Semantik eines urbanen Raums*, Urban Spaces 3. Berlin: De Gruyter.

Sokolicek, A. 2009. Zwischen Stadt und Land: Neues zum Magnesischen Tor in Ephesos. *Jahreshefte des Österreichischen Archäologischen Instituts* 78, 321-347.

Sokolicek, M. 2010. Chronologie und Nutzung des Magnesischen Tores von Ephesos. *Jahreshefte des Österreichischen Archäologischen Instituts* 79, 359-381.

Steskal, M. 2010. *Das Prytaneion in Ephesos*, Forschungen in Ephesos 9, 4. Wien: Verlag der Österreichischen Akademie der Wissenschaften.

Steuernagel, D. 2020. The Upper Agora at Ephesos: an Imperial forum?, in: Schowalter, D., Friesen, S., Ladstätter, S., Thomas, C. (eds.). *Religion in Ephesos reconsidered: archaeology of spaces, structures and objects*, Novum Testamentum Suppl. 177. Leiden: Brill, 93-107.

Thür, H. 1996. Ein dorischer Torbau am Staatsmarkt von Ephesos, in: Blakolmer, F., Krierer, K.R., Krinzinger, F. (eds.). *Fremde Zeiten: Festschrift für Jürgen Borchhardt 1*. Wien: Phoibos Verlag, 345-361.

Thür, H. 2007a. Wie römisch ist der sogenannte Staatsmarkt in Ephesos?, in: Meyer, M. (ed.). *Neue Zeiten – neue Sitten: Zu Rezeption und Integration römischen und italischen Kulturguts in Kleinasien*. Wien: Phoibos Verlag, 75-90.

Thür, H. 2007b. Das Gymnasion an der oberen Agora in Ephesos, in: Christof, E. and Schwarz, G. (eds.). Πότνια Θηρῶν*: Festschrift für Gerda Schwarz zum 65. Geburtstag*, Veröffentlichungen des Instituts für Klassische Archäologie der Karl-Franzens-Universität Graz 8. Wien: Phoibos Verlag, 403-414.

Wankel, H. (ed.) 1979-1984. *Inschriften von Ephesos*, Inschriften griechischer Städte aus Kleinasien 8. Bonn: Habelt 1979-1984.

Wilberg, W. and Keil, J. 1923. Die Agora, in: Österreichisches Archäologisches Institut (ed.). *Forschungen in Ephesos* 3. Wien: Österr. Verlagsgesellschaft Ed. Hölzel, 1-168.

Notes on contributor

Dirk Steuernagel - Institute of Classical Archaeology, University of Regensburg (present). Studies of Classical Archaeology, Ancient History, Latin Philology, Auxiliary Sciences of History at Frankfurt/Main and Hamburg; PhD Hamburg 1995; Habilitation Frankfurt 2002; Full Professor of Classical Archaeology at Regensburg 2010-; Director of 'Centre for Classical Studies' at Regensburg 2012-; Principle Investigator of the Graduate School 'Metropolität in der Vormoderne' at Regensburg 2017-; research project on the Upper Agora at Ephesos (funding by DFG 2014-2018).

STPAS: Scales of Transformation in Prehistoric and Archaic Societies

The book series 'Scales of Transformation in Prehistoric and Archaic Societies' (STPAS) is an international scientific series that covers major results deriving from or being associated with the research conducted in the Collaborative Research Centre 'Scales of Transformation: Human-Environmental Interaction in Prehistoric and Archaic Societies' (CRC 1266). Primarily located at Kiel University, Germany, the CRC 1266 is a large interdisciplinary project investigating multiple aspects of socio-environmental transformations in ancient societies between 15,000 and 1 BCE across Europe.

Volume 1
Das Jungneolithikum in Schleswig-Holstein
Sebastian Schultrich | 2018
ISBN: 9789088907425
Format: 210x280mm | 506 pp. | Language: German | 43 illus. (bw) | 103 illus. (fc)
Keywords: Late Neolithic, Single Grave Culture, Corded Ware Culture, transformation, solid stone axe, battle axe, fragments of axes | Jungneolithikum, Einzelgrabkultur, Schnurkeramische Kultur, Transformation, Felsgesteinäxte, Streitäxte, Axtfragmente

Volume 2
Embracing Bell Beaker
Adopting new ideas and objects across Europe during the later 3rd millennium BC (c. 2600-2000 BC)
Jos Kleijne | 2019
ISBN: 9789088907555
Format: 210x280mm | 300 pp. | Language: English | 91 illus. (fc)
Keywords: archaeology; Late Neolithic; Bell Beaker phenomenon; settlement archaeology; innovation; network analysis; mobility; prehistoric potter

Volume 3
Habitus?
The Social Dimension of Technology and Transformation
Edited by Sławomir Kadrow & Johannes Müller | 2019
ISBN: 9789088907838

Format: 210x280mm | ca. 235 pp. | Language: English | 15 illus. (bw) | 65 illus. (fc)
Keywords: European prehistory; archaeology; habitus; technology; transformation; social dimension; ethnoarchaeology

Volume 4
How's Life?
Living Conditions in the 2nd and 1st Millennia BCE
Edited by Marta Dal Corso, Wiebke Kirleis, Jutta Kneisel, Nicole Taylor, Magdalena Wieckowska-Lüth, Marco Zanon | 2019
ISBN: 9789088908019
Format: 210x280mm | ca. 210 pp. | Language: English | 29 illus. (bw) | 43 illus. (fc)
Keywords: Bronze Age, domestic archaeology, household archaeology, daily life, routine activities, diet, waste, violence, health, natural resources, food production

Volume 5
Megalithic monuments and social structures
Comparative studies on recent and Funnel Beaker societies
Maria Wunderlich | 2019
ISBN: 9789088907869
Format: 210x280mm | ca. 450 pp. | Language: English | 114 illus. (bw) | 246 illus. (fc)
Keywords: Megalithic graves, monumentality, Funnel Beaker Complex, ethnoarchaeology, Sumba, Nagaland, social organisation, cooperation

Volume 6
Gender Transformations in Prehistoric and Archaic Societies
Edited by Julia Katharina Koch & Wiebke Kirleis | 2019
ISBN: 9789088908217
Format: 210x280mm | ca. 500 pp. | Language: English | 114 illus. (bw) | 58 illus. (fc)
Keywords: academic fieldwork; gender archaeology; social archaeology; environmental archaeology; history of archaeology; Mesolithic; Neolithic; Bronze Age; Iron Age; Europe; South-west Asia; Central Asia

Volume 7
Maidanets'ke
Development and decline of a Trypillia mega-site in Central Ukraine
René Ohlrau | 2020
ISBN: 9789088908484
Format: 210x280mm | ca. 312 pp. | Language: English | 141 illus. (bw) | 93 illus. (fc)
Keywords: settlement archaeology; prehistoric archaeology; early urbanism; geophysical survey; paleodemography; Trypillia; mega-site

Volume 8
Detecting and explaining technological innovation in prehistory
Edited by Michela Spataro & Martin Furholt | 2020
ISBN: 9789088908248
Format: 210x280mm | ca. 250 pp. | Language: English | 22 illus. (bw) | 37 illus. (fc)
Keywords: archaeology; prehistory; technology; innovation; invention; tradition; chaîne opératoire; knowledge acquisition; knowledge transfer; Neolithic; Bronze Age; Iron Age; ethnography; ceramic; metal; bone

Volume 9

Archaeology in the Žitava Valley I

The LBK and Želiezovce settlement site of Vráble

Edited by Martin Furholt, Ivan Cheben, Johannes Müller, Alena Bistáková, Maria Wunderlich &
Nils Müller-Scheeßel | 2020

ISBN: 9789088908972
Format: 210x280 | ca. 350 pp. | Language: English | 50 illus. (bw) | 157 illus. (fc)
Keywords: European Early Neolithic; LBK, settlement patterns; social organization; social conflict; village and neighbourhood structures; burial rites; enclosure; excavation report

Volume 10

Hellenistic Architecture and Human Action

A Case of Reciprocal Influence

Edited by Annette Haug & Asja Müller | 2020

ISBN: 9789088909092
Format: 210x280mm | ca. 212 pp. | Language: English | 38 illus. (bw) | 29 illus. (fc)
Keywords: Classical archaeology; Hellenistic architecture; agency; perception